Asexuality, Relationships, and Identity Formation

Valerie Q. Glass

Asexuality, Relationships, and Identity Formation

Best Practices for Affirmative Care

Springer

Valerie Q. Glass
JFK School of Psych & Social Sciences
National University
San Diego, CA, USA

ISBN 978-3-032-22856-7 ISBN 978-3-032-22857-4 (eBook)
https://doi.org/10.1007/978-3-032-22857-4

This Springer imprint is published by the registered company Springer Nature Switzerland AG
The registered company address is: Gewerbestrasse 11, 6330 Cham, Switzerland

Acknowledgments

With a profound and expansive heart, my greatest support and strength throughout my research and writing process has been my daughter, Jordin Glass. Several years ago, during the pandemic, 8th grade Jordin and I were having a conversation. I was exploring a few research directions and she wholeheartedly and passionately suggested studying asexuality. It was a term we discussed in my home as the two of us frequently shared elements of our own identity journeys. From that moment, she has been an unwavering supporter—listening to my constant musings around book ideas, challenging my thinking, and providing invaluable feedback. As an adult now, she has embraced reviewing chapters of this book and providing constructive feedback along the way. Jordin has a way of looking at the world that has always been beyond her years and her own self-reflection and critical thought have been invaluable to this project.

I also want to thank some amazing colleagues for their thoughtful inspiration and review of this book. First, thanks to Anney Tsuji-Lyons, my colleague from National University who provided me with frequent check-ins, validation, and support throughout this project. I am also grateful to Nora Tucker Betz, a clinician and an MFT graduate from Adler University, who devoted a great deal of time and energy into providing feedback. Finally, I want to thank Stephanie Gilak, a doctoral student at Adler University, for her incredible insights and for reviewing a draft of this book.

Finally, words cannot fully express the deep and intense devotion I feel towards the asexual participants who have been part of the projects that have cumulated into this book. Every one of them met me with enthusiasm, support, pride, and more philosophical intellect than I could have ever imagined. I have learned so much from these interactions and will be forever grateful for the personal and professional awareness that has evolved from my interaction with them. The participants entered the interview space and were vulnerable with me almost immediately. They wanted to share their stories and I was immediately captivated by each and every one of them. Many of them commented on how pleased they were that asexuality was given a platform and that their voices were being heard. I felt challenged and humbled in these expectations and worked hard to provide a space to let their thoughts shine and be absorbed by all that are willing to listen.

In order to protect confidentiality and privacy, all participants in this study were assigned a pseudonym. Any information that might identify participants (e.g., names, geographical locations, or other notable identifiers) was removed from the data transcripts. Participants signed National University Institutional Review Board releases before the research process began and were given full authority to end participation at any time or remove any of their comments from the final transcript. Participants were informed of the possible publication of their responses and graciously approved this presentation of the final research results.

Ethics Approval Ethical approval and consent to participate: The study was approved by the institutional review board of National University. There were two iterations of data collection and two IRB approvals (IRB-FY24-25-849 and IRB2020-858). Informed consent was obtained from all individual participants included in the study. All procedures performed in studies involving human participants were in accordance with the Helsinki declaration as revised in 2013 and its later amendments.

Competing Interests The author has no competing interests to declare that are relevant to the content of this manuscript.

Contents

About the Author

Valerie Q. Glass, PhD, is a professor of marriage and family therapy (MFT) at National University (USA), a licensed marriage and family therapist, and an AAMFT approved supervisor. She played a key role in developing an *LGBTQIA+ Couple and Family Specialization* for MFT master's students at National University. With nearly three decades of research on queer individuals, couples, and families, Dr. Glass has contributed significantly to shifts in discourse around family and identity in the social sciences. In addition to research, she maintains a clinical practice where she specializes in working with queer clients. Currently, Dr. Glass resides in South Carolina.

Beyond her professional pursuits, Dr. Glass enjoys spending time with her young adult daughter, being part of nature, engaging in creative writing, and involving herself in the lives of as many dogs as possible—especially her own dachshund/lab mix named Luna.

Chapter 1
Introduction to Asexuality and Affirmative Care

Asexuality is an often misunderstood and under researched sexual orientation. Mental health disciplines and medical fields rarely offer any education or awareness on asexuality. Schneckenburger et al. (2024) state, "globally, asexuality is the most poorly understood sexual minority. Asexuality is often regarded with suspicion, lack of recognition, and delegitimization" (p. 319). Let's change that! My goal in this text is to provide you with information that will increase your awareness of asexuality overall, help you better understand asexuality, and, hopefully, push thinking forward in ways that embrace, validate, and affirm all ways people experience desire, sex, and romance. We will explore social messages that exist around sexual attraction, romantic attraction, and intimacy, as well as build a stronger foundation of understanding asexuality to better provide affirmative care to individuals on the asexual spectrum.

Consider this scenario:

Charley and Joanie have begun couples therapy. Their stated goal is communication issues. Charley and Joanie have been married for 21 years and seem to have a responsive and respectful connection in the therapy room. They shared that they have two teenage children and will be empty nesters soon. They have proactively built hobbies and social networks to meet these future transitions. The therapist dives in with some questions and topics that range from times when they have not felt as close to how they fell in love. Even through difficult moments, the couple is supportive of one another, and they check in with each other constantly to make sure their needs are getting met. The therapist goes through two sessions and cannot seem to uncover what it is that seems to be the root of the issue for the couple (they report no infidelity, they are respectful and listen well to one another, they seem to have resolved any emotional difficulties between them, etc.).

At the start of the third session, the therapist says, "I am really impressed with the two of you, it seems to me that you are connected to one another, talk through issues well, and you are loving and affectionate with each other" (as the therapist notes Charley's hand on Joanie's leg and Joanie sitting close and facing Charley

V. Q. Glass, *Asexuality, Relationships, and Identity Formation*,
https://doi.org/10.1007/978-3-032-22857-4_1

when they talk). The therapist states that they listen to one another, respond, use "I" statements, and genuinely seem to have the same goals and direction. The therapist shares, "I am just checking in because I am not clear yet what the main thing that you are struggling with is and what that brought you to therapy." There is silence, as a feeling of shame and secrecy enters the room. Both Charley's and Joanie's eyes begin to water. Joanie starts to weep, which leads to Charley scrunching his body up a bit in the chair. It is obvious that there is some pain in there for some reason. The therapist patiently allows for that pain to enter the room and says gently, "Joanie, can you share with me where the tears are coming from?" She speaks quietly through tears, "He just never finds me attractive, he never wants to be physical with me, we've been together all these years, but he never looks at me the way I want him to." She continues to release some feelings and deep hurts of her past. She shares that, as an adolescent, she was teased because of her weight, and now she is finding she never feels attractive and never feels good enough for Charley. Charley shares that he feels nothing but strong love for Joanie and struggles to know what she needs and how to give it to her. He shares, "I think maybe I have something wrong with me or, like a low libido or something." His eyes gaze downward, his emotions seep of guilt and shame. He is stammering through his words and says he sometimes does not feel like "a real man" and "never has." They share that sexual intimacy is very uncommon and always has been. Through quiet gulps, Charley says, "I don't think we've had sex in a year, it is all my fault too, I don't know what is wrong."

Pause...

As a reader of this book, you may have immediate reactions to Charley and Joanie's situation, probably both clinically and personally. Maybe you are part of a relationship that has had sexual ups and downs for reasons that you can pinpoint (e.g., medication shifts, busy lives, depressive episodes, etc.). Maybe you are a person who identifies sexual intimacy as critical to your life, and you are reacting to this scenario as "awful for Joanie." Maybe your head starts to wonder "Has Charley been checked out medically? There must be something wrong." Maybe you have a reaction to gender—"how can a man not be interested in sex?" Or, maybe, you are on the asexual spectrum and parts of Charley's experience really resonate with you. Consider what came up for you when you read the scenario. What assumptions did you make, and where did those assumptions stem from?

We will come back to Joanie and Charley in a moment, before that, I want to introduce you to the road map of this book. The cumulative *we*—our societies, our discourses—create specific social scripts and expectations that evolve into an undercurrent of what is considered acceptable. This norm that is created deems what is outside that norm as either invisible, problematic, sinful, broken, and/or unhealthy. Queer identities frequently fall out of the norm and are often seen as something to change or fix. This book will propel asexual sexual orientations to the forefront through the challenging of social scripts that continue to pathologize queer identities (inclusive of asexual identities). I feel that discourse has intentionally and/or unintentionally contributed to an othering/pathologizing process, and language evolution is a major component of understanding the process of othering and moving beyond being othered. Queer affirmative care models arose in mental health communities to address the historical prevalence in mental health fields that pathologized queer identities and/or rendered them invisible. Ultimately, this book will provide a background of asexual experience and identities, challenge social scripts that delegitimize asexuality, and create an affirming lens for recognizing asexuality as a healthy and fulfilling identity.

Introducing Queer Affirmative Care

Queer affirmative care is an undercurrent (hopefully a strong and mighty undercurrent) that is part of most helping fields. Essentially, queer affirmative care provides an *affirming* space for people of all sexual orientations and gender identities. Affirmative care spaces are safe spaces where clients can feel embraced during the vulnerable process of disclosing identity, understanding oneself, and living authentically.

In Chap. 6, I will present an ***asexual affirmative care model*** that will expand on queer affirmative care. Queer affirmative care is an approach to working with LGBTQIA+ persons in helping professions. Affirmative therapy was initially developed in the 1970s as a direct result of mental health fields shifting language that previously identified those with same-sex attraction as having a mental health disorder (Herek & Garnets, 2007). The evolution of affirmative care embraces experiences of queer persons and starts with a recognition of internalized homophobia and heterosexism within the practitioner. It creates a positive and welcoming stance with all patients of all genders and sexual orientations (Giammattei & Green, 2012; McGeorge et al., 2015; McKinney et al., 2020; Rock et al., 2010). Affirmative models stress that practitioners explore their assumptions and biases. Assumptions around identity or experience are often rooted in socially constructed language and meaning. It challenges practitioners to explore these social constructions in their own lives and the lives of their clients. Affirmative therapy also highlights the importance of considering intersectionality (Golden & Oransky, 2019), building cultural competency around diverse queer experiences (Rock et al., 2010), and helping sexual and gender minorities "meet important developmental milestones and achieve a positive self-identity" (McKinney et al., 2020, p. 176).

In summary, queer affirmative care includes the following aspects:

1. **Cultural competency**—Cultural competency is an awareness and an understanding of a community, a group, or differences (Bittle & Anderson, 2023). When I think about cultural competency, I recognize that *competency* of a difference cannot ever be achieved. No person can be fully competent in a group of humans. For example, no matter how much I am a part of queer communities, I cannot ever say I am fully competent of queer experiences because there are so many differences within queerness. That being said, I do bring in the idea of cultural competency to queer affirmative care in a different way. I think of cultural competency as a starting place in building relationships with those different

from yourself. If you encounter a person, for example, who is from a religious background that you know nothing about, you might do some research on this religion. It would not mean that you would assume you knew everything about this person's background, but it might help you with language and pinpoint questions that you might ask. A background in queer communities, in queer history, in queer terminology, in queer theory, in social challenges, in political challenges, in the history of queer experiences in mental health, etc. are critical to queer-affirming care. This is what I think of when I think of cultural competency—more of a background than a full competency. Those providing queer affirmative care should seek out learning opportunities for things they are less familiar with. They should read research and books to be informed, they should immerse themselves in queer events, art, films, theater, etc. to understand queer challenges, queer strengths, and queer cultures and communities. Familiarity provides a sense of comfort and awareness of strengths and challenges that queer people may be facing.

2. **Cultural Humility**—Cultural humility takes cultural competency to another level, by recognizing that we cannot know everything and there are nuances and uniquenesses in all people (Hook et al., 2017). It is about approaching clients in a humble way where you let them teach you about who they are and how they view the world.
3. **Social Justice**—Social justice is an extension of cultural competency to external sources by challenging oppression, power, and privilege (Moussawi & Vidal-Ortiz, 2020). It is being an advocate for our clients in and out of the therapy space. Affirmative therapists are aware of the impacts of social injustices, marginalization, and prejudices that queer clients are experiencing and speak up against homophobia in our personal encounters and/or in political or policy arenas. Social justice can provide community support connections to clients or help them locate services that will also provide affirmative care (Murphy, 2022).
4. **Self-awareness**—Self-awareness is, in my opinion, the most important clinical tool we have (Allen, 2023). I feel this is even more important when working with marginalized identities. I have been a visible and active part of the queer community for over 35 years. I am constantly reflecting on my own power and privilege, doing research, learning more, learning from clients, etc. Despite this very active awareness, an occasional unexpected bias or judgment passes through my brain. We are products of the social constructions that are part of our daily environments, and it takes a life-long committed process to actively consider these moments, sit with them, and challenge them. This work is never complete.

When you think about Joanie and Charley's scenario, consider how queer affirmative care could be applied to their situation? The ingrained social messages might inform our clinical direction—here is this heterosexual couple that has been married for years, but they struggle with sex—let's apply a sex therapy technique, consider past trauma, maybe make sure Charley has been evaluated medically. Could these be good clinical directions? Maybe. But, how might these possible directions be leaving out queer affirmative care? Has the clinician considered that they might be impacting the direction of therapy through social expectations or their own narrative of what relationships look like? Can the therapist dive in and ask questions about the couple, their dreams, their histories, and their desires? Do you think this cultural humility might create a safe, open space for queer identities (inclusive of asexual identities) to be supported?

I plan to take you on a bit of an asexual affirmative care journey throughout this book to help you consider how you might best approach and understand Joanie and Charley. The goals of this book include:

- Providing a historical and research-based cultural competency on asexuality.
- Exploring possible assumptions or areas of ignorance when it comes to asexuality.
- Challenging social constructions around sex, sexual attraction, and romantic attraction.
- Providing an overview of asexual identity formation.
- Considering the role of asexuality in the context of relationships.
- Creating a dialog that starts the advocating process for clinicians with asexual clients.
- Presenting clinical thoughts, theories, tools, research, and case examples to support working with asexual clients.
- Finally, I am integrating "self" (my own "self") into this book and want to be transparent about that. This insertion includes my own identity as an asexual person (demisexual), my own work with asexual clients, and my own contexts and perspectives.

Introducing Asexuality

Imagine this scenario. You are a young adult and were invited to go to a dance club with a group of new friends. You spend the day getting ready, picking out an outfit that helps you feel confident. You admire your outfit—it is something that feels artistic to you and aesthetically pleasing to the eye. You are really excited about getting to know this group of friends that you are heading to the club with. They are all artistic, and the little time you have spent with them has involved deep conversations and vulnerability, something you admire in people.

You are at the club, hanging out together at the side of the dance floor. You are talking and laughing with your new friends as much as you can above the loud music. You and one friend are having a detailed discussion about your similar music tastes. At some point, this individual's attention was diverted, and you glance in the direction of where his attention seems to be focused. Your mind starts thinking about what he might be interested in, maybe the lights on the floor and the aesthetic of the club. You admire some fashion choices of the people around you. While you are lost in thought, the rest of your peer group has started to look where your original friend was looking, it seems they are looking toward an individual on the dance floor. You gaze in that direction to join in. The woman is purposefully dancing seductively and keeps looking over and smiling at the friends in your group. She is wearing clothing that accentuates her curvy body and flirts using her gaze and body movements with a couple of individuals in the peer group. Your thoughts about her are: "that dance move requires a lot of flexibility, she must have some dance training" and "her eyeliner is perfectly accentuating her eye shape and color" and "I wished I had the platform shoes with rhinestones that she is wearing." You feel you are admiring her in similar ways that your friends are, her style, her abilities, even her personality stands out. But you soon realize *your* thoughts of this woman differed a great deal from the friend group's thoughts.

The peer group moves toward the outdoor deck and you follow. There is a lot of commotion, excited voices, and discussion among your new friends. You hear, "oh, man, I can't take it!" and "whew, I need a cold shower!" Another person responds, "for real, I needed to get out and get some cool air!" The rest of the group is responding to this conversation with head nods, laughter, and "um-hum!" or "right!" types of comments. You are completely lost at what the heck they are talking about. You are listening to get the gist and see if you can join in the fun, but nothing is making sense in what they are saying, but they sure are passionate and animated about it. You nod and smile to fit in, but are still waiting for something to click. Someone notices your lack of reaction and says "hey, did you see her?!" Your brain knows there was a lot of "hers" in the dance room, and you still are guessing you missed something. The person says, "did you not see that woman dancing in the tight bright blue top?" You know it is the woman you were thinking about, it is just your reaction differs. You nod, but more in a matter-of-fact way, not in the "oh my gosh" way that your peers have responded to her. The group continues their conversation, and you go into your head thinking something is wrong with you, again. This type of interaction feels common for you. Their conversation moves to words like "sexy" and "hot" and these are things that you do not feel; you can appreciate her style and her skill, but nothing took you to a sexual headspace. This kind of thing happens to you a lot, your friends get crushes and talk about sexual conquests and their huge attractions. You are never quite sure how to be part of these conversations.

This type of scenario is common among a lot of asexual individuals. There is often a disconnect between typical social visual cues that lead others to feel physical attraction toward a person. These differences can create situations for asexual individuals that leave them feeling different than their peers or, as some might reflect, it makes them feel like something is wrong with them (initially). For many individuals on the asexual spectrum, they start some internal searching about these differences and work to try and understand. For some, it might mean sexual activity and dating to try and fit in and experience what others experience. For others, it might mean checking in with doctors or therapists about these things that they are noticing. For some, they may come across the language around asexuality and feel ah-ha moments that the language actually explains what they are experiencing.

I have also explained it to people like this, I ***love*** chocolate chip cookies. It would be really difficult for me not to eat a chocolate chip cookie if it was given to me. I think about them at times when I haven't had one for a while. If I smell them or see them, my senses are awakened. I just really want one badly. Do you have any foods that do this for you? That awaken your senses, and you can't deny those sensory desires?

On the flip side of that, I ***like*** pecan pie; it is a decent dessert. If someone has a pecan pie and is asking me if I want a slice, I could take it or leave it. I might enjoy it if I decide to eat it, but it might just be like "eh" to me. If I smell it, see it, or people are talking about it, I don't have the need or desire to get pecan pie in that moment. And, I can go years without thinking about it. This is how I explain my own sense of *my* version of asexuality. For most people on the asexual spectrum, their lives, when it comes to sexual attraction, are kind of like me and the pecan pie. It (sexual attraction and sexual desire) is something that doesn't evoke the same kind of energy as non-asexual-spectrum people experience when they see a particular person (or piece of pecan pie) in front of them. For me, I equate chocolate chip cookies with how I think people who are not asexuals might feel—if it is there, if the idea is there, it sounds really good to them and hard to resist. Additionally, they are thinking about chocolate chip cookies a lot. These descriptions are merely simple, generalized, symbolic ways to describe asexuality from my own musings. This book will dive into asexual spectrum experiences to provide a more inclusive breadth of asexuality. The ultimate goal of this book is to provide a deeper sense of asexual competence for clinicians and practitioners (or really anyone who wants to know).

In Western cultures specifically, sexual desire, romance, and sexual activity are socially constructed to look a certain way—we must all be having good, satisfying sex regularly (mind you, there are often heteronormative messages around sex too that are specific to what that looks like), and romance is a majorly important part of being a human. The message is that if you do not experience the world as a particular romantic or sexualized being, doing and enjoying sex and sexual desire in one particular way, there must be something wrong with you. These messages not only negate the inner worlds of many asexuals, but also many others who may vary from these expectations for other reasons.

Introducing Key Constructs

This entire book is about defining asexuality, and my hope is that you leave this book with a broad definition of the term asexuality that allows you to understand and embrace each asexual's experiences as unique and deeply personal to them. Some people might even argue that labels and language are constraining in some ways. I do want to recognize that to be the case for some and that fluidity (moving in and out of desires and experiences) is a real thing. However, I recognize that, for many people, language legitimizes experiences, and labels can help people outside that experience better understand. This is the paradigm I am working from. In this chapter, I will begin by presenting some specific constructs around asexuality as a foundation for the discussion overall. If this language is new to you, it might be of use to bounce back and forth between this section as you go through the book to remind yourself of the definitions of these terms, as there are many of these terms used in quotes by participants and in research. I have also included a glossary at the end of the book that highlights much of the language used throughout this book and in many asexual communities.

First, there are four primary concepts that I want to introduce here that are significant to this book and in asexual communities. These constructs warrant a deep dive before moving ahead: (a) asexuality, (b) allosexuality, (c) amatonormativity, and (d) the split attraction model. These terms will be revisited as the book progresses and the impact of language is explored; however, having a basic understanding of these four terms is foundational to much of what you will see in this book as a whole.

What Is Asexuality?

Most research on asexuality defines asexuality as a sexual orientation that identifies a continuum of experiences; the primary uniting experience that defines asexual spectrum identities is not feeling sexual attraction (Boegart, 2015). Pause there for a moment and take in the statement "asexuality is a sexual orientation." Much like gay, lesbian, bisexual, heterosexual, and the list goes on, asexuality is about attraction and who a person is attracted to (or not attracted to) sexually and romantically. Asexuality is part of a person from birth, part of their DNA, and not a result of other events in their lives. Most asexuals feel that their sexual orientation is innate—something they are born with (Gupta, 2017). For some asexual spectrum people, sexual attraction is more variable; we will dive into some of the language around those distinctions in a moment.

Lack of sexual attraction is a major aspect of asexual identities. Russell (2023) states: "sexual attraction, sexual desire and sexual behaviour are different processes. Sexual behaviour indicates a choice, or intention, and is generally under one's control. Sexual attraction, on the other hand, is not a choice" (p. 92). Sexual attraction is like a draw, a pull, or a deeper sense of want and it is just something that does not feel the same for asexuals (Brunning & McKeever, 2021).

There has been an evolution to defining asexuality. Bogeart published a book in 2012, *Understanding Asexuality*, which highlights the complex word "attraction" (p. 15) and how this idea of attraction can be "deconstructed" (p. 15) into four ways of being attracted. They identify the following (p. 15):

A = Attraction and arousal—When there are physiological responses to seeing or being touched by a person.
B = Behavior—Behavior is what a person actually does or does not do when it comes to sexual behaviors.
C = Cognition—This concept describes what a person is thinking about (e.g., fantasies about sex and/or romance).
D = Desire—Desire explains a person wanting to engage in certain behaviors (e.g., sexual or romantic).

Bogeart (2012) summarized that asexuality is the "lack of sexual desire" (p. 26), noting that without this piece, the other elements (A, B, & C) are not possible. Van Houdenhove et al. (2014) described asexuality in this way: "(a) absence of sexual behavior, (b) absence of sexual attraction, (c) self-identification as asexual, or (d) a combination of these" (p. 177). Though there are asexuals that have little or no interest in sexual activity, it is less common in present day to identify a lack of sexual behavior as a linking point for asexual identities because this piece is so variable in the asexual spectrum. I think one key element to describing asexuality is that one has never experienced sexual attraction (or done so variably) (Bogeart, 2015). Most asexuals can look back at their adolescence and recognize that they felt different than their peers who were seeking out crushes and doting over teen heartthrobs.

The idea of a lack of sexual attraction is commonly expressed as the definition of asexuality. Asexuality Visibility and Education Network (AVEN—asexuality.org) remains one of the present-day guides to public awareness and education on asexuality. They identify three common definitions of asexuality:

1. An asexual person does not experience sexual attraction.
2. An asexual person experiences little or no sexual attraction.
3. An asexual person does not have intrinsic/innate desire for partnered sex (asexuality.org).

In my own research on asexual individuals and what I often see in blogs, social media, and research is that asexuals feel connected to other asexuals and how they describe their own feelings and emotions around sexual attraction. This felt connection is part of the identity process—the understanding of oneself as asexual. Asexuals often self-identify as asexual based on a connection with other asexual individuals who report feeling similar experiences around attraction, intimacy, and sex (MacNeela & Murphy, 2015). Chasin (2013) described their experience as an asexual, noting, "it was not a definition of asexuality per se that struck me or led me to call myself asexual; it was the incredible sense that these people—members of the asexual community—sounded like me" (p. 405).

As a person on the asexual spectrum, this all resonates with me. I feel like the experiences of other asexuals fit with my own experiences, how they describe their adolescence, how they describe their desires—just feels like it fits me. A lot of it, for me, comes down to the fact that I do not find myself making any sense of those frequent conversations that I have been part of all my life where people are commenting on physical attraction (e.g., "omg, look at the body on her," "that guy is hot," or "those tight jeans"). I am totally lost in these conversations and find myself pausing and trying to think about what people are saying and what they mean, almost like I just am not connecting to something like others do. This experience I have mirrors what I hear other asexual people experiencing.

For people who are not asexual, this lengthy definition might sound contrived; however, keep in mind that if you have never imagined a world without chocolate chip cookies (or your inserted favorite food here), and never known what it is like to *not* desire them, or think about them, or even never considered that other people were not equally as into what you were experiencing. It is likely difficult to understand this like-minded, ah-ha feeling of connection asexuals feel in talking with other asexuals. This feeling is difficult to articulate to non-asexuals. Do you have a food that you absolutely cannot stand and just cannot wrap your head around when someone tells you it is their favorite food? Like, you have tried to like it, but just cannot find the appeal? I think sometimes this is how I view my own asexuality. Like, if someone says they cannot stand chocolate chip cookies, that would be very confusing to me. I think that people who are not asexual are sometimes confused because they never considered that a person might not feel the way they do or desire something the way they do. I also get it on another level! I define myself as a romantic demisexual—I experience romantic attraction (and even sexual attraction when a bond is formed). When I meet aromantic asexuals, it can take me a moment to get around the fact that they do not experience romantic attraction or sexual attraction—because it is different from my own experience. It is like a mini-dive into my brain and a reminder—oh, yes, we experience this thing differently! (Note that I am early in presenting terminology here—I will explain in a moment). Also, keep in mind that just because we (practitioners) may not have the same identity, perspective, or experience as our clients, it does not mean that we can't provide affirming care! A critical part of cultural humility and affirming care is the recognition that there are things we do not understand.

Sherronda J. Brown (2022) wrote a book that considers asexuality and how culture and messages around sex are so prevalent. They discuss some challenges asexuals have navigating these social elements as they process their own asexual identity. In addition, Brown, who describes asexuality through a Black asexual lens, examines the intersectional lenses of Blackness and asexual-ness within a "sex-obsessed culture" (p. 2). I appreciated Brown's perspectives on defining asexuality. They state,

> People on the asexual spectrum, also called ace, experience little to no sexual attraction and/or little to no sexual desire, and these things are not evidenced by either the presence or absence of sexual arousal or activity. Even though 'lacking sexual attraction or desire' is the widely accepted general definition, I do not understand asexuality to be defined by this 'lack.' It is not about being without sexuality, though some may choose to describe themselves this way. I believe it is more true to say that asexuality is defined by a relationship to sex that is atypical to what has been decided on by society as normative, and that atypical nature is marked by varying degrees of sexual attraction and desire (p. 2).

I value this look at asexuality and how it embraces the spectrum of experiences under the asexual umbrella. Additionally, this definition re-frames the stereotype of all asexuals being "non-sexual" and recognizes the variability in how people experience sexual attraction, romantic attraction, or sexual desire. I feel by removing "lack" from the definition, we can still recognize asexuals as sexual beings if they feel that is also part of them, and it de-pathologizes this vision of lacking something "normal."

How many people are asexual? There is no easy answer to this question. Because the label asexuality is a rather new way of defining this particular sexual orientation and because of the variability of how people experience their own asexuality, it is unclear how many people might fit under the asexual umbrella. In the early 2000s, there were some thoughts that asexuality existed in about 1% of the population;

however, more recent research has suggested higher numbers, maybe more like 6% of the population (Bogeart, 2004; Brunning & McKeever, 2021; Hille, 2023). Some people experience asexuality as fluid, and some asexual identities (e.g., graysexuals, aceflux, and demisexual) report varying degrees of sexual attraction. Asexuality is not a choice or a condition. There are some biases that might consider asexuality to be celibacy, a medical issue, or trauma; however, asexuals report that this attraction part is just who they are and have felt they were consistently (Sherrer, 2008).

The term *broken* is echoed in research on asexual identities as terminology used, at times, by asexual persons who are still grappling with their identity and also by external individuals who are describing asexuals (Flanagan & Peters, 2020; MacNeela & Murphy, 2015; Mandigo & Kavar, 2022). As some asexuals start to navigate relationships, they may begin to recognize that something does not fit for them when it comes to attraction. In these moments, when viewing others around them experiencing something different, many asexuals report feeling *broken* or like something was medically or emotionally wrong with them (Gupta, 2017). At times, asexual people seek out counseling or medical intervention to "fix" something they perceive may be wrong (Flanagan & Peters, 2020). Medical and mental health professionals often incorrectly pathologize the experiences of asexuals. Asexuality should not be considered a disorder (Boegart, 2015; Flanagan & Peters, 2020). Research indicates no major differences in asexuals and the general population in sexual functioning, sexual response, mental health, or trauma (Boegart, 2015). In fact, many asexuals report being happy and content not experiencing sexual attraction or sexual experiences in the way that allosexual people do (Chasin, 2013).

Identities Under the Asexual Umbrella

In general, other than defining oneself as asexual, I typically hear demisexual or graysexual as common asexual spectrum identities. That being said, there are many identities and labels that I will describe below that are part of the asexual spectrum of experiences and identities.

Ace—another word used to describe asexual (Mandigo & Kavar, 2022).

Asexual Spectrum/Aspec—commonly used word to describe people who define themselves as under the asexual umbrella of experiences (Mandigo & Kavar, 2022).

Aceflux/Acefluid—Refers to a person who may describe their asexual orientation as more fluid or shifting (Young, 2023). They might describe moments of feeling a lack of sexual attraction in their life, and other moments where this feeling does not exist.

Aegosexual—An aegosexual may describe themselves as not really having a desire to engage in sexual activity with a person, but does experience arousal from content, masturbation, or fantasy (Young, 2023).

Apothisexual—When a person is repulsed by sexual activity or even sexual content (Young, 2023). Some apothisexuals describe a sense of feeling physically repulsed (e.g., nauseous).

Aroace—A person who is both asexual and aromantic.

Cupiosexual—A cupiosexual asexual desires a sexual relationship despite not feeling sexual attraction (Young, 2023).

Demisexual/Demi-asexual/Demiace—An individual who only experiences sexual attraction to a person once they form an emotional bond or connection (Hille, 2023). I hear a lot of demi people (including myself) say "I am asexual, until suddenly, I am not." Demisexuals may make up about 12% of asexuals (Copulsky & Hammack, 2023).

Graysexual/gray-asexual/grayace—An individual who only experiences sexual attraction in very specific circumstances (Hille, 2023). Some of the ways that graysexuals share these experiences can include: maybe feeling some sexual attraction but not really a desire to act on it, only feel sexual attraction at specific times, with specific people, or under specific circumstances, maybe infrequently feel sexual attraction, or maybe feel like sexual attraction just is not important to them. Graysexuals may make up about 14% of asexuals (Copulsky & Hammack, 2023).

Fraysexual—A person who feels sexual attraction toward those that they do not know well and sexual attraction fades the more they get to know the person (Young, 2023).

Lithosexual—A person who feels sexual attraction; however, they don't want others (or the person they are attracted to) to feel it back (Young, 2023).

There are other less common microlabels out there that fit under the asexual umbrella and, likely, over time, there will be more labels that help people better articulate their identity.

What Is Allosexuality?

Essentially, allosexuality is anything that is not asexuality. It is the most commonly reported sexual orientation where one experiences sexual desire. Yes, the idea that there are two binary identities (asexuality and allosexuality) is oversimplifying human diversity (Russell, 2023), but it is a jumping-off space for describing a difference. Both asexuality and allosexuality are spectrums of identities. But, generally speaking, there is a distinction that exists on those spectrums.

Consider this scenario, you are walking down the street and notice a person who is very sexually attractive to you. You might notice things going on in your body that let you know that your body is reacting to this person. Your mind might be bringing in fantasy, you might feel a sense of warmth or tingling, your body might actually become physically aroused in some ways. You know this is normal for you and is frequently represented in social discourse, so you don't think much about it really.

Your friends often talk about these experiences, you see people having similar experiences on TV and in the movies, and it is a fairly regular occurrence for you. It is considered the norm in Western cultures to experience this. This is allosexuality. A majority of people fall into this category of identity.

Overall, allosexuality is when a person responds to physical attractiveness in a way that can feel arousing, bring a sense of desire, and/or feel internally notably different than just seeing or admiring something pretty or attractive without a sexual overlayer. Not surprisingly, research identifies that asexual people that partner are less likely than allosexual people to pick persons based on appearance and more likely to consider personality and interests (Edge & Vonk, 2024). There seems to be an elemental difference between how asexuals and allosexuals navigate the world when it comes to attraction and what that means to them.

One thing that I would like to point out is that allosexual people (like asexual people) vary a great deal when it comes to sexual attraction, sexual desire, romantic attraction, fantasy, relationship goals, etc. Even more importantly, a person's desire and experience with sex and romance can shift throughout their lifetime. As a relationship therapist, I have met so many people who have vastly different experiences with libido, desire, sexual experiences, and romantic experiences. One couple may come in constantly angry at each other, but share with me that they have sexual intercourse more than once a day and both are happy and this is their norm. I might have the most loving, intimate couple, and they tell me that they only have sex about once or twice a year—and they are happy, and this is their norm. And, both of these couples are allosexual. I have people in relationships with different levels of libido—which can be challenging, but some people work it out nicely and others come to therapy to figure out the best way to connect when they have a different felt need. There is no one way to be allosexual and, despite the binary that I often use throughout this book (asexual ←→ allosexual), I do not feel that our identities are always that clear cut. Also, I feel like even with a person who may not have that much interest in sex or a low libido, that does not mean they would fall into the asexual identity; it is that lack of sexual attraction and the connection to other asexuals that defines this difference for most asexuals.

What Is Amatonormativity?

Amatonormativity is the assumption that all people desire a specific kind of love and partnership and that this partnership is socially valued more than any other relationship (Brake, 2012). I think of amatonormativity as the expectations put on people that you will fall in love, be romanced, have amazing sexual experiences, and society will celebrate those things. In some ways, it is the Disney Princess dream of finding Prince Charming and living happily ever after while society cheers you on. I think of 1980s sitcoms that often centered around families—the parents were always in-love, they expressed satisfaction in intimacy, and they held power in society being a "strong couple." This type of relationship was seen as the social ideal. The image of coupling, the "mom, dad, 2.5 kids, white picket fence" image, has left a legacy that spirals into a social construction that achieving this type of relationship is the only way to be happy. Children and teens in these sit-coms would negotiate crushes, dating, romance, and even sexual experiences in similar (and expected) ways. The first kiss of many young characters is celebrated by families, peers, and communities—it is an expected part of growing up and expected to feel a certain way. These expectations and the social discourse around the expectations are amatonormative. Amatonormativity can be limiting to all people because of human differences in experiences and desires. What if an allosexual individual does not want that first kiss at the party, despite being attracted to an individual there? It puts them in a difficult space at times because of the narrative that this is expected. In this book, I often refer to amatonormativity when I am discussing the challenges that asexuals feel when they may not desire the expected romantic and sexual scripts that social structures have defined.

What Is the Split Attraction Model?

Despite the lack of feeling sexual attraction, asexual people report variability in sexual experiences, sexual responses, and romantic desires (Glass, 2022). A commonly utilized construct in asexual communities is the ***split attraction model*** (Diamond, 2003; Galupo et al., 2014; Lund et al., 2016; Van Houdenhove et al., 2014). The split attraction model highlights that people can experience *sexual attraction* and/or *romantic attraction* separately or differently. For example, one person may feel both sexual attraction and romantic attraction for someone, another person may not experience sexual attraction but does experience romantic attraction, and another person may not experience sexual attraction or romantic attraction. These variations are frequently discussed in asexual communities and are often captured through the use of microlabels. Microlabels specify internal group uniquenesses and variabilities. These microlabels further increase how asexuals (and even those outside asexual spectrums) describe their experiences. Some of the information I present in this book includes data from research interviews I have done with asexuals and their partners. These participants often defined themselves in terms of sexual interest microlabels (e.g., sex averse, sex indifferent, and sex favorable) and romantic orientation microlabels (e.g., panromantic, biromantic) (I will expand on these in a bit). The split attraction model is one paradigm for looking at unique experiences of asexual individuals.

If you are a person who considers partnering, what is it about a person that you are drawn to? What are you "attracted" to about people? Maybe this is not as simple as chocolate chip cookies vs. pecan pie. Continuing on my obsession with chocolate chip cookies, what if you asked me "what is it about chocolate chip cookies that you find so appealing?" That is a loaded question, maybe the dripping, warm chocolate chips that melt in my mouth? Maybe that cozy, snuggled-up comfort I feel when I am eating them? Maybe the fond memories of connection in baking with my mother? Maybe the moment I almost burn my mouth because they are right out of the oven? Heck, I can break that down into a lot of things! When it comes to love, connection, and intimacy—what is attraction? When I have been partnered, what is it that attracts me to that person? I would imagine most asexual people would say they were not drawn to a person (at least initially) because of their sexual attractiveness.

I had an allosexual client say to me recently about an ex-spouse, something like, "we have nothing in common really, we argue a lot, he actually has always been unkind to me—but, oh my gosh is he hot!" After that, I had to sort of shake my head and wake up a bit, realizing that some allosexual people can build a begin and sustain a relationship where sexual attraction is primary. This example helps me describe the way attraction works differently for everyone. The *split* in the split attraction model is the recognition that there are two kinds of attraction, romantic attraction and sexual attraction. In this example above, this client felt a sense of sexual attraction when she first met her husband, and this likely led to a feeling of romantic attraction—this romantic attraction, at the end of the relationship, was fizzling out, but that physical attraction was still prevalent. I think of a person who may have a friends-with-benefits relationship, and they might feel only a sexual attraction toward that person, but not really a romantic attraction. Many asexuals share that they have romantic attraction, but not sexual attraction. Often, the language around the split attraction model can be comforting and add to asexuals' understanding of their identity (Mandigo & Kavar, 2022). Those asexuals with romantic attraction may desire to have the romantic connection to a person, for example, talking, snuggling, buying flowers, holding hands, walking along the beach at sunset, sharing stories and feelings with each other, etc., but they may not be looking at that same person saying, "he is hot!" Individuals of all sexual orientations can experience attractions in different ways. Maybe a gay male is both sexually and romantically attracted to men, but also sexually attracted to women. I have met a lot of heterosexual women who share that they have been sexually attracted to women, but do not care to have a romantic relationship with a woman. I would argue that the *split* in the split attraction model will continue to split in even more inclusive ways—as many people report other types of attractions (e.g., aesthetic, platonic, sensual, etc.) (Winer, 2025). I am sure this split attraction may become a plural attraction through research and discussions.

As a practitioner, bringing in the split attraction model can really help a lot of clients consider things differently. Think back at Charley and Joanie—if this couple started to view the intensity of Charley's romantic attraction to Joanie (even though sexual attraction feels a bit differently to him), this might help the couple really start to understand the areas that they *do* connect and remind Joanie of how attracted he is to her—it is just that it looks a little differently than the way that she is attracted to him. For many asexuals who have located terminology, understood their identity as asexual, and have found community—the split attraction model is frequently discussed as a way to differentiate and describe who they are.

Sexual Interest Microlabels

Some asexual people identify with certain sexual interest microlabels. Keep in mind that although asexual people identify under the "lack of sexual attraction" definition, this does not always mean a lack of sexual desire (Agrawal et al., 2025). Lack of sexual attraction is not the same as a lack of sexual desire. In fact, arousal can occur naturally (just maybe differently) for most asexuals. So, when it comes to defining a person's interest in sexual activity, some sexual interest microlabels have evolved, these are (Agrawal et al., 2025):

Sex-repulsed—Typically, a person who labels themselves as sex-repulsed has a very negative reaction to sexual activity. For some, this can be a physical reaction.
Sex-averse—Those who are sex-averse tend to just not really be drawn to sexual activity.
Sex-indifferent/sex-neutral—Many asexuals describe a feeling of being open toward sexual activity but maybe not considering it.
Sex-favorable/Sex-positive*—Sex-favorable asexuals tend to appreciate and desire a sexual relationship.
(*Note: "sex positive" can also mean that a person supports and is committed to presenting a positive climate for everyone about their own bodies and their own sexuality. Often asexuals use this term to also define their personal attitudes towards feeling comfort and desire around sexual experiences).

Research is all over the place when it comes to how many asexuals identify or fit into these categories (Clark & Zimmerman, 2022; Singh, 2017). In general, most asexuals seem to fall into sex-favorable or sex-neutral identities. I have seen ranges for sex-favorable around 39% (Singh, 2017) and sex-neutral or sex-indifferent 41–55% (Clark & Zimmerman, 2022; Singh, 2017). This leaves about 10% or so identifying as sex-averse or sex-repulsed, though I have seen numbers in this category as high as 38%. I think the accuracy of these numbers is a bit difficult because they are subjective, and microlabels are not always used by all asexuals. Exact numbers are not all that important if you consider the spectrum or experiences and fluidity that can occur within behaviors and experiences.

Romantic Interest Microlabels

Often, asexuals use microlabels to define their own identity with regard to romantic attraction. Some of the following labels are listed below. Remember that the split attraction model opens up this idea of romantic attraction as separate from sexual attraction. Asexuals use these microlabels frequently, but keep in mind that they can also fit allosexuals.

Aromantic—is a person who does not experience romantic attraction. About 29–34% of asexuals define themselves as aromantic (Copulsky & Hammack,

2023; Tessler, 2025). An aromantic asexual reports not feeling romantic or sexual attraction.

Aromantic spectrum (A-spec)—can describe a person who mostly does not experience romantic attraction, but can include variations of that experience.

Alloromantic—a person who has a romantic identity or romantic attraction. About 2/3 of asexuals describe themselves as having a romantic orientation (Tessler, 2025).

Heteroromantic—a person who identifies as having romantic attraction to persons of a different gender.

Homoromantic—a person who identifies as having a romantic attraction to persons of a similar gender.

Biromantic—a person who identifies as having a romantic attraction to more than one gender.

Panromantic—a person who identifies as having a romantic attraction to all genders. Gender is not a factor in attraction.

Polyromantic—a person who identifies as having a romantic attraction to multiple genders.

Omniromantic—a person who identifies as having a romantic attraction to all genders, but still considers gender a defining aspect of their romantic attraction.

Grayromantic—a person who identifies as experiencing romantic attraction in certain circumstances.

Demiromantic—a person who identifies as experiencing romantic attraction only when a deep emotional connection is formed.

Again, language evolves, and I am sure there are many others that are not part of this list.

Other Important Constructs

A few other terms are presented here that will be brought up throughout this text.

Acephobia—The fear or hatred of asexuality or asexual people. Acephobia can come out as microagressions or discrimination that implies a person is not "normal" or their sexual orientation is not valid (Brown, 2022). Asexuals who share their identity with others frequently hear "oh, you just haven't been with the right person"—delegitimizing or erasing asexuality as a whole. Brown (2022) states: "We are often dehumanized, seen as failures of humanity" (p. 25).

Aesthetic attraction—Viewing a person in a way that appreciates their appearance, but this isn't rooted in sexual attraction (Fine, 2023).

Alterous attraction—when an individual describes a love they have toward a person that does not necessarily fit into traditional definitions of romantic or sexual attraction (Young, 2023).

Non-desire—A notable lack of feeling desire for another person that is a contradiction to heteronormative, allonormative, amatanormative expectations (Fine, 2023).

Queerplatonic/queerplatonic relationship (QPR)—A QPR is a relationship that may not fit into the sexual, romantic, or social norms of a "relationship"; however, they are equally as valid, committed, and intimate relationships (Young, 2023). It is important to note that QPRs are different than "friendships" (which are also equally valid and important)—there is a level of commitment and connection that those in QPRs feel that defines this type of relationship in its own category.

Sexual normativity—the idea that all people have sexual desires and have a need to act on these desires (Schneckenburger et al., 2024).

Squish—a "non-romantic, non-sexual desire for a potential friend" (Fine, 2023, p. 165). Kind of like a crush, but not a romantic or sexual feeling.

Okay, as I mentioned, this terminology may feel a little dense. For many, a lot of these constructs might be new. It is perfectly fine to flip back and forth or take a look at the glossary in the back as you take in the rest of this book.

A Note about Intersectionality In my own research on asexuals and in a majority of the studies I have read on asexuality, most (not all, but most) participants seem to be White and from Western countries. Additionally, much of the research out there on asexuality has sought participants from similar locations (e.g., the Asexuality and Visibility Education Network—AVEN or social media associated with AVEN groups) (Hille, 2023). This leaves the evolving social science field looking at asexual perspectives that are largely White, Western, and middle class.

A couple of researchers have presented experiences of Black asexuals in Western cultures (e.g., Brown, 2022; Foster et al., 2019); these discussions are less common in research, social media, asexual spaces, and even Black queer spaces. Similarly, other cultural, ethnic, and racial differences are rarely noted in current asexual research. Very little research has been done on asexual communities in non-Westernized areas; however, more recently, Lu and Chui (2025) have brought research to light that explores asexual experiences in China. There is some asexual research growing in India (Agrawal et al., 2025; Chatterjee & Rastogi, 2024). Additionally, An and Kim (2024) bring asexual identity formation themes from a sample of South Korean asexual participants. One study I came across examined asexuals globally (Chan & Leung, 2023). These researchers explore the context of these non-Western cultures and the intersections of asexuality. Remarkably, despite cultural differences in these other studies, there are a lot of overlaps in findings from asexual research studies in Western cultures; however, these non-Western studies on asexuality are still emerging. I am thrilled to see this area of research continue to grow, expand, and include many perspectives.

I feel like, instinctively, asexuality is a sexual orientation equally represented in all humans. I do think that, as a sexual orientation, maybe more White/less diverse communities are defining and describing their asexuality in *White* and *Westernized* language, undoubtedly, leaving voices out. I am frequently curious about the role of intersectionality when it comes to asexuality. I will be the first to critique all that I present here in this book moving forward because, at this point, asexual intersections outside of my own (White, middle class, American) are still emerging in research. I think about, for example, the over-sexualized images and exploitation of Black people in my country and know that I cannot center myself in the context of being a Black asexual person and how that context could impact asexual identity formation or the experiences of Black asexual individuals in the context of relationships. Brown (2022) presented their perspectives on being Black and being asexual in their book *Refusing Compulsory Sexuality: A Black Asexual Lens on Our Sex-Obsessed Culture*. In this book, Brown connects slavery and the objectification of Black bodies in the United States to asexual identity (specifically for those asexuals who are also Black). I highly recommend this book and this perspective, and hopefully do it justice as I highlight parts of it throughout this book.

Consider other intersections and asexuality, like disability, gender, and age (Hart-Brinson et al., 2024). The social stereotypes of those with disabilities being non-sexual can impact how a person views their own asexuality and how others view them, creating an entirely different experience of identity formation. Gender and expectations of sexual behavior will be discussed more in Chap. 3; however, the ideas of masculinity and sex drive and domination or femininity and submissive and willing (or the pure virgin image) can certainly impact asexual experiences. Age and generation are also intersectional aspects of asexual identities that have not been researched specifically. Asexuals are locating the language to describe their identity at younger ages—likely due to more visibility among younger generations (Brozowwski et al., 2025). This difference could significantly impact the experiences of an asexual person in their 60s compared to an asexual person in their 20s.

So, as part of this book, I am doing something that I never thought I would do, I am presenting from my perspective and making that transparent. I value difference and will embrace and open dialog throughout this text in hopes the conversation continues and new voices can be added. I will be mindful and integrative with what is out there and work to continue to create space for all voices. Being that research is largely not out there that represents multiple intersectional asexual perspectives, there are a lot of voices that are currently left out of the dialog on asexuality and, hence, left out of this book.

Finally, as we jump in to considering asexual affirmative care, I want to leave this chapter with a couple of assumptions I make in crafting this book:

1. Asexuality is not necessarily about the presence or lack of sex (Dawson et al., 2018); however, so much of how to explain asexuality is housed within this social language of sex, sexual intimacy, sexual desire, and sexual attraction. It is somewhat impossible to leave out the language and discussion around sex. It feels like I have to describe what asexuality is not (not what it is) because it is not the norm, and we live in a sexualized world.
2. Another assumption that I feel is important to mention is that I think language is a major force in how we see ourselves, how we understand what is around us,

and, ultimately, a tool that I feel can lead to great positive change (as a therapist, but also out of the therapy room). Language is a key factor in identity formation for many asexual people and queer people overall. Being able to use words to describe who we are is a powerful thing.

3. This book is about asexual affirmative care; the root of the information I present is to grow and learn as practitioners. This intentional immersion in asexual journeys provides a greater understanding of asexuality, therefore, a more affirming approach to working with asexuals.
4. Finally, this book is about me. In many ways, this makes me biased, and in many other ways, it makes me informed. My story is woven into the fabric of all the voices I present here. I am a therapist by profession, a researcher, an educator, and an asexual. This is the context from which I begin the art of this book and sharing these stories.

References

Agrawal, N., Shainy, M. R., Sebastian, J., Srivastava, A., & Scoats, R. (2025). "Sex without sexual attraction?": Perceived sexual experiences of Indian sex-favourable asexuals. *Psychology & Sexuality*, 1–21. https://doi.org/10.1080/19419899.2025.2518977

Allen, K. R. (2023). Feminist theory, method, and praxis: Toward a critical consciousness for family and close relationship scholars. *Journal of Social & Personal Relationships, 40*(3), 899–936. https://doi.org/10.1177/02654075211065779

An, H., & Kim, E. (2024). Unveiling the stressful experiences faced by asexual individuals in South Korea: A consensual qualitative study. *Psychology & Sexuality*, 1–16. https://doi.org/10.1080/19419899.2024.2408018

Asexual Visibility and Education Network (AVEN). (2022, February 1). https://www.asexuality.org/

Bittle, A., & Anderson, V. N. (2023). As human as anybody else: Attitudes toward asexual people. *Psychology of Sexual Orientation and Gender Diversity*. https://doi.org/10.1037/sgd0000652

Bogaert, A. F. (2004). Asexuality: Prevalence and associated factors in a national probability sample. *The Journal of Sex Research, 41*(3), 279–287.

Bogaert, A. (2012). *Understanding asexuality*. Rowman and Littlefield Publishers.

Bogaert, A. F. (2015). Asexuality: What is it and why it matters. *Journal of Sex Research, 52*(4), 362–379. https://doi.org/10.1080/00224499.2015.1015713

Brake, E. (2012). *Minimizing marriage: Marriage, morality, and the law*. Oxford University Press.

Brown, S. (2022). *Refusing compulsory sexuality: A Black asexual lens on our sex-obsessed culture*. North Atlantic Books.

Brozowski, A., Chopik, W. J., Weidmann, R., Oh, J., & Weaver, J. R. (2025). Demographic and experiential characteristics of asexual individuals and associations with well-being. *Archives of Sexual Behavior: The Official Publication of the International Academy of Sex Research, 54*(2), 575–588. https://doi.org/10.1007/s10508-024-03068-0

Brunning, L., & McKeever, N. (2021). Asexuality. *Journal of Applied Philosophy, 38*(3), 497–517. https://doi.org/10.1111/japp.12472

Chan, R. C. H., & Leung, J. S. Y. (2023). Experiences of minority stress and their impact on suicidality among asexual individuals. *Journal of Affective Disorders, 325*, 794–803. https://doi.org/10.1016/j.jad.2023.01.025

Chasin, C. J. D. (2013). Reconsidering asexuality and its radical potential. *Feminist Studies, 39*(2), 405–426. https://www.jstor.org/stable/23719054

Chatterjee, N., & Rastogi, K. (2024). Exploring the psycho-social experiences of asexuals in India. *Journal of Psychosexual Health, 5*(4), 263–265. https://doi.org/10.1177/26318318231221927

Clark, A. N., & Zimmerman, C. (2022). Concordance between romantic orientations and sexual attitudes: Comparing allosexual and asexual adults. *Archives of Sexual Behavior: The Official Publication of the International Academy of Sex Research, 51*(4), 2147–2157. https://doi.org/10.1007/s10508-021-02194-3

Copulsky, D., & Hammack, P. L. (2023). Asexuality, graysexuality, and demisexuality: Distinctions in desire, behavior, and identity. *Journal of Sex Research, 60*(2), 221–230. https://doi.org/10.1080/00224499.2021.2012113

Dawson, M., Scott, S., & McDonnell, L. (2018). '"Asexual" isn't who I am': The politics of asexuality. *Sociological Research Online, 23*(2), 374–391. https://doi.org/10.1177/1360780418757540

Diamond, L. M. (2003). What does sexual orientation orient? A biobehavioral model distinguishing romantic love and sexual desire. *Psychological Review, 110*(1), 173–192. https://doi.org/10.1037/0033-295X.110.1.173

Edge, J., & Vonk, J. (2024). A Comparison of mate preferences in asexual and allosexual adults. *Archives of Sexual Behavior: The Official Publication of the International Academy of Sex Research, 53*(1), 17–24. https://doi.org/10.1007/s10508-023-02723-2

Fine, J. (2023). From crushes to squishes: Affect and agency on r/AskReddit and r/asexual. *Journal of Language and Sexuality, 12*, 145–172. https://doi.org/10.1075/jls.22004.fin

Flanagan, S. K., & Peters, H. J. (2020). Asexual-identified adults: Interactions with health-care practitioners. *Archives of Sexual Behavior, 49*(5), 1631–1643. https://doi.org/10.1007/s10508-020-01670-6

Foster, A. B., Eklund, A., Brewster, M. E., Walker, A. D., & Candon, E. (2019). Personal agency disavowed: Identity construction in asexual women of color. *Psychology of Sexual Orientation and Gender Diversity, 6*(2), 127–137. https://doi.org/10.1037/sgd0000310

Galupo, M. P., Mitchell, R. C., Grynkiewicz, A. L., & Davis, K. S. (2014). Sexual minority reflections on the Kinsey Scale and the Klein Sexual Orientation Grid: Conceptualization and measurement. *Journal of Bisexuality, 14*(3–4), 404–432. https://doi.org/10.1080/15299716.2014.929553

Golden, R. L., & Oransky, M. (2019). An intersectional approach to therapy with transgender adolescents and their families. *Archives of Sexual Behavior, 48*(7), 2011–2025. https://doi.org/10.1007/s10508-018-1354-9

Giammattei, S. V., & Green, R.-J. (2012). LGBTQ couple and family therapy: History & future directions. In J. Bigner & J. Wetchler (Eds.), *Handbook of LGBT-affirmative couple and family therapy* (pp. 1–22). Taylor & Francis.

Glass, V. Q. (2022). Queering relationships: Exploring phenomena of asexual identified persons in relationships. *Contemporary Family Therapy: An International Journal, 44*, 344–359. https://doi.org/10.1007/s10591-022-09650-9

Gupta, K. (2017). "And now I'm just different, but there's nothing actually wrong with me": Asexual marginalization and resistance. *Journal of Homosexuality, 64*, 991–1013. https://doi.org/10.1080/00918369.2016.1236590

Hart-Brinson, P., Tlachac, M. L., & Lepien, E. (2024). Contradictions in experiences of compulsory sexuality and pathways to asexual citizenship. *Sexuality & Culture: An Interdisciplinary Journal, 28*(1), 187–213. https://doi.org/10.1007/s12119-023-10110-1

Herek, G. M., & Garnets, L. D. (2007). Sexual orientation and mental health. *Annual Review of Clinical Psychology, 3*, 353–375. https://doi.org/10.1146/annurev.clinpsy.3.022806.091510

Hille, J. J. (2023). Beyond sex: A review of recent literature on asexuality. *Current Opinion in Psychology, 49*. https://doi.org/10.1016/j.copsyc.2022.101516

Hook, J. N., Davis, D., Owen, J., & DeBlaere, C. (2017). *Cultural humility: Engaging diverse identities in therapy*. American Psychological Association. https://doi.org/10.1037/0000037-000

Lu, R., & Chui, H. (2025). Counseling aces: Experiences of asexual clients in China. *Archives of Sexual Behavior: The Official Publication of the International Academy of Sex Research*, 1–19. https://doi.org/10.1007/s10508-025-03148-9

Lund, E. M., Thomas, K. B., Sias, C. M., & Bradley, A. R. (2016). Examining concordant and discordant sexual and romantic attraction in American adults: Implications for counselors. *Journal of LGBT Issues in Counseling, 10*(4), 211–226. https://doi.org/10.1080/15538605.2016.1233840

MacNeela, P., & Murphy, A. (2015). Freedom, invisibility, and community: A qualitative study of self-identification with asexuality. *Archives of Sexual Behavior, 44*, 799–812. https://doi.org/10.1007/s10508-014-0458-

Mandigo, D. M., & Kavar, L. (2022). The experience of male asexuality: A phenomenological inquiry. *Qualitative Report, 27*(2), 488–508. https://doi.org/10.46743/2160-3715/2022.5213

McGeorge, C. R., Carlson, T. S., & Toomey, R. B. (2015). Assessing lesbian, gay, and bisexual affirmative training in couple and family therapy: Establishing the validity of the faculty version of the affirmative training inventory. *Journal of Marital & Family Therapy, 41*(1), 57–71. https://doi.org/10.1111/jmft.12054

McKinney, R., Desposito, M., & Yoon, E. (2020). Promoting identity wellness in LGBTGEQIAP+adolescents through affirmative therapy. *Journal of LGBT Issues in Counseling, 14*(3), 176–190. https://doi.org/10.1080/15538605.2020.1790464

Moussawi, G., & Vidal-Ortiz, S. (2020). A queer sociology: On power, race, and decentering Whiteness. *Social Forum, 35*, 1272–1289. https://doi.org/10.1111/socf.12647

Murphy, M. J. (2022). Heteronormativity and ethics in the treatment of LGBTQ clients. In R. Harvey, M. J. Murphy, J. J. Bigner, & J. L. Wetchler (Eds.), *Handbook of LGBTQ-Affirmative couple and family therapy* (pp. 45–57). Routledge.

Rock, M., Carlson, T. S., & McGeorge, C. R. (2010). Does affirmative training matter? Assessing CFT students' beliefs about sexual orientation and their level of affirmative training. *Journal of Marital and Family Therapy, 36*(2), 171–184. https://doi.org/10.1111/j.1752-0606.2009.00172.x

Russell, J. (2023). The sex lives of asexuals. In *Erotically queer: A pink therapy guide for practitioners* (pp. 59–74). https://doi.org/10.4324/9781003260608-5

Scherrer, K. S. (2008). Coming to an asexual identity: Negotiating identity, negotiating desire. *Sexualities, 11*(5), 621–641. https://doi.org/10.1177/1363460708094269

Schneckenburger, S. A., Tam, M. W. Y., & Ross, L. E. (2024). Asexual competent practices in healthcare: A narrative review. *Journal of Gay & Lesbian Mental Health, 28*(3), 314–334. https://doi.org/10.1080/19359705.2023.2214528

Singh, P. (2017). A study of trends observed in self-identified 'asexual' people. *Journal of Sexual Medicine, 14*, e302. https://doi.org/10.1016/j.jsxm.2017.04.696

Tessler, H. (2025). Aromanticism, asexuality, and relationship (non-) formation: How a-spec singles challenge romantic norms and reimagine family life. *Sexualities, 28*(1/2), 514–535. https://doi.org/10.1177/13634607231197061

Van Houdenhove, E., Gijs, L., T'Sjoen, G., & Enzlin, P. (2014). Asexuality: Few facts, many questions. *Journal of Sex & Marital Therapy, 40*(3), 175–192. https://doi.org/10.1080/0092623X.2012.751073

Winer, C. (2025). Splitting attraction: Differentiating romantic and sexual orientations among asexual individuals. *Social Currents, 12*(3), 215–230. https://doi.org/10.1177/23294965241305170

Young, E. (2023). *Ace voices: What it means to be asexual, aromantic, demi or grey-ace*. Jessica Kingsley Publishers.

Chapter 2
Asexuality: History, Background, and Contemporary Issues

For many, asexuality is new and obscure. This is hardly the case; asexuality has been historically prevalent, despite the terminology around asexuality being somewhat new. In writing this book or in telling people that I am a researcher of asexuality, I tend to get this glazed-over look from most people and am often curious what they are thinking—are they dismissing asexuality, is it not part of their world, or is it something that they just do not understand? Maybe a little of all of those. I think queer communities do embrace the language and recognize that asexuality is unique. However, many, even in queer communities, do not quite understand what asexuality is all about. I think that many non-asexual people overall struggle to understand what asexuality means and tend to lump it into a category of people who just are not interested in sex.

Not surprisingly, there are a lot of misguided thoughts on asexuality. One research study found that participants were less favorable of people who lack sexual conquest behaviors or flirty behaviors (Bittle & Anderson, 2023)—which could be characteristics of some asexual people. One major finding from this research was that people who chose to be celibate for a period of time were rated higher than those who were not interested in sexual experiences (Bittle & Anderson, 2023). The results of this study noted a bias around the expectations of people feeling sexual regularly. The vast experiences of asexual individuals can be confusing to some allosexuals. Some asexuals are super romantic and yearn for relationships. Some asexuals really enjoy sexual activity. Some asexuals are involved in polyamorous relationships. Some asexuals are part of kink communities. True, some asexuals are not comfortable with sexual relationships or are indifferent to them, and some may not be interested in romantic relationships; however, this is only a sub-set of those who consider themselves under the asexual spectrum.

This chapter will provide discussion on the historical roots of asexuality through mental health and medical research. I will tie in the split attraction model as a key model for considering asexuality and variations of attraction. Finally, I will introduce current global research on asexuality.

V. Q. Glass, *Asexuality, Relationships, and Identity Formation*,
https://doi.org/10.1007/978-3-032-22857-1_2

History

With a lack of language on asexuality throughout history, much of what is presented, prior to labeling asexuality, is theoretical or assumptive. Even without language, asexuality has been present throughout history and labeled or viewed in a variety of ways. Bogaert (2015) surmised some historical (e.g., Emily Bronte, Issac Newton) and fictional (e.g., Sherlock Holmes and Sheldon Cooper from Big Bang Theory) individuals who may have been asexual because of some of their characteristics. These individuals may have led single lives or not been consumed by romantic or sexual thoughts, rather they put their energies into intellect or art.

As a term and orientation, asexuality appears to have evolved from research during the late 1970s and early 1980s (Johnson, 1977; Storms, 1979, 1980). Some of the earliest mentions of asexuality suggest that scientists and theorists were a little puzzled by the idea of "lacking sexual desire" (Johnson, 1977, p. 96). Johnson described, in 1977, that science broadly defined asexuality as "ranging from unexpressed sexuality to the absence of sexual desire" (p. 96). As the evolution of language found its way into science, researchers would notice some differences in sexual attraction, but were a little clunky describing these findings.

In a chapter of the book, *The Sexually Oppressed* (Gochros, & Gochros eds., 1977), Johnson presents a discussion on asexuality that challenges readers to veer away from previously held belief systems around lacking sexual desire that are rooted in either devotion to religion (e.g., celibacy) or as a result of trauma. She also identifies and opposes an undercurrent of social expectations that women experience around sex and sexual expression that are impactful to all people. Her work challenged pathologizing notions of asexuality, and she was committed to questioning social discourses around sexuality.

Storms (1979) was one of the earlier researchers who focused on asexuality. They researched same-sex attraction and integrated asexuality as a description in their findings. Storms researched erotic fantasies of homosexuals (using Storm's word here for those who identify as having same-sex attraction) and heterosexuals. Not surprisingly, they found that homosexuals fantasized about same-sex sexual relationships and heterosexuals fantasized about sex with someone who was not their gender. However, Storms also found a sub-set of people who "scored low on both dimensions" of "heteroeroticism and homoeroticism" (p. 790). They labeled this subset of individuals *asexual*; however, they did not necessarily hypothesize much about these distinctions, they simply expressed their existence.

These early publications are notable in the recognition that there was something different when it came to attraction that was not completely understood by research at that point. Additionally, these theorists and researchers begin to question that humans have one way of feeling sexual attraction. These ideas of asexuality challenged social belief systems and expectations.

Asexuality—Mental Health and Medical Background

I have been in the field of marriage and family therapy for over 25 years. Throughout my professional career, I have attended dozens (maybe hundreds) of conferences and trainings. One thing that I still often hear during discussions on working with couples is the opinion that, in order to be a healthy couple, a particular type and frequency of sexual activity is critical. Sometimes this idea is stated outright, sometimes it is implied. Additionally, there is a sense in couples' work, that if there is a difference in partners when it comes to desire or libido—that the less sexual partner should adapt to meet the sexual needs of the other partner. I find these messages that exist to be really outdated and reflect a one-sided way of looking at relationships and intimacy. Also, I find these messages to promote an oppressive feeling around sex overall that might not have anything to do with a person's asexuality (e.g., a lesser libido or maybe a medical or medicinal shift in desire). Why would we, as relationship therapists, challenge our clients to give up their bodies to meet this socially described script of necessity? There are researched roots in these expectations of sex as critical to happiness; these roots exist in language and social discourse, but also come directly from historical messages in medical and mental health research.

Let's consider historical messages in mental health and the impacts of these on present-day clinical work with asexuals. Maybe a good place to start is the book *Psychopathia Sexualis* by Richard von Krafft-Ebing in the late 1800s (2011). During the late 1800s, there was a growth in medical and research interests around the idea of "sexual deviance" (Federici, 2025, p. 83). von Kraft-Ebing worked in a psychiatric hospital at the time and began researching sexual disorders. Much of what von Krafft-Ebing and other sexologists did at the time was dive into anything related to sex that did not fit the Christian/Westernized idea of what was appropriate. As a result, these foundational studies noted a "deep concern about non procreative sexual practices" (Federici, 2025, p. 87). Any sexual experiences or desires that were not procreative were identified as "mental diseases" (Federici, 2025, p. 87), "pathological" (Federici, 2025, p. 95), or "insane" (Federici, 2025, p. 92). Asexuality, though unlabeled as that at the time, was part of this pathological categorization. von Krafft-Ebing (2011) found ten individuals within his research who were noted as having no sexual desire; he labeled this group of people "anaesthesia sexualis." This lack of sexual desire was considered a dysfunction and a notable medical condition. People who had no desire were seen as mentally defective. Additionally, von Kraft-Ebing discussed possible origins of these "pathological" sexual issues in medical and/or early traumas and also considered ways to fix these "mental diseases."

This leads us to Freud. How could we talk about sexuality and mental health without at least touching on Freud and the impact of some of what Freud theorized has had on sexuality overall? Of course, I say this sort of tongue-in-cheek. However, Freud's psychoanalysis is influential to mental health and continues to impact mental health care and our understanding of mental health to this day. Because asexuality was not a clear concept at the time of Freud, we can only surmise from his other perspectives what he might have said about having a lack of sexual attraction. Freud (1905) pathologized same-sex sexual attraction and blamed this attraction on unconscious unresolved conflicts (e.g., Oedipus Complex) or traumatic events from childhood. Freud seemed to consider homosexuality to be a mechanism of development—a sexually underdeveloped individual (Drescher, 2015). His messages about differences in fantasy, attraction, and sexual experiences are embedded in the recognition that there is only one way to be a human (and that is to be a sexual human) and all variation or deviance from this requires intensive psychoanalysis.

I will go more into the connection between language and identity later in the book, but some of the early sexologists (like von Krafft-Ebing) and early mental health contributors (e.g., Freud) contributed language or deviance that fed into religious persecution of what were identified as pathological sexual issues (Federici, 2025), while also concurrently contributing to the medicalization and treatment of non-procreative sexual practices. These ideas were present in Western medical and psychological paradigms in the early 1900s. The presence of these messages further imposed a sense of morality or sinfulness to certain correct ways and incorrect ways of being sexual (Oosterhuis, 2012). These messages have seeped into the foundational core of current medical and religious communities. In addition, legal systems have created laws and identified crimes based on these different sexual behaviors that are labeled "deviances" or "pathologies."

On a more positive note, the more von Kraft-Ebing dove into the topics of sexual differences, long after his 1886 book was published, he advocated more for those who experienced sex in various ways (Oosterhuis, 2012). He even disagreed with the criminalization of sexual variant behaviors. Despite this, the foundation for the language of pathologizing sexual behaviors had been put into motion. One might also argue that von Kraft-Ebing's work may have concurrently opened the door to future research (e.g., Kinsey) and provided a sense that there was no *one way* to be when it comes to sexual desire.

Let's fast forward from these late 1800s and early 1900s medical and mental health messages and consider the impact of Alfred Kinsey (Kinsey et al., 1948, 1953). In the late 1940s and early 1950s, Kinsey presented research on sexuality in a more objective and less pathologizing way (Brown & Fee, 2003; Bullough, 1998). He attempted to provide a biological basis for sexuality that was not connected to moralism, psychological, or unconscious roots (Brown & Fee, 2003; Kinsey et al., 1948, 1953).

One of Kinsey's major contributions was the development of the Kinsey sexual orientation scale (Kinsey et al., 1948, 1953). This is a 0–6 point scale of sexual orientation. Kinsey felt that 10% of the population fell into an "exclusively homosexual" (a "O" on the scale) and 10% were "exclusively heterosexual" (a "6" on the scale) and everyone else fit somewhere on a continuum of "varying levels of same- and other-sex attraction and sexual behavior" (Galupo et al., 2014, p. 409) (or 1–5 on the scale). The reason that this scale is of specific importance to asexuality is that Kinsey noted there were people who did not fit in the scale because they lacked sexual attraction, he labeled these individuals as "nonsexual" and created a category he called "X" to define these individuals. His research noted that about 1.5% of his participants fell into this category (Kinsey et al., 1948). This might be the first time asexuality was noted as a specific orientation of sorts in modern day science.

Not having lived in the 1950s, my vision of that time is likely skewed by my parents' recounting of their memories and watching 1950s sitcom re-runs. I can only imagine the impact of Kinsey's research overall during that time. Sexuality at that time was riddled with expectations and morality—that really discounted biological perspectives. Kinsey opened a door to looking at differences in sexual attraction that could be viewed in less pathological ways. I can only imagine the parents in *Leave it to Beaver* or the *Father Knows Best* family contributing to the expectations around sexual behavior that both were secretive and indirect, but also, likely supported this idea that there was one healthy way to approach sexuality (hcteronormative, only in marriage, and meeting male/husband needs).

In many ways, much of our medical and mental health fields are still stuck in the early Freudian or von Kraft-Ebing theoretical versions of sexuality. And, to say the least, religions (most notably Christian religions) have fed back into these early theories in a cyclical pattern of identifying normal versus abnormal, while putting abnormal in a category that equates with sinful behaviors that must be controlled. Thankfully, this pattern of creating pathologies around sexual attractions, desires, and intimacies has led to the unfolding of language and science that labels and ultimately embraces these differences in sexuality. I feel like this movement has allowed asexuals (and other queer people) to better understand themselves and hope for a future unraveling of our understanding of asexual identities through visibility and education.

Diagnostic and Statistical Manual

I feel this could not be a book for practicing practitioners if I didn't jump in and talk a little about the impact of the DSM (Diagnostic and Statistical Manual) (American Psychiatric Association, 1952, 1980, 1987, 1994, 2000, 2013, 2022) on queer communities. The DSM is a tool still commonly used by mental health professionals to diagnose mental illness. The DSM has been utilized in the mental health fields to separate normal mental health from abnormal mental health. In fact, insurance companies often will not pay for mental health services unless a person somehow fits into the abnormal diagnostic category based on the DSM. The DSM is a tool that categorizes and defines mental health, emotional health, and learning differences. For mental health professionals, those with mental health issues, school systems, workplace environments, family, friends, and well, anyone—these categorizations can be helpful to understanding the common ways people might experience certain diagnoses. A DSM diagnosis can lead to evidence-based tools for helping people achieve success as they navigate possible challenges. I think in an ideal world, the DSM would provide language that people could try on as a way of understanding themselves or helping others to understand them. The problem, as I see it, is that the

DSM has led to major pathologizing and furthering that understanding of normal and abnormal—and can get these things incorrect (particularly when it comes to sexuality and identity), because in reality, we all live in a spectrum of experiences.

Here is an example of what I mean. On the one hand, you could have a person who has struggled all of their life feeling sad and empty. They share their struggle to find joy in any activity and wish they could just sleep all the time. Maybe they would get a diagnosis of depression from the DSM (American Psychiatric Association, 2022) and feel a sense of relief. This finally gives them an understanding to why they have been feeling the way they have. They can start to see what has helped others in their situation and maybe the language around depression is something that they own and understand about themselves as they navigate their future. On the other hand, this diagnosis of depression could lead to other things—maybe an internal deepening of not feeling "good enough" because the person does not see their way out of it, maybe there is a stigmatization of those in the medical field that cause them to dismiss some of their issues, maybe family and friends see them as weak or abnormal and this can cause isolation or feelings of inadequacy. Certainly, there are advantages and disadvantages to labels. None-the-less, the DSM is widely used in all mental health fields and has been highly regarded as a top-notch, research-based diagnostic tool.

I have seen parts of the evolution of the DSM over the last 3–4 decades and the impacts of creating pathologizing diagnoses on queer people (American Psychiatric Association, 1952, 1980, 1987, 1994, 2000, 2013, 2022). I will take a little bit of book space here to talk about the history of the DSM, in particular, the pathologizing of queer people, and then circle back around to asexuality and how the DSM can impact those who may be asexual.

In 1952, when the DSM was first published, "homosexuality" was listed as a "sociopathic personality disturbance" (as cited in McHenry, 2022, p. 2). In this version of the DSM some other sociopathic personality disturbances that were lumped together with homosexuality (under the broader category of "sexual deviation") (American Psychiatric Association, 1952, p. 38) were antisocial reaction, dissocial reaction, sexual deviation, and drug addiction (American Psychiatric Association, 1952). Additionally, homosexual was under the sub-category of sexual deviation with also included "transvestism, pedophilia, fetishism, and sexual sadism (including rape, sexual assault, and mutilation)" (American Psychiatric Association, 1952, p. 39). I can clearly see the lingering links to these lumped together categories creating fear and stigma toward queer persons in our present-day Western world, language is powerful. It is not uncommon to hear some politicians and public figures fearfully describe transgender individuals going into bathrooms and arguing that this will cause sexual assault. The foundation of connecting gender and sexual diversity in with pedophilia and rape is DSM language that has been hard to shake.

In the 1950s, during these early versions of the DSM, the era in the United States that embraced the nuclear family ideal and was shocked at Kinsey, seemed to comfortably embrace that homosexuality was something scary and wrong within a person. There are videos from the 1950s out there, for example, *Boys Beware* (Sid Davis Productions) that were designed to present education to coming-of-age young men in the 1950s about the "dangers" of "homosexuality." In this particular video, a young teen is stalked by a gay man, making the gay man out to be a predator. The message to young men was to avoid homosexuality at all costs. I am imagining the DSM I (American Psychiatric Association, 1952) fed into this cycle of fear (impacting legal standards and persecution) and still exists as an undercurrent in many Western communities despite efforts to change these stigmas.

Between 1952 and 1973, homosexuality (and transvestitism) remained under this umbrella term of personality disorders (Drescher, 2015; McHenry, 2022). In the early 1970s, queer activists protested and disrupted meetings of the American Psychiatric Association (APA). They argued that much of the classifications in the DSM did not take into account science, like Kinsey's study, which considered sexual orientations as natural variants among humans. The DSM was blamed in part for the hostile climate toward queer people (Drescher, 2015). Additionally, a group of individuals within the American Psychiatric Association fought for and challenged this classification of homosexuality, stating that "homosexuality is a normal variant of human sexuality" (APA document, n.d., p. 1). Despite much resistance in the APA, homosexuality was removed as a pathologized mental health condition in 1973, and homosexuality was defined as only being a pathologized condition if a person wanted to change their orientation (Drescher, 2015). Hectors (2023) described, "the official story of homosexuality's departure from the DSM is one of science advancement, social consciousness and normalization" (p. 19).

The shift in language that happened in the DSM began a social construction process in many Western countries that impacted legal/criminal laws, laws protecting queer people in work and school settings, militaries began opening up to out queer members, laws around marriage and family rights shifted, even religious institutions have shifted their perspectives in some areas (Drescher, 2015). But this shift in what is pathologized and what is not in terms of sexual orientation and gender identity is still occurring (I would argue especially for asexuals, but we will get to that in a minute). Keep in mind, gender identity disorder is still under the DSM in the current version (Drescher, 2023). The DSM IV TR, the current version of the DSM, suggests gender dysphoria has a pathological connection to childhood trauma and reflects a sense of rigidity in gender roles that—anything outside of that—is a "disorder" (Hectors, 2023). Additionally, critics of the categorization of the DSM and queer identities state that gender and sexuality disorders in the current DSM rely "on uniform and normalized notions of gender and sexuality" (Hectors, 2023, p. 25).

Asexuality and the DSM Do medical and mental health professionals sometimes view asexual experiences as pathological or a mental or physical health concern? You bet! This view is prevalent, and, in my own research, many asexual participants shared stories about physicians or therapists urging them to seek medical treatment or invalidating asexuals' experiences as real. Officially, asexuality has been removed as a disorder in the current DSM; however, the DSM houses a lot of language that can be applied to asexual experiences, that, one would argue, might get in the way of practitioners helping clients become aware of asexuality as a way to describe what they feel.

In earlier versions of the DSM (prior to DSM V), a labeled sexual dysfunction was hypoactive sexual desire disorder (HSDD) (Bogaert, 2006). HSDD still exists as a diagnostic category in the current International Classification of Diseases (ICD 11), the major medical diagnostic guidebook. This diagnosis is defined by a lack of sexual interest or desire and noted medical problems (e.g., medication, hormone issues, menopause, etc.) as contributing to HSDD. Despite the clinical language shift in the present DSM, this terminology is still used in clinical and medical research. Not surprisingly, this research rarely mentions asexuality as a possibility and describes everything from medication fixes (Barakeh et al., 2025; de Oliveira et al., 2024), sex therapy (Tetik & Yalcinkaya Alkar, 2023), sex education (Luo et al., 2023), and counseling (Kingsberg & Simon, 2020) as ways to aid one with this "condition."

In the DSM V, HSDD has shifted in language to *sexual dysfunction* (American Psychiatric Association, 2022; Hinderliter, 2015). Two categories of sexual dysfunction that specifically evolved from HSDD are *female sexual interest/arousal disorder* and *male hypoactive sexual desire disorder*. In the DSM V and the DSM V TR, buried in deep among the criteria for *female sexual interest/arousal disorder* is the statement:

> Distress may be experienced as a result of the lack of sexual interest/arousal or as a result of significant interference in a woman's life and well-being. If a lifelong lack of sexual desire is better explained by one's self-identification as 'asexual,' then a diagnosis of female sexual interest/arousal disorder would not be made (American Psychiatric Association, 2022).

Additionally, the DSM V TR has a statement about *male hypoactive sexual desire disorder*, "if the man's low desire is explained by self-identification as an asexual, then a diagnosis of male hypoactive sexual desire disorder is not made" (American Psychiatric Association, 2022). I am pleased that the language of asexuality has been addressed here; however, I do not feel research has caught up with the distinction between asexuality and genuine HSDD. I find it especially interesting that you can do a quick research glance at any of these sexual disorders and find a tremendous amount of research that considers the origins of these sexual dysfunctions and the researched methods for aiding in these dysfunctions with very little (if any) acknowledgment of asexuality as a possibility. Additionally, this research on sexual dysfunction takes an allo-centric approach—essentially, providing the message that anything that is a barrier to sexual arousal, sexual relationships, or sexual attraction is important to tackle and solve. Furthermore, these diagnostic categories can leave out intersex, nonbinary, and transgender experiences—as they only consider the gender binary in the two disorders.

So, what is the line? According to the classifications and the definitions, even with the inclusion statement of asexuality, based on the imposed DSM definitions, it is difficult to differentiate between what is a dysfunction and what is not in terms of the DSM's classification of sexual desire (Hinderliter, 2015). Research does indicate that in order for asexuality to be considered a mental health issue is if it causes "clinically significant personal distress" (Brotto & Yule, 2017, p. 621). Most asexuals report they do not feel a sense of distress about their lack of sexual attraction, particularly once they have located language and understanding (Brotto et al., 2010). This understanding of self is unlike those with labeled sexual dysfunctions that often report distress.

All this to say, current research does indicate that asexuals (along with other sexual and gender minorities) do experience minority stress that can impact their mental health (Chan & Leung, 2023). A global research study on the impact of minority stress on asexuals found that 2/3 of asexuals reported experiencing minority stress. Some experiences included "verbal aggression," "inappropriate personal questions," "attempts or suggestions to 'fix' and 'cure' them," and "verbal harassment" (Chan & Leung, 2023, p. 801). Minority stress can impact a person's physical and mental health, as well as their interpersonal relationships. Some research has noted that there could be slight differences in depression and anxiety among asexuals when compared to heterosexuals (Yule et al., 2013). We could surmise that this increase in depression and anxiety could be related to minority stress, inclusive of challenges asexuals might face navigating their identity uniquenesses in an allosexual world. The larger picture when it comes to the DSM classifications for gender and sexual minorities has led to statements like "being gay is not the issue, but the stress a person receives from being teased is" or "being transgender is not the pathology, it is the dysphoria that can come from how people around the person are treating them." In the end, the DSM, which is designed to categorize, label, define, and describe mental health, has a strong historical presence in current Western culture. The impacts and the evolution of language around certain uniquenesses can be both liberating and confining.

Biological Research

Mental health and medical health are often intertwined when it comes to research. The medical community has been quick to label a lack of sex drive, lack of desire, or lack of sexual attraction as a medical issue (Bogaert, 2015). Research on sexual dysfunction in medical fields seeks out a solution, the quick fix, the medication, or surgery that will solve these "sexual problems." I will present a short history of some of the medical research that has been done in this area, not to further stigmatize asexuals or to even suggest that variations in desire are inherently an illness—but to share what is out there that practitioners or medical professionals still often lean on. Creating a dialog about what asexuality *IS* can arise from what it *IS NOT*. I think that there is a huge space for education and competency in asexuality in both medical and mental health fields that is not met. My purpose of diving into this research is to share the atmosphere around differences in sexual arousal, sexual attraction, and sexual interest that fall back on medicalized care rather than seeing the bigger picture.

Medical research over the last 50–75 years has presented one perspective on normal and abnormal sexuality. Much of the present-day research is rooted in some of the assumptions made by Masters and Johnson's (1966) research. Masters and Johnson completed a large-scale study that measured sexual arousal, orgasm, and response.

This study introduced a sexual response cycle that included excitement, plateau, orgasm, and resolution. In contrast, this research labeled anything that did not fit this sexual response cycle as *sexual dysfunction* or *abnormal*. On the one hand, this pivotal work increased the awareness of biology and science as it pertains to sexual functioning; it also suggested that any variation was pathological and even critical to overcome.

The medical field continues to identify medical issues with sexual functioning as "dysfunctions" that occur in each of the stages that were identified by Masters and Johnson. Medical disorders in sexuality are labeled in the arousal stage of functioning, the orgasmic stage, and the resolution. The most commonly noted sexual dysfunctions are low sexual desire (39% of those with sexual dysfunction), sexual arousal (26%), and orgasm challenges (21%) (Gari et al., 2020). Many individuals experience great distress and are impacted by sexual dysfunctions that are medically relevant. Some causes of sexual dysfunctions can include certain diseases, certain medications, fluctuations in hormones, pain, and mental health. It is possible that an asexual person could have sexual dysfunctions (at the same rate as allosexual persons). In one study, for example, 86.5% of asexuals reported they had no difficulties with sex or sexual functioning (Milani et al., 2023). Asexuality is not a sexual dysfunction, and yet medical fields may commonly dismiss patient experiences as a sexual dysfunction when they hear something like "I am not experiencing arousal" or "I am not interested in sexual relationships," which may not be at all medical related.

Two commonly discussed sexual disorders that are sometimes inappropriately considered or applied to asexuals are female sexual dysfunction and male sexual dysfunction (SAID). In my research for this book, I encountered study after study that used language that could incorrectly lump asexuals into serious medical conditions if the medical professional was unaware of asexuality. For example, the first couple of sentences of a 2025 research study stated:

> Impairments in sexual desire and arousal are some of the most common health concerns, reported by up to a third of women. When these impairments are long-lasting and significantly distressing, they can constitute Female Sexual Interest/Arousal Disorder (SIAD)...Problems with low desire are associated with a range of negative conditions including relationship distress and low quality of life. Given the prevalence and potential impact of SIAD, efficacious interventions are needed (Mahar et al., 2025, p. 188).

This type of discussion around sexual interest and arousal is typical in the medical and mental health literature. I am clearly aware that sexual disorders do exist and are very real things for many individuals. That being said, I cannot help but look at this paragraph and note the strong language around the urgency and distressing nature of lacking sexual desire. I am also aware that many asexuals have experiences with medical professionals putting these sexual dysfunction labels on them. The aforementioned study does not even discuss asexuality as an option or possibility in gathering participants or in their findings; this seems to be common in sexual dysfunction research. I will mention that this study utilized a CBT tool to help women and noted that these tools lessened the participants' sense of distress around sexual experiences.

The causes of SIAD are explored throughout research—e.g., sleep (Andersen & Tufik, 2025), thyroid issues (Salari et al., 2024), diabetes (Msolly et al., 2025), eating disorders (Hess & Spacirova, 2025), trauma (Weiss et al., 2023), and menopause (Jahangirlfar et al., 2023). It is not that this research is not important to many women; however, the lack of attention to distinguishing asexuality from these research samples or focusing on asexuality in the discussion or findings could lead to biases among medical professionals who may encounter a patient who says, "I am just not interested in sex." Rather than evolving the conversation into exploring asexuality as a possible sexual orientation, medical professionals might be quick to consider what they are saying as a disorder and dismiss or even pathologize what a person's experience is.

Interestingly, some research tackles the differences in asexuality as a sexual orientation and sexual dysfunctions. Brotto and Yule (2017) researched asexuals and compared their experiences to allosexual individuals who reported "low desire" (on the sexual dysfunction scale)—and found some key variations. Asexuals were more likely to have engaged in sexual activities and to have an active fantasy life than those allosexuals who had "low desire." Additionally, those with "low desire" rated higher in distress measures than asexuals.

I had a participant, an asexual, sex indifferent, woman who was 53 at the time of the interview describe that she did not find the label of asexuality until the age of 46. She is in a marriage of 25 years. Prior to locating the label of asexual, she described herself as "being performative" and stated, "I carried a lot of rage." It impacted her marriage, her own sense of guilt and shame, and was just overwhelming to her not understanding what was going on and why she had such a different experience in her sexual life. She often stressed throughout the interview the importance of education for medical and mental health professionals so that those younger asexuals can figure things out much sooner. She stated she hopes for more asexual visibility…

> …mostly so that young people know that (they) can look at that as something they can explore as they are trying to figure themselves out to see if it fits. I certainly would have appreciated that as a young person…I really want young people to know they can go into adulthood with open eyes and not hurt themselves the way I hurt myself.

She stated that her relationship and her personal identity are stronger after figuring out her identity and making peace with it.

This participant did not go into her medical background; however, I can only infer that her sexual desires and attraction were not discussed with physicians, or they never suggested asexuality as an option. The lack of knowledge and awareness in medical communities is something that would benefit other asexuals coming through medical or mental health care.

Are Asexuals Biologically or Genetically Different?

I mentioned earlier that research on asexuality seems to suggest no differences in sexual functioning when compared to allosexuals (Brotto & Yule 2017; Van Houdenhove et al., 2014). Research has started to take a stab at some of the genetic or biological differences between asexuals and allosexuals. This is an area of research (much like research on genetic differences with other sexual orientations) that I feel is limited and difficult to make any assumptions about at this point. But I will present a little on what is out there.

In one study on visual preferences, researchers examined how asexual and allosexual people responded to faces (Edge & Vonk, 2024). They found that, overall, asexual people (of all genders) favor more "feminine looking" faces of people of all genders (Edge et al., 2024). These researchers hypothesized that this might be related to social messages in society that suggest more masculinized individuals are equated with being more sexual. Though this is just a theory based on the results, the study does leave the door open to inherent and distinct differences in allosexual and asexual people.

Another study used eye-tracking testing and found that allosexuals look at erotic images for much longer periods of time than asexual people (with allosexual people gazing at these images for about five times longer than asexual people) (Milani et al., 2023). Bradshaw et al. (2021) found similar results; they examined eye gazing of women when shown erotic and neutral images. Participants were in two groups—asexuals and those who have been diagnosed with Sexual Interest/Arousal Disorder. They noted that asexual women looked at erotic images for less time than allosexual (diagnosed with Sexual Interest/Arousal Disorder) women. These research studies suggest a clear difference between asexuality and a medically noted disorder.

There is research support that indicates that sexual attraction and romantic attraction are distinct ways of viewing the world and play a role in how people pick partners (Scheller et al., 2024). An asexual individual is less likely than an allosexual person to place emphasis on a particular type of appearance or on sexual compatibility. Results suggest that visual attraction can play a role in allosexuals' decision to partner with a person and maybe this is not something that asexuals consider in the same way.

One research study looked at arousal in male participants. Skorska et al. (2023) found that when cisgender males were presented with erotic images, asexual males experienced less arousal than allosexual males (using a penile plethysmograph that measures penial arousal). Interestingly, this same study found that asexual and allosexual males have similar arousal levels when it comes to sexual fantasy. This could support the idea that asexuality is more about a lack of visual sexual attraction and less about desire to engage in sexual experiences.

Yule et al. (2014) found that more asexuals were left-handed. Additionally, these researchers found a correlation between asexuality and where a person falls in birth order (e.g., the more older siblings, the more of a likelihood a person was asexual).

Again, these findings are preliminary to theoretical guesses around the genetic variability that can exist with sexual orientations.

One area of research regarding asexual sexuality was exploring reasons for self-pleasure. In a research study on masturbation that compared asexuals and allosexuals, a couple of distinctions have been noted (Yule et al., 2017). Asexuals often report slightly different reasons for masturbation than allosexuals. For example, allosexuals report more fantasy or arousal to visual cues as reasons for masturbation, whereas asexuals more commonly report tension release, relaxation, or just boredom as common reasons for masturbation (Bogaert, 2015; Yule et al., 2017). That being said, research in this area is limited, and I fear jumping into bias when I recognize the variability of asexuality.

Other research looked at fantasy and the unique differences among asexuals when it comes to fantasizing. Asexuals typically fantasize less than allosexuals (about half of reported numbers from allosexuals) (Yule et al., 2017). Research noted that among asexuals, 80% of men and 65% of women report engaging in fantasy, which is less frequent than allosexual counterparts. Asexuals are less likely that allosexuals to have fantasies be individual focused or visual focused (e.g., the sex appeal of another person) and, at times, more focused on romantic activities (kissing, cuddling, etc.). Also, in another research study, asexual women were less likely to experience arousal from erotic images (Brotto & Yule, 2011).

It is critical to note that all of these body reactions and biological differences that have evolved in the research also indicate a spectrum of experiences and behaviors within asexuals (Bogaert, 2015; Brotto & Yule, 2017; Yule et al., 2017; Van Houdenhove et al., 2014). I would caution anyone at this point to make bold assumptions around any of this research. As practitioners, communicating and listening to clients and diving into their perspectives and experiences is still key to understanding.

Another area of focus in some asexual research explores connections between autism and asexuality. Anecdotally, in neurodivergent groups and in asexual groups, the topic of the connection between neurodivergence and asexuality is frequently brought up. There is speculation that there is a link; however, scientifically, this link has not been uncovered. Some asexual researchers note that it seems many of their participants noted neurodivergent identities; however, it is speculative (not scientific) that there is a connection. Given the spectrum of autistic traits and the spectrum of asexual identities, not to mention the lack of genetic or biological research on these two areas make a clear connection inconclusive. In my own research, I have found that many of my asexual participants (about 50%) have self-reported autism and/or neurodivergence.

Some research has directly addressed the connection between autism and asexuality (Attanasio et al., 2022; Bush et al., 2021; Chan & Hung, 2025; Ramirez et al., 2024; Ronis et al., 2021). Chan and Hung (2025) found in a group of 10,419 asexual participants, about 34% identified possible autism (7% diagnoses, 9% self-diagnosed, and 18% who considered they might be autistic). Given these self-reported responses, this rate of autism in asexuality is much higher than autism in the larger population (which is reported to be about 1%). Additionally, this study found that autistic asexuals were more likely to label themselves as aromantic than non-autistic asexuals. Ronis et al. (2021) found that about 5% of people on the autism spectrum also self-identified as asexual. Additionally, some research suggests that some of the elements of autism, for example, difficulty in social interactions and differences in how they view emotional interactions, could lead to an incorrect identification as asexual (Ramirez et al., 2024). Overall, research in the area of the connection between autism and asexuality has been variable and inconclusive (Attansio et al. 2022; Bush et al., 2021). But, I would argue, still an interesting thing to consider.

Split Attraction Model

In Chap. 1, the split attraction model was defined. I will continue to build on this idea because I believe parceling out sexual and romantic attractions has been especially validating for many asexuals. Here, I will touch on the current research that supports the idea of the split attraction model and how it can be a way to describe the experiences of all people. Just a quick reminder of the split (romantic and sexual) and the meanings of these.

Romantic Attraction

Tessler (2025) stated,

> Romantic attraction can be defined by physiological responses such as 'butterflies in the stomach' or the idea that 'I can't get them out of my mind,' but can also be defined using cultural scripts such as wanting to go on a date with someone or envisioning a future married life with that person (p. 515).

When I think about romantic attraction, I think about myself and the gitty feelings that I sometimes get thinking about a particular person. That excitement I feel thinking about holding their hand or snuggled on the couch together. I think that yearning in the stomach feeling for a romantic dinner, a marriage proposal, a wedding day fantasy, or even smiling at thinking about spending old age together can fit under this idea. Many asexuals (not all) feel a sense of romantic attraction despite not really experiencing sexual attraction.

Sexual Attraction

Sexual attraction is a key word or assumption that differentiates many asexuals, as asexuality is defined by experiencing little or no sexual attraction (Tessler, 2025). Sexual attraction is a sense of desire that one feels for another person (Winer, 2025). For most allosexuals there is no distinction between sexual and romantic attractions—for example, an allosexual person may experience sexual and romantic attraction with the same person at the same time, not really differentiating the differences in the moment.

Research on Split Attraction

When you think about someone you care about or love in non-romantic and non-sexual ways, this could be a friend, family member, or partner. Think for a moment about all the pieces of that relationship that lead to your feelings for them. For example, I have a teenaged daughter, my feelings run really deep for her and if I start to parcel it out, I can think of so many facets that create that connection (or feeling of love). I enjoy her intellect and how she looks at the world. I think she is an aesthetically beautiful person and admire her beauty, she creates and I am drawn to her artistic endeavors. There is a maternal/nurturing side of me that feels like I am in her corner at all times. I like how she challenges my brain. I could go on forever, but my point is that there are people in our world that we have feelings for (that are not romantic or sexual in nature) that we can highlight all these multiple ways we love them. Love is not just one thing and does not look one way. If I think of other people I love, I would have possibly very different ideas, for example, maybe I love a person because of the humor and laughter we share. Or, I may love a person because of their ability to solve analytical problems.

So, let's throw into this equation the idea of relationships. If you have been in a romantic relationship or partnership before where love was part of this relationship, think through the aspects of this relationship that drew you to it. You might say something like "oh my gosh, when I saw him, I thought—he is so hot!" or "there was a night where she kissed me under the moonlight and I fell for her" or "when I really need a shoulder to cry on, they are there for me" or "we just have so much fun together" or "sexually, we just connect, and it is so comfortable" or "their deep brown eyes just pull me in"—on and on…think about what your brain is saying as you read this about any past relationships that you might have had.

This whole set up to say—look at ALL the ways we experience and get gratification from all relationships! Even if we focus on partnerships or romantic relationships, it is likely that people love each other for so many different reasons that are not just sexual. Research has evolved to identify unique experiences of attraction. In many psychology and sociology courses, Sternberg's Love Triangle theory (Sternberg, 1997) is taught. This theory describes three parts of (romantic) attraction: intimacy, passion, and commitment. Sternberg also identified that romantic love begins with a more passionate connection, and this leads to a more romantic committed ("companionate") connection as time progresses in the relationship. Sternberg did not necessarily parcel out these terms as he considered all these forms of love to be within the person feeling them. I think research on split attraction takes some of these ideas a step further by recognizing types of attractions and the way people feel differs from one person to the next.

As research has evolved on asexuals, what seems to be common is the idea that there are different ways to view attraction and relationships. Scherrer (2008) identified that asexuals feel and experience sex and attraction very differently; some may be more interested in romance, others might experience sexual attraction in some circumstances. Winer (2025) explored the split attraction model and the experiences of 77 asexual participants. They found that many asexuals (68 out of the 77 participants) fully integrated some of the language of the split attraction model into their asexual identity. For example, a participant might say, "I am an aromantic asexual" (e.g., no sexual or romantic attraction) or "I am a heteromantic asexual" (e.g., they have romantic attraction toward a person of a different gender, but not sexual attraction), or "I am a panromatic demisexual" (a person with romantic attraction to all genders, but only experiences sexual attraction when there is a deep bond formed). The combinations are endless here, but they certainly provide internal insight and language to use with potential partners.

The split attraction model can be applied to both allosexual and asexual individuals. An allosexual person, for example, may experience sexual attraction and romantic attraction to women, but also report romantic attraction toward men and nonbinary individuals. Or maybe a person only experiences sexual attraction and not romantic attraction. 99.1% of allosexuals in one study reported having a romantic orientation (Clark & Zimmerman, 2022). Clark and Zimmerman (2022) did a research study comparing allosexual and asexual individuals on sexual attraction and romantic attraction. Their research highlighted that, of allosexuals, 82% were sex favorable and 89% had romantic attraction. This compares 37% of asexuals who reported they were sex favorable and experienced romantic attraction.

Tessler (2025) explored the nature of sexual and romantic attraction among asexuals and how these parts of their identity inform their connections, partnering, and/or relationships. Tessler noted a theme of "untangling sex, romance, and family" (p. 526) where participants presented their perspectives on relationships and how these can vary depending on an persons' romantic or sexual attractions. For example, an alloromantic asexual may seek out a romantic relationship, or an aromantic asexual may define family as a connection to a QPR.

Summary

I would like to think that the movement toward research on split attraction and some of those inherent differences that people experience overall will continue to prosper. I think, when it comes to gender and sexual orientation, most of the research has led to the idea that there is only one way to experience things and everything else must be a problem. When I think of research history, I think—wow, something to build on! I can feel a sense of pride in knowing that Kinsey's or Masters and Johnson's research has created language and conversation that has moved the mental health field and the medical field into new places. I do see that our medical and mental health fields are steeped in allosexual norms and expectations. These messages impact those of all sexual orientations and can present a difficult environment for asexuals to learn about who they are separate for a sexual norm that is labeled as one healthy way to experience sexual attraction, arousal, and intimacy.

A Global Perspective

I want to add some relevant research directions. As I mentioned at the start of this book, so much of the research on asexuality is written by White, Western researchers, and most participants seem to be White and from Western cultures. I did want to take a little space here and share some of the research that has been growing recently in other communities and cultures. There are a couple of research studies on asexuality that highlight asexual experiences in non-Western communities; these are sparse; however, I feel they are especially notable. Because there is little research outside Westernized perspectives, taking a glance into this research provides a slightly different perspective. There are a great deal of findings within these studies that mirror Western research on asexuals, with some differentiations. There are three studies that I want to highlight, one study from China (Lu & Chui, 2025), one study from India (Agrawal et al., 2025), and another study from South Korea (An & Kim 2024).

Lu and Chui (2025)

Lu and Chui (2025) explored counseling experiences of Chinese asexuals. Their research highlighted some possible contextual elements of asexuals living in Chinese communities. The authors discuss obligatory feelings and social messages around getting married and having children that exist in Chinese cultures. This sense of obligation is connected to philosophical messages of passing down one's bloodline and building on genetic family expectations. Chinese culture is rooted in collectivism, and part of this value includes preserving cultural elements and historical presence. Lu and Chui discussed the possibility that those who do not fit these cultural expectations of family could risk disappointment or even being disowned by family. These expectations led Lu and Chui to consider the mental health of asexual Chinese participants—specifically how they report navigating their asexual identity in the midst of cultural expectations and what engagement in mental health services might look like.

To answer these questions, Lu and Chui interviewed 10 Chinese asexuals using a phenomenological lens. Thematic findings included:

(a) "Identity exploration" (p. 2220)—participants discussed *ah-ha* moments of discovery when locating the language of asexuality.
(b) "Identity negotiation" (p. 2220)—participants were challenged with knowing this part of who they are, feeling good about it, and balancing that with disclosure and the impact of that disclosure.
(c) Seeking mental health services—why and how participants sought services.
(d) "Satisfying experiences in counseling" (p. 2223)—these included openness of clinician, non-judgment, empathy, awareness of identity formation, and how this was helpful in asexual identity development.
(e) "Unsatisfying experiences in counseling" (p. 2223)—these included lack of awareness (of asexuality), lack of willingness to understand asexuality, and counselor microaggressive moments or insensitivity.

On the one hand, some of these findings (which I will explore in more depth in future chapters) mirror some of the experiences of asexuals in Western research studies. Lu and Chui explain that the added challenges of being in a collectivist culture can be impactful to those of all minority sexual orientations. Part of being in collectivist communities includes a sense of conformity and an expectation of individuals to meet community expectations. These added components should be considerations of clinicians who are working with these identity intersections.

Agrawal, Shainy, Sebastian, Srivastava, and Scoats (2025)

Agrawal et al. (2025) explored the phenomenon of participants in India who identified as sex-favorable asexuals. The research goal was to better understand asexuals' relationship with sexual activity and sexual desire. The authors discussed an atmosphere of discreetness and negative constructs around sex and sexuality in India that can impact sexual identity overall. Additionally, those of sexual and gender minorities in India are often faced with discrimination in health care. The authors noted that asexuality is not a well-known orientation in India, making it challenging for those who may be experiencing that sense of being different that many asexuals feel, but not having the language or connection to community to validate those feelings.

The research highlighted sexual pleasure, specifically among Indian asexuals (Agrawal et al). There were 15 participants interviewed for this research study. The researchers sought an understanding of how Indian sex-favorable asexuals perceive both self-pleasuring activities and sexual activities with partners. Some of the findings from this research included:

(a) Asexuals defined their interest in sexual activity with partners despite not experiencing sexual attraction. Participants shared a biological desire and/or an emotional bond in sexual activity that was not based on visual attraction.
(b) Asexuals experienced an identity process. Participants noted early in life that they felt different from peers when it came to sexual attraction. These differences led them to explore these nuances in their identity and consider the terminology of asexual.
(c) Asexual participants experienced both "extrinsic and intrinsic" (p. 9) factors that were related to sexual experiences with partners. These could include feelings of peer pressure, societal pressure, or even wanting to feel close to a partner.
(d) Asexual participants reported that, at times, they left sexual experiences with partners with feelings of discomfort.
(e) Asexual participants varied in self-pleasure activities. Some participants did engage in self-pleasuring and noted biological drives, stress relief, and body comfort as leading to self-pleasuring. Some participants shared they had little interest in self-pleasure.
(f) Asexual participants discussed allonormative messages that led to their expectations that romance and sexual relationships would make them feel like "a complete person" (p. 11). However, the participants had struggled with not identifying with what they felt was expected.

The authors discussed the importance of cultural context in the lives of their participants. One finding specifically seemed relevant to Indian cultural contexts. Participants often shared (in fact, authors note all participants indicated this) that sex was something that was "happening to them" (p. 15). I will discuss some aspects of consent in Western culture later in this book; however, it is notable that this language used by Indian asexuals may have different roots and expectations than those of asexuals in Western cultures. This idea of consent and asexuality would be interesting to flesh out from multiple cultural perspectives.

An and Kim (2024)

The final study I would like to call attention to here is a study from South Korea (An & Kim, 2024). The researchers explored asexuality in South Koreans and considered cultural context. The authors present contextual variables of sexual minorities in South Korea, stating the Confucianism sets a background around specific family structures that are acceptable (e.g., heterosexual marriage with a focus on passing down genetic lineage). Additionally, sexual orientations, other than heterosexual, are often discriminated against in South Korean communities. Conversations in public around sex and sexual orientations are frowned upon. These messages leave a lot of Korean people who identify as sexual and gender minorities struggling with legal protections, harassment, discrimination, and mental health challenges.

Researchers noted one of the prevailing reasons for their research project was to build visibility of asexuality in South Korea—being that asexual research is mostly on asexuals in Westernized countries, asexual experiences in other areas contribute to a deeper invisibility.

The purpose of An and Kim's research was to explore specific stressors of asexuals in South Korea. The researchers used consensual qualitative research for their analysis. Participants in this study included 12 adult asexuals who grew up in South Korea. Some of the findings mirror findings in Western research on asexuality. South Korean asexual participants mentioned some social expectations and standards that imply marriage and sexuality that they found stressful and challenging. The authors hypothesize that allornomativity is pervasive across the globe and plays a major role in asexuals' understanding of self and navigating their identities in allonormative environments.

What differs in An and Kim's research was that South Korean asexual participants reported a sense of invisibility that might be more profound than those in Western cultures. This invisibility might be due to language differences. The authors note that "sexuality" does not translate the same in Korean—leaving it difficult to translate "asexuality" in a meaningful and resonating way. Additionally, even when asexual South Koreans do research and understand the construct of asexuality as it fits for them, there is still a lot of confusion, misunderstanding, and lack of awareness in the larger Korean communities about asexuality.

I appreciate the cultural contexts of these emerging global studies on asexuality. As we continue to build on our knowledge of asexuality overall, I think that considering the impacts of these culture-specific messages will only help our understanding of asexual strengthen. I think what stands out to me the most in considering global perspectives is that it reminds me that the inner voice that I have that, despite all this research I have done, holds on to some of the early messages of asexuality not being real or being a pathology. Thank goodness that inner voice is very, very quiet now, but it still slides in there once in a while. What I feel when I read these global studies is a solidarity—a recognition that asexuality is worldwide, it is human, it is real, and it is legitimate!

References

Agrawal, N., Shainy, M. R., Sebastian, J., Srivastava, A., & Scoats, R. (2025). "Sex without sexual attraction?": Perceived sexual experiences of Indian sex-favourable asexuals. *Psychology & Sexuality*, 1–21. https://doi.org/10.1080/19419899.2025.2518977

American Psychiatric Association. (1952). *Diagnostic and statistical manual of mental disorders* (1st ed.).

American Psychiatric Association. (1980). *Diagnostic and statistical manual of mental disorders* (3rd ed.).

American Psychiatric Association. (1987). *Diagnostic and statistical manual of mental disorders* (3rd ed., rev.).

American Psychiatric Association. (1994). *Diagnostic and statistical manual of mental disorders* (4th ed.).

American Psychiatric Association. (2000). *Diagnostic and statistical manual of mental disorders* (4th ed., text rev.).

American Psychiatric Association. (2013). *Diagnostic and statistical manual of mental disorders* (5th ed.). https://doi.org/10.1176/appi.books.9780890425596

American Psychiatric Association. (2022). *Diagnostic and statistical manual of mental disorders* (5th ed., text rev.). https://doi.org/10.1176/appi.books.9780890425787

An, H., & Kim, E. (2024). Unveiling the stressful experiences faced by asexual individuals in South Korea: A consensual qualitative study. *Psychology & Sexuality*, 1–16. https://doi.org/10.1080/19419899.2024.2408018

Andersen, M. L., & Tufik, S. (2025). Sleep disorders and sexual function in women. *Maturitas, 199*, 1–8. https://doi.org/10.1016/j.maturitas.2025.108625

APA Document. (n.d.). Homosexuality and sexual orientation disturbance: Proposed change in the DSM II. chrome-extension://efaidnbmnnnibpcajpcglclefindmkaj/https://pages.uoregon.edu/eherman/teaching/texts/DSM-II_Homosexuality_Revision.pdf

Attanasio, M., Masedu, F., Quattrini, F., Pino, M. C., Vagnetti, R., Valenti, M., & Mazza, M. (2022). Are autism spectrum disorder and asexuality connected? *Archives of Sexual Behavior, 51*(4), 2091–2115. https://doi.org/10.1007/s10508-021-02177-4

Barakeh, D., Mdaihly, H., & Karaoui, L. R. (2025). Pharmacotherapy of hypoactive sexual desire disorder in premenopausal women. *The Annals of Pharmacotherapy, 59*(2), 148–161. https://doi.org/10.1177/10600280241253273

Bittle, A., & Anderson, V. N. (2023). As human as anybody else: Attitudes toward asexual people. *Psychology of Sexual Orientation and Gender Diversity*. https://doi.org/10.1037/sgd0000652

Bogaert, A. F. (2006). Toward a conceptual understanding of asexuality. *Review of General Psychology, 10*(3), 241–250. https://doi.org/10.1037/1089-2680.10.3.241

Bogaert, A. F. (2015). Asexuality: What is it and why it matters. *Journal of Sex Research, 52*(4), 362–379. https://doi.org/10.1080/00224499.2015.1015713

Boys Beware, Sid Davis Production, YouTube. (n.d.). Retrieved 30 July, 2025, from https://www.youtube.com/watch?v=9-kj1YopL9s

Bradshaw, J., Brown, N., Kingstone, A., & Brotto, L. (2021). Asexuality vs. sexual interest/arousal disorder: Examining group differences in initial attention to sexual stimuli. *PLoS One, 16*(12). https://doi.org/10.1371/journal.pone.0261434

Brotto, L. A., Knudson, G., Inskip, J., Rhodes, K., & Erskine, Y. (2010). Asexuality: A mixed-methods approach. *Archives of Sexual Behavior, 39*, 599–618. https://doi.org/10.1007/s10508-008-9434-x

Brotto, L. A., & Yule, M. A. (2011). Physiological and subjective sexual arousal in self-identified asexual women. *Archives of Sexual Behavior: The Official Publication of the International Academy of Sex Research, 40*(4), 699–712. https://doi.org/10.1007/s10508-010-9671-7

Brotto, L. A., & Yule, M. (2017). Asexuality: Sexual orientation, paraphilia, sexual dysfunction, or none of the above? *Archives of Sexual Behavior, 46*, 619–627. https://doi.org/10.1007/s10508-016-0802-7

Brown, T. M., & Fee, E. (2003). Alfred C. Kinsey: A pioneer of sex research. *American Journal of Public Health, 93*(6), 896–897.

Bullough, V. L. (1998). Alfred Kinsey and the Kinsey Report: Historical overview and lasting contributions. *The Journal of Sex Research, 35*(2), 127–131. https://www.jstor.org/stable/3813664

Bush, H. H., Williams, L. W., & Mendes, E. (2021). Brief report: Asexuality and young women on the autism spectrum. *Journal of Autism and Developmental Disorders, 51*(2), 725–733. https://doi.org/10.1007/s10803-020-04565-6

Chan, R. C. H., & Hung, F. N. (2025). Sexual, romantic, and community experiences of individuals at the intersection of autism and asexuality. *Archives of Sexual Behavior*. https://doi.org/10.1007/s10508-025-03170-x

Chan, R. C. H., & Leung, J. S. Y. (2023). Experiences of minority stress and their impact on suicidality among asexual individuals. *Journal of Affective Disorders, 325*, 794–803. https://doi.org/10.1016/j.jad.2023.01.025

Clark, A. N., & Zimmerman, C. (2022). Concordance between romantic orientations and sexual attitudes: Comparing allosexual and asexual adults. *Archives of Sexual Behavior: The Official Publication of the International Academy of Sex Research, 51*(4), 2147–2157. https://doi.org/10.1007/s10508-021-02194-3

de Oliveira, L., Vignozzi, L., Giraldi, A., Varod, S., Corona, G., & Reisman, Y. (2024). What women want? The state of the art regarding the treatment of young women with hypoactive sexual desire disorder. *Pharmacology, 109*(2), 69–75. https://doi.org/10.1159/000535587

Drescher, J. (2015). Out of DSM: Depathologizing homosexuality. *Behavioral Science, 5*(4), 565–575. https://doi.org/10.3390/bs5040565

Drecher, J. (2023). Special report: Evolving controversies in the treatment of gender dysphoric/incongruent minors. *Psychiatric News, 58*(6). https://doi.org/10.1176/appi.pn.2023.06.6.27

Edge, J., & Vonk, J. (2024). A comparison of mate preferences in asexual and allosexual adults. *Archives of Sexual Behavior: The Official Publication of the International Academy of Sex Research, 53*(1), 17–24. https://doi.org/10.1007/s10508-023-02723-2

Edge, J., Vonk, J., & Welling, L. (2024). Asexual individuals report high preferences for femininity in male and female faces. *Psychology & Sexuality, 15*(3), 398–414. https://doi.org/10.1080/19419899.2023.2293760

Federici, A. (2025). Echoes of Krafft-Ebing's Psychopathia Sexualis in scientific periodicals: Sexual and mental pathology in late nineteenth- and early twentieth century medical discourse. *Lea, 7*, 81–98. https://doi.org/10.36253/lea-1824-484x-16030

Freud, S. (1905). *Three essays on the theory of sexuality* (Trans. James Strachey). Basic Books.

Galupo, M. P., Mitchell, R. C., Grynkiewicz, A. L., & Davis, K. S. (2014). Sexual minority reflections on the Kinsey Scale and the Klein Sexual Orientation Grid: Conceptualization and measurement. *Journal of Bisexuality, 14*(3–4), 404–432. https://doi.org/10.1080/15299716.2014.929553

Gari, R., Al-Kafi, A., & Costescu, D. (2020). Evaluation of common sexual dysfunctions and treatment outcome in a Canadian sexual medicine practice. *Journal of Sexual Medicine, 17*(7), S241–S242. https://doi.org/10.1016/j.jsxm.2020.04.284

Gochros, H. L., & Gochros, J. S. (1977). *The sexually oppressed*. The Associated Press.

Hectors, A. (2023). Homosexuality in the DSM: Critique of depathologisation and heteronormativity. *New Zealand Sociology, 38*(1), 18–28. www.saanz.net/wp-content/uploads/2023/03/03_Hectors_Homosexuality-in-the-DSM_NZS-Special-Issue-2023_final.pdf

Hess, T., & Špacírová, Z. (2025). Sexual dysfunction in women with eating disorders: Systematic review and meta-analysis. *European Eating Disorders Review., 33*(5), 879–894. https://doi.org/10.1002/erv.3189

Hinderliter, A. (2015). Sexual dysfunctions and asexuality in DSM-5. In S. Demazeux & P. Singy (Eds.), *The DSM-5 in perspective: Philosophical reflections on the psychiatric Babel* (pp. 125–139). Springer Science + Business Media.

Jahangirifar, M., Fooladi, E., Davis, S. R., & Islam, R. M. (2023). Menopause symptoms, sexual dysfunctions and pelvic floor disorders in refugee and asylum seeker women: a scoping review. *Climacteric, 26*(4), 373–380. https://doi.org/10.1080/13697137.2023.2173572

Johnson, M. T. (1977). Asexual and autoerotic women: Two invisible groups. In H. L. Gochros & J. S. Gochros (Eds.), *The sexually oppressed* (pp. 96–109). The Associated Press.

Kingsberg, S. A., & Simon, J. A. (2020). Female hypoactive sexual desire Disorder: A practical guide to causes, clinical diagnosis, and treatment. *Journal of Women's Health, 29*(8), 1101–1112. https://doi.org/10.1089/jwh.2019.7865

Kinsey, A. C., Pomeroy, W. B., & Martin, C. E. (1948). *Sexual behavior in the human male*. Saunders.

Kinsey, A. C., Pomeroy, W. B., Martin, C. E., & Gebhard, P. H. (1953). *Sexual behavior in the human female*. Saunders.

Lu, R., & Chui, H. (2025). Counseling aces: Experiences of asexual clients in China. *Archives of Sexual Behavior: The Official Publication of the International Academy of Sex Research*, 1–19. https://doi.org/10.1007/s10508-025-03148-9

Luo, L., Huang, J., & Li, H. (2023). Characteristics of Chinese women in need of enhanced sexual health attention and at risk of hypoactive sexual desire disorder. *BMC Women's Health, 23*(1), 1–12. https://doi.org/10.1186/s12905-023-02357-5

Mahar, E. A., Stephenson, K. R., & Brotto, L. A. (2025). A randomized controlled trial of online mindfulness and cognitive-behavioral interventions for sexual interest/arousal disorder in women: eSense. *Behaviour Research and Therapy, 188*, 1–13. https://doi.org/10.1016/j.brat.2025.104732

Masters, W. H., & Johnson, V. E. (1966). *Human sexual response*. Little, Brown, and Company.

McHenry, S. E. (2022). "Gay is good": History of homosexuality in the DSM and modern psychiatry. *American Journal of Psychiatry Residents' Journal, 18*(1), 4–5. https://doi.org/10.1176/appi.ajp-rj.2022.180103

Milani, S., Zhang, J. Y., Zdaniuk, B., Bogaert, A., Rieger, G., & Brotto, L. A. (2023). Examining visual attention patterns among asexual and heterosexual individuals. *Journal of Sex Research, 60*(2), 271–281. https://doi.org/10.1080/00224499.2022.2078768

Msolly, S., Bornaz, E., Abdesslem, H., Ounaissa, K., & Amrouche, C. (2025). Evaluation of sexual disorders in diabetic women before menopause: Associated factors and determinating thresholds. *Georgian Medical News, 360*, 51–56. PMID: 40466693.

Oosterhuis, H. (2012). Sexual modernity in the works of Richard von Krafft-Ebing and Albert Moll. *Medical History, 56*(2), 133–155. https://doi.org/10.1017/mdh.2011.30

Ramirez, A. G., Dela Cruz, H. M. C., Mangalus, A. R., Mirador, M. K. T. R., Reyes, H. G. V., & Tamondong, W. B. (2024). Love on the different spectrum. *Academic Journal of Psychology and Counseling, 6*(1). https://doi.org/10.22515/ajpc.v6i1.9941

Ronis, S. T., Byers, E. S., Brotto, L. A., & Nichols, S. (2021). Beyond the label: Asexual identity among individuals on the high-functioning autism spectrum. *Archives of Sexual Behavior, 50*(8), 3831–3842. https://doi.org/10.1007/s10508-021-01969-y

Salari, N., Heidarian, P., Jalili, F., Babajani, F., Shohaimi, S., Nasirian, M., & Mohammadi, M. (2024). The sexual dysfunction in women with thyroid disorders: a meta-analysis. *BMC Endocrine Disorders, 24*(1), 1–7. https://doi.org/10.1186/s12902-024-01817-9

Scheller, M., de Sousa, A. A., Brotto, L. A., & Little, A. C. (2024). The role of sexual and romantic attraction in human mate preferences. *Journal of Sex Research, 61*(2), 299–312. https://doi.org/10.1080/00224499.2023.2176811

Scherrer, K. S. (2008). Coming to an asexual identity: Negotiating identity, negotiating desire. *Sexualities, 11*(5), 621–641. https://doi.org/10.1177/1363460708094269

Skorska, M. N., Yule, M. A., Bogaert, A. F., & Brotto, L. A. (2023). Patterns of genital and subjective sexual arousal in cisgender asexual men. *Journal of Sex Research, 60*(2), 253–270. https://doi.org/10.1080/00224499.2022.2071411

Sternberg, R. J. (1997). Construct validation of a triangular love scale. *European Journal of Social Psychology, 27*, 313–335. https://doi.org/10.1002/(SICI)1099-0992(199705)27:3<313::AID-EJSP824>3.0.CO;2-4

Storms, M. D. (1979). Sexual orientation and self-perception. In P. Pliner et al. (Eds.), *Advances in the study of communication and affect, Vol. 5: Perception of emotion is self and others* (pp. 165–180). Plenum Press.

Storms, M. D. (1980). Theories of sexual orientation. *Journal of Personality and Social Psychology, 38*, 783–792. https://doi.org/10.1037/0022-3514.38.5.783

Tetik, S., & Yalçınkaya Alkar, Ö. (2023). Incidence and predictors of low sexual desire and hypoactive sexual desire disorder in women: A systematic review and meta-analysis. *Journal of Sex & Marital Therapy, 49*(7), 842–865. https://doi.org/10.1080/0092623X.2023.2208564

Tessler, H. (2025). Aromanticism, asexuality, and relationship (non-) formation: How a-spec singles challenge romantic norms and reimagine family life. *Sexualities, 28*(1/2), 514–535. https://doi.org/10.1177/13634607231197061

Van Houdenhove, E., Gijs, L., T'Sjoen, G., & Enzlin, P. (2014). Asexuality: Few facts, many questions. *Journal of Sex & Marital Therapy, 40*(3), 175–192. https://doi.org/10.1080/0092623X.2012.751073

von Krafft-Ebing, R. F. (2011). *Psychopathia sexualis; The case history* (Trans. D. Fall). Solar Books. (Original work published 1886).

Weiss, J., Steil, R., Priebe, K., Lindauer, P., Kleindienst, N., Fydrich, T., & Müller-Engelmann, M. (2023). Sexual dysfunctions in women with posttraumatic stress disorder following childhood sexual abuse: Prevalence rates according to DSM-5 and clinical correlates. *Archives of Sexual Behavior: The Official Publication of the International Academy of Sex Research, 52*(8), 3365–3378. https://doi.org/10.1007/s10508-023-02652-0

Winer, C. (2025). Splitting attraction: Differentiating romantic and sexual orientations among asexual individuals. *Social Currents, 12*(3), 215–230. https://doi.org/10.1177/23294965241305170

Yule, M., Brotto, L., & Gorzalka, B. (2013). Mental health and interpersonal functioning in self-identified asexual men and women. *Psychology & Sexuality, 4*(2), 136–151. https://doi.org/10.1080/19419899.2013.774162

Yule, M. A., Brotto, L. A., & Gorzalka, B. B. (2014). Biological markers of asexuality: Handedness, birth order, and finger length ratios in self-identified asexual men and women. *Archives of Sexual Behavior: The Official Publication of the International Academy of Sex Research, 43*(2), 299–310. https://doi.org/10.1007/s10508-013-0175-0

Yule, M. A., Brotto, L. A., & Gorzalka, B. B. (2017). Sexual fantasy and masturbation among asexual individuals: An in-depth exploration. *Archives of Sexual Behavior, 46*(1), 311–328. https://doi.org/10.1007/s10508-016-0870-8

Chapter 3
A Focus on Language and the Impact of Socially Constructed Messages

Oftentimes, I hear some non-queer people (and some queer people) roll their eyes at "LGBTQIA2S+" and the ever-evolving nature of how queer identities are defined, included, and embraced. I was watching a lesbian comedian on YouTube the other day (Urzila Carlson), and she said something along the lines of "we (queer communities) don't even know what all these letters mean." The focus on this parceling out of language and identity is sometimes seen as a joke to some. In more serious ways, language is a frequent commentary in queer communities—about what we call ourselves, what do our identities mean, and how do we legitimize ourselves. For me and many asexuals, bringing in the "A" (asexual) within the LGBTQIA2S+ identity can feel validating and creates visibility and acceptance of asexuality as a legitimate sexual orientation (Mollet & Lackman, 2018). Note that there has been some debate that the "A" in this anacronym stands for "ally" and some community recognition that this is indeed for "asexuals" and that the anacronym should not apply to those who are not part of gender and sexual minorities, for the sake of this book and the evolution of these letters, I am stating the *a* is for *asexual*. Cowan and LeBlanc (2018) state, "labels we use for people shape what actions and roles they perform, and how those actions then change the accepted meanings of the labels" (p. 30). I am certain that many of those who identify under the other letters feel a sense of recognition when their identities are added and welcomed. Language and the evolution of queer language are key components of this chapter and how this evolution of language can impact asexual (and other queer) individuals.

The lack of knowledge or the dismissal of something is as oppressive and marginalizing as being outright, vocally discriminatory (Cuthbert, 2022). Asexuality is one of the most invisible and misunderstood identities. Arguably, this lack of awareness and knowledge leads to a large portion of people not understanding their uniqueness as a valid and complete identity. An asexual participant in one of my research interviews stated, "I needed to understand why I was so confused my entire life…because I am never in the story, ever." She felt her asexual identity was invisible because it was not represented anywhere, and she had not found language

V. Q. Glass, *Asexuality, Relationships, and Identity Formation*,
https://doi.org/10.1007/978-3-032-22857-4_3

earlier in life to embrace what she felt internally. Additionally, language impacts the social structures around a person and the expectations of those structures. I feel that language can be a vehicle for awareness.

The more we know about queerness overall, the more we realize how fluid and variable it can be. In my own personal journey, I was once "gay" in the 1980s (note: I am a cisgender, demisexual, lesbian, female)—we were known as the "gay community." Eventually, there was a little mini-shift, and we would sometimes be the "gay and lesbian community." You might hear "transsexual" or "bisexual" here and there, but still it was usually the "gay community" for the throughout the 1980s and 1990s. In the early 1990s, there was a sort of social constructionist language recognition of "why is it the *gay and lesbian community* rather than the *lesbian and gay community*." This shift possibly had to do with the feminist movements and people questioning sexist, male-dominated perspectives. I remember hearing "why is it that gay *men* come first?". I have also heard, anecdotally, that this shift was partially because of the AIDS crisis at the time and the way the queer community thanked lesbians for joining in this fight, by putting their "letter" first. Either way, a more focused effort on "lesbian and gay" rather than "gay and lesbian" evolved. So, I owned this shift and proudly claimed the identity of "lesbian"—who I was internally didn't change, but the language around me changed in good ways, ways that allowed me to honor my womanness and my romantic attraction to women at the same time. I remembered feeling a sense of ownership and pride in embracing my femininity, my womanly presence, and my strengths while also having language that identified some of the elements of my sexual orientation. The shift in language around being a woman and a lesbian provided language for me to flourish even more so than I was when I was "gay" (which was a bit limiting to my parts of self).

Bisexual and transgender ("B" and "T") became part of our queer letters, somewhere in the mid to late 1990s. For a while, we were GLBT communities and then became LGBT communities. Over the last 20 years or so, there is an increasing awareness of fluidity and queer spectrum identities that more fully allow people to express and understand who they are through language. And, it is important to say that the continued inclusiveness of the "letters" embraces variability and identity. Holding on to the terminology of *queer* allows us to recognize that we are connected in our minority gender identities and sexual orientations, as different than the norm, while the letters break down and validate many of the separate queer identities.

My youth likely differs a great deal from present-day queer identity experiences. The information that exists at the click of a button brings so much language and connection to queer experiences and queer communities. Even in my research, it seems that asexual participants over about 40 did not have the language to explain their asexuality until later in life, whereas the younger asexuals I interviewed learned of asexuality in their teens or early adulthood. Online communities are vast and provide knowledge and support in the present day in ways I probably can't even fully understand, being from a different time period.

So, fast forward to 2025—now, I am able to label myself, if I am being fully embracing—as an asexual and lesbian identified person, but also demisexual, graysexual, panromantic, homoromantic, and queer, and I lie somewhere between sex-indifferent and sex-favorable. It feels good to be able to embrace all my queer identities and better understand myself and the nuances in who I am more clearly. I value that the "A" (asexual) part of my identity shows up in the "letters" and know that so many of my parts of self are valid. What does all that mean? Let's get to it. This chapter is all about language. I argue that language in our worlds and our communities is incredibly impactful to who we are and how we view ourselves.

As a therapist, I am constantly hearing from clients who share stories of how language has impacted their lives. For example, I have a client with attention deficit disorder (ADHD), and she often shares with me that, throughout her whole life, people have told her that she is "a lot" or "too much." These words haunt her and impact her when she is trying to engage with others—that underlying fear that she will not be embraced because of this part of self. The language of being "a lot" has such a negative connotation that she has felt she needs to change or adjust who she is in social situations so that those words are not part of how people view her. In a slightly positive look at languaging, the terminology of ADHD has helped to a degree, because it has allowed her to put language to this part of herself. Language created, for her, a way to internally process what was actually happening in moments when she had a lot of different kinds of energy or why others may see her differently (because they don't have ADHD and it doesn't make sense to them). Language also allows her to explain to people what is happening (e.g., "I have ADHD, so my mind is sometimes all over the place"). The language allows her to connect with other people who have similar experiences and know she is not alone. But the language that is used often (being "a lot") also cuts deeply to her and has the undercurrent message that she should not be this way. She is constantly aware of her behavior and adjusting to meet this contrived norm of not being "too much." The socially constructed normality around being a "calm, focused" person is internalized by many with ADHD and comes out through language that is "othering" and feels negative. These words can be harmful to those just trying to exist and be who they are. Othering, ignoring, and dismissing are all ways language is used to marginalize, to make people feel less than.

Each of my clients, no matter their background, shares stories like this in a variety of forms. In fact, each person reading this likely has a history where words have described them in ways that feel harsh or uncomfortable, words that may describe parts of who we are in ways that let us know when we are out of the acceptable range of behavior—according to some constructed sense of what is normal and what is not. As a child, I was often told that I was quiet. In some ways, that was a good thing. When teachers said it—it meant that I was a "good child," this subtle message on report cards and in hallways when others were talking led me to feeling that I was this well-behaved kid. The same teachers, however, might say that I needed to speak up more in class or engage more with my peers. These narratives left me battling my internal reflective self all my life. How could I find a way to embrace this part of myself when there were ways this quietness was "bad" and ways this was "good?" I am sure you can think of narratives that have infiltrated your identities, and the way the world sees you may have clouded how you see yourself. It is also through language that I started to own my qualities and words like "reflective," "intuitive," "observational," and "empathetic" took over those "bad" and "good" social terms and allowed me to own those parts of self as I saw them, not how others applied them to me.

In all this discussion on language, this chapter will take a journey into some of those more ingrained social perspectives that infiltrate our daily language in ways that affect queer people. Words are impactful. If there is not a word for something—it is often invisible, if there is a negative word for something—it is something that often feels like it should change, if there is a positive word for something—be prideful of it. It is one thing to tell me as a child that I am shy—another thing to tell me I am weird or awkward. Words have been used to tell people they are unhuman or disgusting because of who they are. Language exists that calls certain behaviors or experiences sinful, which spirals into internal identity confusion that can lead to guilt or fear, or can go completely against all that makes a person who they are. This use of language can lead to lifetimes of hiding, of internal strife, or of complete rejection.

The evolution of language can begin with messages within language that may be invalidating, pathologizing, or even de-humanizing (particularly in queer communities). Think back at the discussion of the DSM and pathologizing language of sexual differences that have been impactful on everyone. The use of the term *homosexual* as a blanket term of people who were not heterosexual was common and acceptable 50 years ago; currently, this construct feels uncomfortable and demeaning to many queer individuals because of the historical meaning of same sex attraction as rooted in medical or mental health issues (Matsick et al., 2022). Language (such as the use of the word *pride* or even the symbol of the rainbow) can sometimes shift and empower. Even my use of the term *queer* in this book would have been frowned upon 20 years ago. It has become for many a word that symbolizes community, connection, hope, and self-respect.

This chapter will begin by considering the roots of language as a way to deconstruct the messages being sent to asexuals (specifically those of us in Western cultures). Ultimately, this chapter will conclude by specifically looking at asexuality and the evolving language around asexuality. My goal is to highlight the historical impacts of language on sexuality and identity. More importantly, I hope to share with the readers the importance of re-languaging as a way to deconstruct those negative messages and feel a sense of understanding, connectiveness, identity, and pride.

In the early 1990s, I entered college at the *University of North Carolina at Greensboro* and began my own personal language deconstruction around gender and sexuality. I attended the university during the time that John D. Emilio was in the faculty. He is a leading historian of sexuality (see *Intimate Matters: A History of Sexuality in America* by D'Emilio & Freedman, 1997). On top of my exposure to this book and my desire to read every page carefully and thoroughly, I rushed to all the psychology and women's studies (now gender studies) courses available to me. My unspoken inner goal was to begin to understand more how our society had become (and continues to be) so hostile, angry, and demeaning toward genders, sexual orientations, sexual behaviors, and any difference that it does not deem suitable. And, as a therapist, I continue to seek out this understanding as I am constantly aware of the power of both positive and negative languaging and the deep, internalized impacts of language.

I will bring a great deal to this chapter, but I recognize there is so much more I could bring. This complex interwoven connection between history, cultural expectations, and language is vast and ever-changing. I have made the decision to somewhat look at this intersection from my own perspective, with the recognition that others can likely apply this to their backgrounds and the meaning-making involved in their own context. All that to say, being a White, middle-class, cisgender, queer woman in the United States, the context of language that I see around me has very much been influenced by Christian belief systems, so I will start there. From this context, I will explore the language and meanings that have arisen out of these belief systems that are frequently applied to gender, relationships, and sex/sexuality. Finally, I will consider the impact of all this background language noise on asexuals. It is no surprise that there is a plethora of historical analysis on language and meaning with regard to queerness, sexuality, and gender. Rather than presenting an encyclopedia of historical shifts and belief systems that have impacted present day, I will provide a briefer summation of some of the key areas that I feel, from my research, have significantly impacted language around asexuality (and, in some respects queerness as a whole). I feel an unpacking of messages around gender and relationships is vital to better understanding asexual experiences.

Religion and Expectations

One asexual that I interviewed (Sage) joked, "I think the church should love asexuals because they are all about celibacy and abstinence."

So, where do I decide to start—religious influences. Given that I am in the United States, and the Western cultures are heavily influenced by Christianity, this is my initial focus. I am not trying to leave out the hundreds of unique ways that people connect to spirituality; rather, my focus is a direct reaction to where I see these larger messages in my community and the spiraling influences of these messages even into many other religious, spiritualities, and non-secular communities. Messages and language from Christian faiths have been used to demean queer people in current history. Additionally, Christian interpretations have been historically used to control sexual behaviors and *acceptable* ways of being in relationships. Even though the United States was founded on religious freedom, the impact of Christianity on larger social constructions, laws, education, and policy is undeniable. Zehra et al. (2023) state:

> …religious teachings emphasize the binary nature of gender and heterosexual relationships, often leading to less acceptance of LGBT individuals. This perspective, grounded in traditional interpretation of sacred texts, contributes to the marginalization and stigmatization of LGBT people in many societies (p. 28).

In other words, some people who do not fit into other people's interpretation of Christian messages are seen as sinful, ungodly, and not worthy. The messages that we all hear as an undercurrent to what is appropriate sexually or in relationships become part of social expectations that can lead to inner and external judgment.

In my research with asexuals, one message that I often heard was that there was this bizarre confusion for some who were part of Christian communities (as younger people and even into adulthood). There was discussion of how, as asexuals, they felt that they were doing the right (the most Christian) thing. They were not lusting after others and, in many cases, maybe even not engaging in sex. This part of their asexual identity helped them feel like they were doing what their church communities would approve of. One participant in my research described the messages of sex and sexuality that she received in Catholic school throughout her childhood and stated, "I just thought I was doing a really good job…being a Christian…waiting until marriage." Rothblum et al.'s research (Rothblum et al., 2019) explored asexual participants who shared that, when they were younger, they found comfort in the Christian communities because of the no dating and no sex focus. It is almost like these Christian messages provided a bit of a supportive reasoning that permitted them not to have to mask parts of their identities among more sexually interactive peers. It gave some asexuals a socially acceptable reason for not wanting a romantic and/or sexual relationship.

Oddly, Christian messages around sex indicate that before marriage, you should not want to engage in sex at all, in fact, lusting, dating, any kind of sexual contact is sinful until marriage (Bogaert, 2004). Flash forward to marriage—it is expected to be this immediate transition, you are supposed to have sex (plenty of it), satisfy male partners, and—get this—enjoy it! What a complex message for some asexual individuals to battle, especially if they are unclear or unaware of their asexual identity until after marriage. For a period of their life, they may have felt like a "good Christian" and suddenly, at marriage, they may not be able to meet these expectations put upon them. One couple I interviewed, Kai (an asexual) and their partner Jacob (an allosexual), spent time telling me about the messages of Christianity that have impacted them. Kai discussed their background growing up in a Christian church. They stated,

> There is so much pressure, people talk about purity culture, it is this thing that tells you that sex is bad, but they don't really know about the part that comes after, because it is like, sex is bad until you are married and then once you are married, you are supposed to do it as much as your husband wants to and have as many children as you can and if you don't like it, too fucking bad. That is where a lot of asexuals run into problems…it compounds the feeling of 'I am broken,' 'there is something wrong with me,' 'I am not fulfilling God's purpose for me.'

Like Kai, many asexuals feel a similar message, no matter what their religious upbringing is.

Some of the major Christian messages that are part of the legal and moral undercurrent of Western communities include:

- Men initiate sex (Stevenson & Hiebert, 2021)

- Men "have high levels of desire" (Stevenson & Hiebert, 2021, p. 61)
- Women are "both the object and subject of desire" (Stevenson & Hiebert, 2021, p. 62), they are responsible for tempting men and at fault for men's indiscretions, yet their own desires are "less than" and should not be considered.
- Women are property and must remain pure only for future husband (Stevenson & Hiebert, 2021).
- For women being a virgin at marriage is the expectation. This message has been echoed in different forms throughout history, abstinence, purity culture, etc.
- Lust is considered an "evil of the flesh" (Stevenson & Hiebert, 2021, p. 62)
- Sex should be about procreation (Stevenson & Hiebert, 2021).
- Waiting until marriage is "a beautiful gift" (Stevenson & Hiebert, 2021, p. 64) and will be outstanding once the gift is opened.
- Mixed messages on masturbation, however, evangelical Christian messages are against self-pleasuring activities (Stevenson & Hiebert, 2021).
- Mixed messages on pornography; however, there are some messages that this is acceptable for males (Stevenson & Hiebert, 2021).
- Same sex attraction and same sex physical experiences are sinful (Zehra et al., 2023).

In Western communities, we are doused with these Christian messages of sexuality, no matter what our religious backgrounds are. Zehra et al. (2023) state:

> Religious beliefs also shape cultural norms and societal expectations regarding gender and sexuality, thus contributing to homophobia and transphobia. In many societies, religious doctrines influence the definition of acceptable and unacceptable behaviors. Traditional gender roles and heteronormativity are often rooted in religious beliefs. When people deviate from these norms, they may face rejection, discrimination, or violence (p. 31).

It is likely that if you are a mental health professional in Western communities, you have worked with many clients who are navigating Christian messages that identify how they are expected to experience sex and sexuality. These ideas are deeply rooted. I have seen many clients in my practice, some who have not even come from homes that they would describe as religious or Christian, describe background language around sex and sexuality that has clear, strict rules of normalcy (Stevenson & Hiebert, 2021). Deviance from this normalcy can lead to trauma and sense of shame and guilt, particularly for women and girls (Leonhardt et al., 2020; Stevenson & Hiebert, 2021). Overall, there can be a sense of confusion, self-blame, or inner negotiation when it comes to sex and pleasure (Leonhardt et al., 2020). Flanagan's (2024) research highlighted some of the messages women get that discount their own sexual desires. They share voices of women who were surprised, for example, that women had orgasms or masturbated, because so much of the context of sex was focused on males and their gratification.

Despite these foundational messages, there has been growth in some Christian communities that do play a role in shifts when it comes to understanding sex and sexuality overall. Consider the impact of medical awareness. Minimally, research on the human body indicates that arousal is a natural, biological response, which challenges many of the messages that have been provided this Christian foundation of expectations. Research has shown that education can play a role in helping people view these messages from different angles by bridging factual elements of sexual behavior (Flanagan, 2024). In addition, some Christian communities have been working to create a welcoming environment and language that embraces all sexual orientations and gender identities (Hugues & Rouse, 2023; Zehra et al., 2023).

Consider, for example, an impactful term to many (in particular asexuals), the terminology around *frigidity* (Thurmond & Levin, 2023). Frigidity, as a term, is rooted in Christianity and used to describe a person (typically a woman) who has a lack of sexual desire (Brown, 2022). This term evolved into describing certain areas of mental health. Freud linked this construct of frigidity to a woman's unconscious issues from childhood. The term is not used often in present day, but does still exist. In my research, some asexual participants have shared this sense of, "I thought I was frigid or something," demonstrating how impactful this outdated language can be. Brown (2022) explores the gender and racialized elements of the term frigidity. Frigidity is often applied to White women, suggesting an assumption of non-White races as being opposite to this term—as "savage" (Brown, 2022, p. 91) in terms of sexual desire and conquest. The layered impacts of the microaggressive meanings wrapped up in the terminology of *frigidity* and *savagery* are impactful to asexuals, particularly asexuals who are of other marginalized identities.

Similarly, the term *celibacy* often comes from Christian origins. You might hear people saying, "I am taking a break from sex, I am celibate this year" or something along those lines. The difference between celibacy and asexuality is that celibacy is a choice, and those who choose to be celibate still experience sexual attraction and often desire sexual activity (Brunning & McKeever, 2021). We see the impact of celibacy in higher order Christian religious officials, for example, priests and nuns who forego any sexual desire to connect to God. Does the message of celibacy represent that not engaging in sex is a good thing? Make you more divine? Closer to God? It is quite a mixed message when compared to the more sex-obsessed Western climate, which we will get to in a moment.

Some Christian asexuals (e.g., Dewitt, 2023; Thurmond & Levin, 2023) identify that Christian messages can be homophobic and unsupportive of their identities (Rothblum et al., 2019). As a result of social stigma around religious doctrine, some queer people may find ways to adapt so that they feel safe from the condemnation they may experience in their religious communities (Frey et al., 2021). Some queer people may hide their sexual orientation from others or change their behaviors in some settings in ways that mimic their heteronormative counterparts. These behaviors can include things like, not inviting partners to family or community events, using different terminology for partners (e.g., friend), and monitoring their language and behaviors.

Some people are using language to come to terms with some of these mixed messages from Christianity and the impact on their asexual identity. For example, *Sojourners Magazine*, a magazine devoted to "faith-driven activism" (https://sojo.net/about/about-sojourners retrieved 6/27/15), has published stories from asexual writers' experiences balancing Christianity and asexuality. Dewitt (2023) reflects on the messages that she has felt from Christianity as an asexual person. She states,

> We're inconvenient to remember — on all sides of the political and religious spectrums. To those on the Right, we throw a wrench into the narrative that queerness is just about sexual acts. On the Left, we complicate a sex-saturated, "love is love" attitude that too often turns anemic visions of liberation into compulsory sexuality and romance; in either of those spaces, those of us who don't experience these kinds of attraction are incomprehensible. Christians are often equally unable to imagine a life that is not shaped by romantic and sexual desire (https://sojo.net/about/about-sojourners).

She continues to challenge the assumption that purity culture is ideal for asexual individuals because of the focus on marriage as a sacred and necessary direction. She concludes that her own journey has allowed her to see that God rejoices her asexual uniqueness, stating "I am a manifestation of Love's complex divine revelation." Thurmond and Levin (2023) echo a similar sentiment around the mixed messages that purity culture has presented. They further expand on the gendered messages in Christian teachings of males being expected to be hyper-sexual beings while women are supposed to remain pure until marriage, and upon marriage does not seek pleasure for themselves, only for a man.

Smith (2025) shared her experiences, in a Christian blog, with the language she was presented as a teen and the impact this had on her own sexual identity journey. She brings in the concept of *temptation* and how focused those Christians around her were with the idea of resisting temptation. She shared, "according to my youth pastor, temptation was everywhere, and sexual temptation was something every teenager struggled with" (https://sojo.net/about/about-sojourners). She saw information about this temptation struggle in the media, among her friends, in educational communities, yet she felt something was wrong internally because she did not feel this thing that she was expected to feel.

Legal social tenets evolve with religious views, regardless of the initial intent in the United States to separate church and state. Christian perspectives, a Christian God, and Jesus' teachings remain the foundational components of how the United States seems to identify right vs. wrong, leading to laws based in a morality that are linked to Christian teachings. This evolution of Christianity and language and the meanings applied to some Christian belief systems are impactful to one's sense of self, and those messages lead to bias, prejudice, and even mental health challenges. The mixture of the foundational messages of sex and sexuality that include exact ways that people should experience desire and engage in romantic and sexual relationships does not always fit with other social messages of desire and sexual obsession. For asexuals, neither of these really fit their own sense of self—and navigating identity can be a bit of a journey as a result of sifting through these messages and what does or does not fit.

Media and Expectations

I remember, as a young adult, watching the movie *American Pie* (Weitz, 1999). This movie is a traditional American coming-of-age story, which means that it is full of sexual experiences that are deemed normal for those coming-of-age. I was confused as a teen and young adult about these expectations, because I lived in a world where sex was not talked about freely, where waiting until marriage was what was expected, yet, there was this dichotomy of movies that represented teens who wanted to conquer their virginity and lived their lives as horny messes with only one thing on their mind. This contradictory message was not the only part that confused me. I remember thinking about the characters in the movie and asking myself, "is this normal?" "Is this how I am supposed to be?" "Why do I not experience the world like these characters?" The movie depicts a group of guys who make a pact of sorts to lose their virginity. The whole movie is about sexual conquest, but it starts with sexual attraction, and a lot of it. The teen girls in the film are sexualized based on appearance (or body parts really), all the characters seem to feel sexual attraction; it is a constant conversation. Additionally, sexual experiences are normalized as something all people experience in one way—everyone at that age is only thinking about sex, non-stop. I think these types of movies were pretty common in the 1980s and certainly were impactful in my own journey. I tried to figure out how I fit into this world, for years, to no avail. I think each generation of asexuals can pinpoint media they have consumed in their lives that just confused them more.

In addition to the sexual conquest themes in a lot of media—the impact of sexual messages in the media when it comes to Black, Indigenous, and people of color (BIPOC) is often rooted in oversexualized and hypersexualized themes (Brown, 2022; Castillo et al., 2024; Leath et al., 2021). Often, in the media, BIPOC women's bodies are hypersexualized and objectified with an aggressive and/or violent undercurrent. These presentations can contribute to power dynamics in social scripts that can be detrimental to BIPOC people as they navigate their sexual identities, especially in terms of their queer identities. The media often presents BIPOC masculine images of sex as dominant, forceful, something to fear, and also expendable (Goodwill et al., 2019; Oluwayomi, 2022). When considering the sexualized BIPOC images in the media, finding queer BIPOC representation is also not common and also often not representative of queer BIPOC experiences. Consider being BIPOC and asexual and the extent to which these social scripts differ for this intersectional identity (Brown, 2022). If the media is presenting hypersexualized and forceful images of BIPOC sexual experiences, where does romance, tenderness, nonsexual intimacy, or lack of sexual desire fit in?

On top of this, in present day, nearly every film—drama, action, thriller, or sitcom—has a romance focus. The leading character could be fiercely independent, heroically saving the world, or just making funny jokes, but, in the end, there is almost always a love interest that the audience is waiting to see develop. Try to think about any mainstream media film or show that alludes to the message that, regardless of anything, final romantic relationship is still the most important factor. Even sex (and good sex) is often a critical factor for main characters. These are messages of social normality are embedded in the fabric of storylines in a way that presents romantic and sexual relationships as critical and natural for everyone (Rothblum et al., 2019).

I adore a good romance movie. There is a tenderness and connection between two people that I just find very satisfying, particularly when there is a lesson or challenge involved that the relationship grows to meet. In fact, if you throw in other genres of films, science fiction, thriller, action, I am much more in tune if there is a romantic undercurrent. That being said, so too often (for me), I will put on a movie that looks good, and it starts with a sex scene and my only thought is "geez, again!? Who wants to see all this?" I could care less about any sex in my romance movies, unless they are very tender and more about cuddling and affection. I recognize romance resonates with me and sex really doesn't (at least not in the way it seems to do with most people). Did you know many people like sex scenes in their shows and movies? Watch out, my asexual side is showing. But the terminology around the split attraction model makes sense for me here—I love romance and have deep romantic and emotional connections with people and partners of my past. When I get all cozy into a romance movie, I think about some of my aromantic peers who probably feel like I do—except that romance in movies may seem very overrated to them, much like sex scenes feel in movies to me.

A lack of representation of asexuality in the media leads to a sense of marginalization or invisibility (Hart-Brinson et al., 2024). Think about this—have you seen a popular show or movie with a person who identifies as an asexual? There are rumors of characters being asexual (e.g., Sheldon Cooper in The Big Bang Theory); however, even in these situations, it feels too political or too extreme to actually disclose. The media is behind in a lot of ways when it comes to representations of diverse characters and plots.

Gender and Expectations

Gender constructs are filled with social expectations from constant barrages of language that symbolize appropriate ways to *gender*. I think gendered expectations can be particularly present for romance, sex, and relationships—which are impactful to asexuals particularly, but to all people. Research on the historical presence of gendered expectations is vast. In fact, if we consider Christianity, gender, and language, we could deconstruct encyclopedias of how these message infiltrate Western societies. Unpacking gender from social expectations, sexual expectations, and romantic expectations is bigger than I will tackle here, but do want to touch on it as it might relate to asexual communities.

Masculinity and femininity are social constructs that are fraught with clear expectations that are unattainable by most people. Despite this, social discourse suggests that deviation from these unattainable expectations gives other people the right to challenge, judge, and shun those who do not fit into these molds. We see this daily in the United States, everything from an off-handed remark about "women drivers" to father's "toughening" up their sons through harsh words or experiences.

I can reflect on my own experiences growing up and the messages around sex and romance and how gendered language around this was for me. Just watching Disney—which a majority of Americans do in their childhoods—Disney presents a clear message in every film that I can think of—that women want romance and a prince or prince-like figure to save them, and this makes everyone peaceful and happy. Despite having somewhat progressive parents, the messages of gender were still strong in my home. The messages I heard from family, extended family, and community were that women should listen to men and please them. These messages translated to sexual norms that male expectations of pleasure should be met by women. I am not even sure I ever heard about women's pleasure being part of sexual equations until I was a young adult. Peer conversations were often around "boys should ask the girl out" or "boys should pay for the date." Listening to boys talk about romance, there were often discussions that would objectify my friends (e.g., "look at her rack" or "shake that ass."). The messages I got were that men need sexual pleasure, women are the objects of this gratification, and women should comply if they want the Disney princess romance (otherwise they were condemned to be the ugly step-mom or witch).

Despite a great deal of shifts in gender expectations overall in the last 100 years or so, there still exists rigidity in gender roles when it comes to dating, marriage, and sexual relationships (Burge, 2018; Lamont, 2021). For example, current research shows that, in heterosexual dating, males almost always pay for the meal on the first date (Wu et al., 2021), and there is still an expectation that males will generally take the lead on asking out, sexual initiation, and even proposing (Lamont, 2021). These lingering social messages suggest these gender scripts are deeply rooted and very slow to shift.

Masculinity, in general, has this connotation of hyper-sexuality (Higginbottom, 2024). Men often share this experience of indoctrination around relationships that indicate a high need for sexual activity and an ogling of women. Social constructions of masculinity may include that having sexual experiences will boost a masculine image, while a lack of sexual experiences may take away from a person's manhood. Being an asexual, cisgender male is often the anthesis of this constructed masculine image. Asexual males may work to attain this acceptable image, despite not be feeling the same kinds of attraction as their allosexual peers (Mandigo & Kavar, 2022; Tessler & Winer, 2023). Aromantic asexual men might engage in romantic activities (e.g., poems, flowers, etc.) to meet social expectations without necessarily feeling the romantic feelings behind them. Or, asexual men may follow suit with flirting behaviors or sexual interest for fear of judgment if they do not respond like their peers.

How might these images and expectations of masculinity impact asexuals? Mandigo and Kavar (2022) highlighted that asexual male participants experience a sense of "otherness" (p. 498) because they do not identify with the hypersexual Western cultural expectations put on men. Their participants then identified common language that described their sexual experiences and attraction. The realization that this language speaks to their experiences leads to a more developed sense of "belonging" (p. 500). Asexual men that I have encountered share stories of feeling especially out of place during peer conversations around desire and attraction.

Femininity, romance, and dating are impacted by the image that women should be sought out and conquered. Being flirty, submissive, and demure is part of that image (Burge, 2018; Scappini & Fioravanti, 2022). The heterosexual scripts around sex and gender are impactful to all genders and sexual orientations—as the man as conqueror and woman as submissive prevails (and any other genders are not even considered). These scripts lead to a continuous culture of sexual violence and, at times, an inability to voice needs, desires, and consent becomes complex (Scappini & Fioravanti, 2022). Additionally, there is still a dominant mixed message for many women that judges women for hooking up or engaging in premarital sex, while these things are often celebrated for men (Lamont, 2021). Consider the term *prude* and how this is used as a judgment toward women who are not engaging in sex acts. Some asexuals I spoke with brought up this construct, Jessica shared, "in my early 20s, I was seen as a prude…" She shared a story of a guy she met at a party and told him she wasn't interested in sex. She shared, "later I found how he was telling people that I was a prude…a few guys I have turned down…I know they think I am a prude, it is annoying." Miranda also discussed this image of being a prude,

> There is this perception that demisexual people are just choosy or just prefer to develop a connection and that is just not the case. I think it would be much easier if I could just hook up with anyone I wanted to and not care about getting to know them really well first…demisexual people get a lot of pushback, even from otherwise positive people, they will invalidate our identities entirely or think we are being prudish and that is not it, so it is frustrating.

In both of these participants' accounts, they felt the devaluing of their experience through the negative connotation of the construct of *prude*.

My discussion here is more generally about messages around the gender binary and heterosexual romantic and sexual relationships that exist in larger social messages—rendering intersex, nonbinary, and transgender identities invisible. Jumping into exploring queer relationships and gender diversity can bring about a whole new set of assumptions and expectations, which are still rooted in these Westernized binary ways of looking at gendered expectations in relationships. Moving ahead, I feel the discussion of amatonormitivity and allonormativity is a good next step in this language journey.

Amatonormativity and Allonormativity

It is not a surprise that social messages of gender, religion, and relationships create this symbiotic, systemic, re-cursive influence on expectations. I visualize a conveyer belt of sorts with all sorts of messages going into a machine and popping out something that these messages generated. This is how I symbolically look at *amatornormativity*—the impact of Christian expectations, the role of the media, the messages from history (even scientific history), and the role of what is happening in politics or popular culture have led to this idea of amatonormitivity. Western cultures have been dominated by relationship expectations that are steeped in amatonormative and allonormative language. Just a reminder—

> **Amatonormativity** is the assumption that all people desire a specific kind of love and partnership and that this partnership is valued more than any other relationship (Brake, 2012).
>
> **Allonormativity** is the expectation of allosexuality, that all people will experience sexual attraction and romantic attraction the same way (Brandley & LeMaster, 2025).

These two constructs define oppression directed toward asexuals (and, any others that do not fit these boxes) by *othering*—creating a space where anything that does not fit these ideals (of being in the relationship or feeling sexual and/or romantic attraction) is wrong. The messages are that differences in attraction should be pathologized or anything that isn't allonormative is invisible because of the louder voices of allonormative expectations.

Think for a moment about key, critical, supportive, and/or caretaking relationship in your own life. Maybe mentally consider the top five people in your world that you know are there for you or whose relationship is of most importance to you. It is possible that one of these five people is a spouse or partner. It is possible that you have family members as part of that top five. More than likely at least one of those individuals is someone you know you could not live without and has had a particular impact on you, but it is not a romantic or sexual partner. It is possible that this person plays more of a role in your world than a romantic or sexual partner would. Think more deeply again, what is it these five people give you, what comes to mind that made you think about these five people? Maybe some of the words that come to mind are: companionship, support, concern, assistance, caretaking, affirmation, fun, connection, passion, laughter, kindness, intellectual stimulation… Despite these five people being so integral to your world, our society still seems to place ultimate value only on one type of relationship that includes marriage, sex, and romance. The amatonormative message is that a life-long romantic and sexual partner is put in higher regard than any other type of relationship, and something that you should strive for in order to achieve health and happiness.

One participant I interviewed was from a Latinx background and was sharing her perspectives of allornormative expectations in her community. She stated that "virgin-shaming" was a "tough and persistent" message in her community. She continued,

> (I was) feeling confused during my adolescence because I knew I liked men romantically, but I didn't know if I liked them sexually. Being considered undesirable, or the term used in my country of origin would be 'unfuckable.' I never talked to boys or did anything to draw them to me. I never wore skirts or dresses, or make up, or feminine clothes…I was bullied a lot because of this. People assumed my sexuality, asking me if I was a lesbian and even misgendered me. My culture encourages sex and dating, and being sexy in my society -- virgin equals loser -- and I was treated as such.

The impacts of these amatonormative and allonormative messages were felt deeply by this participant. Additionally, there were ingrained social messages in her community that impacted how others viewed her and led to very hurtful and overwhelming comments.

Amatonormativity is a construct coined by Brake (2012) and means that there is *ONE* kind of love—passionate, loving, romantic, sexual, monogamous—that all people strive for and attaining this relationship will be the key to happiness. Amatonormativity is the idea that one romantic and sexual relationship trumps all others and that "romantic love is the universal goal" (p. 88) of all humans. Brake states, "Our culture focuses on dyadic amorous relationships at the cost of recognizing friendships, care networks, urban tribes, and other intimate associations" (p. 88). Brake is a professor of philosophy and a researcher of polyamorous relationships. Her development of this construct originated as she dove into messages and meanings in social constructs that only allowed for monogamy. The construct of amatonormativity has been an important lens for viewing asexual experiences and desires, deconstructing the social perspective of this view of only one way to be in a relationship. Presently, allonormative belief systems are often at play setting up the stage that there is only one ideal way and that everyone should follow. There is no one way to *sex,* and this is also rooted in heteronormativity and allonormativity.

Amatonormativity and allonormativity also impact non-asexual people. For example, one type of relationship—being single—is seen as problematic in many social contexts. Brake (2012) states "singles are often seen as lacking a sense of responsibility as well as having empty lives" (p. 93). If you take any course on psychology, development, and childhood, you will hear that single parenthood is a major risk factor for everything from increased mental health issues to increased substance use to criminal behavior. We can extend this amatonormative expectation to same sex relationships, non-monogamous relationships, even step-families, divorced individuals, any relationship or lack thereof that doesn't fit the nuclear family perspective is othered or seen as more problematic.

One asexual participant I interviewed, Miranda, shared her own thoughts on social messages and how she has shifted these for herself. She stated,

> I think our culture has so many social pressures that you should be in a relationship or trying to get into a relationship at all times and that really stresses me out, recognizing that I actually do not have to date has made a huge difference in my life satisfaction.

Miranda touches on her own personal journey through a restrictive language and through deconstructing that language in a way that embraces her authenticity—which leads to "life satisfaction."

The constructs of relationships are upheld through social discourse. Brandley and LeMaster (2025) state: "The taken-for-granted assumptions and structures that reinforce allosexuality and alloromanticism as normal are upheld by allornormativity, a system of oppression responsible for the discrimination and violence against people who identify as asexual or aromantic" (p. 285). Additionally, the rooted perceived moralism around this idea of amatonormativity or allonormativity comes out as discrimination in the daily life of those that do not fit the norm, for example, there are legal impacts, educational exclusions, housing limitations, lack of familial support of rituals, lack of representation in the media, the list is endless (Brake, 2012).

One example of the impact of allonormativity is legal precedents. Legal precedents are established by majority belief systems and perceived values. Legalities around marriage impact tax breaks, workplace benefits, and family law (including adoption, wills, healthcare decision making, etc.). These legal impacts omit those that do not fit social rules and expectations. If value is placed in one type of relationship (e.g., marriage that looks one way), all the legal aspects that support this relationship are put into place.

Just a personal reflection that fits into this idea—as a single parent (with no other legal parent in the picture), I remember adding my daughter to my health insurance a few years ago. It is just me and my daughter on my health insurance. There is a significant difference in the yearly cost for each of the three tiers of health insurance: (1) a single person, (2) a married couple, and (3) a "family plan." Even though it was just me and my daughter (two of us)—my only choice is the "family plan." You would think we would have the same options as a "couple" being that there are only two of us. I pay the same for two people that someone might pay for five. This is just one simple personal example of the benefits that are in place that favor only one type of relationship. I do not think this benefit was set up on purpose to discriminate against single parents; however, it is the invisibility of not recognizing my unique family structure that has led to this design that is not fair to my situation, my identity, and my family.

The impacts of these expectations of heteronormativity, allonormativity, and amatonormativity have played a notable role in the lives of most asexuals (Vares, 2022). Vares' (2022) highlights experiences of asexual participants who struggled with not having this normative family ideal and getting the social message that if they did not have a particular type of relationship, they would be "lonely and unhappy" (p. 777). This perspective bleeds into friends and family of Vares' asexual participants who feel quite concerned over the participants' lack of a relationship (even with the participants themselves feel completely happy to not be in relationships). This familial concern rang true with some participants in my own research. One asexual participant I spoke with, Joni, described that asexuals feel a lot of "familial pressure to be mono-normative, heteronormative." There is also, for some participants, a sense of not fitting in or being left out when people are sharing romantic and/or sexual happiness. In my own research, oftentimes, participants would share a sense of guilt over not being "everything" for their partners or feeling like they are missing something. What is this expectation based on? My participants (and those in Vares', 2022 study) do seem to develop new narratives that integrate their asexual identity. I will dive more into this in a couple of chapters when I discuss relationships; however, it is important to mention briefly that the shift in language and expectations around *happiness* and r*elationships* can open the door to many different experiences that a person can value.

These shifts in narratives around relationships were also noted by Brandley and LeMaster (2025). Brandley and LeMaster are communication researchers and theorists who embrace the importance of a critical review of language and communication and the impact of power and privilege that infiltrates language (particularly around queer experiences and identities). They discussed the impacts of allonormativity on asexuals as rooted in oppression and de-humanization. These impacts can lead to internalized and externalized acephobia that gets in the way of asexuals feeling affirmed, welcomed, and that their identity is not valid.

Brandley and LeMaster (2025) also discuss the importance of deconstruction, through "decentralizing allonormativity" (p. 293). This language reconstruction involves education and intentional re-languaging/disrupting messages that there is only one way to be happy—and that looks like a specific kind of romantic and sexual, long-term, monogamous fairy tale ending. I particularly appreciated their insertion of data from a couple of their participants, one who shared "...societies need more awareness and more acknowledgement 'that ace people exist'" (p. 293). And, another who shared that "more information about our (asexuals) experiences' will help denaturalize allonormativity" which can help in the "desexualization of society in general" and leaves room for "so much other right aspects of human relationships" (p. 293). Similarly, one asexual participant I spoke with, Joni, shared, "Once I realized that this (asexuality) was a thing, I could dive into what that meant to me and let my relationships be whatever they could be instead of what society prescribes my relationship to be." The freedom that exists when we start to see outside the norms is incredible.

An aside, in my own journey, I became aware of how social expectations and language influence legal thought and how legal thought feeds back into social expectations. In North Carolina, in the late 1980s and early 1990s, when I began connecting to queer communities, it was illegal for anyone to engage in any sex act that was not "missionary" position and between a male and female (man on top, penis-in-vagina sex). This persecutory law was common conversation among my queer friends. As young heterosexual couples were enjoying all kinds of different sexual experiences (often not "penis and vagina missionary sex"—despite this law), while two people with penises were having to risk prosecution if they were caught in any sexual relationship. Despite the fact that this law outlawed oral sexual activities, even in heterosexual relationships, it was only men having sex with other men who were being persecuted. Queer communities were inundated with messages that we were to remain secret and underground and should not inhabit among heterosexuals. Laws known as *anti-sodomy* laws were used to further repress sexuality and any sex act that was not seen as normal. These anti-sodomy laws applied to everyone (e.g., oral sex was considered a felony for everyone in NC until 2003 when the US supreme court *Lawrence v. Texas* case, which nullified any current state sodomy laws). I remember hearing of undercover agents just waiting in men's bathrooms or gay bars, to catch fellatio between two men in the moment or to be propositioned and whisk them off to jail. It was terrifying. There was a confusion that existed for me then and remains today. How have things evolved to this space where queerness, sexuality, and gender diversity remain languaged in a way that *still* frequently devalues (even criminalizes) ranges of desires and identities that exist in our world? And, what the heck does this mean for asexuality? You might think—well, asexuals are not going to be whisked off to jail for having illegal sex. But, it still comes down to this power of language to equate what is normal in relationships and to place what is not considered normal into persecutory categories.

Social messages often take things that seem undesirable to a few and place them into language that is meant to "take it away"—often through religious persecution or legal persecution, but this runs more deeply into daily language, bias, and prejudice. Allonormativity and amatonormativity provide language that helps us recognize that, as asexuals, the world is putting us in an *other* box that it finds undesirable. This can be a scary place, I have seen heteronormativity and homophobia used toward queer communities for decades—resulting in violence, ostracism, hate, punitive measures, and dehumanizing. As an asexual, it is kind of easy to sit back and hide behind what may not be as much of a visible minority, yet these lingering messages are powerful and privilege certain types of relationships and certain types of sexual engagement. I argue that the language around the DSM, in the medical field, in our legal system, and in daily life is facilitating persecutory messages of allosexuality and amatonormativity that are discriminatory for asexuals, as well as perpetuating messages to allosexual individuals that there is only one way to relationship—limiting many people and their experiences.

Hypersexualization

Hypersexualization, over-sexualization, and compulsory sexuality are common messages in Western worlds. In some ways, these terms fit under amatonormativity and allonormativity, in the sense that sex is considered the ultimate human need that can be met by relationships and romance. I remember taking a college class in marketing back in the 1990s. I remember when the professor stood in front of the class and showed some clearly sexualized advertisements on the old-fashioned light-up projector. Slide after slide of advertisements for soda, alcohol, cigarettes, furniture, even cleaning supplies had sexualized images. The professor spoke proudly because he was able to shock us by pointing out these undercurrent messages (e.g., a nude woman's silhouette hidden in a drip of froth off a beer mug)—"sex sells!" was the concept I remember. What I remember even more was how shocking it was to me that sex was so integrated into the images that I was seeing every day and knowing that research and science identified that if these messages are used, more products will be bought, which obviously led to more and more sexualized (often objectified) images everywhere.

Interestingly, the "sex sells" debate is still playing a role in marketing research, with more current research suggesting sexualized advertisements have little or no influence on purchasing (Ciuvat et al., 2023; Stewart et al., 2023). One current research finding implies that people can be put-off by sexual images that are used to sell because of the objectifying and sexist elements of those images (Hertel et al., 2025; Hosen et al., 2025). Other research has honed-in on certain aspects of older studies—for example, people seem to recall sexualized advertisements or recognize them (an earlier theory for including sex in advertising), but are not necessarily connecting these with specific products or purchasing more of those products (Wirtz et al., 2018). Advertising is not my area of expertise; however, I do find it interesting that these shifts have occurred in the research, yet I am guessing that "sex sells" is still a common marketing lesson. These recent trends that indicate that sex may not actually sell do not seem to impact the amount of sexualized ads that exist. Additionally, in my world, in my experience, television commercials, video game covers, social media advertisements, heck, and even phone puzzle games are filled with sexual images, presumably in an effort to sell a product. Research on sexual content in the media suggests this to be true as about 85% of motion pictures and 82% of television shows contain sexual content (Ward et al., 2014).

Most asexuals report feeling like the world around them is hypersexualized and that there is too much of an emphasis on sex all around them (Gupta, 2017; Higginbottom, 2024). Brown (2022) discussed the impacts of "compulsory sexuality" (p. 7). She highlights (almost what seems contrary to the religious messages discussed above) the expectation that society has around sexual experiences, sexual desire, and the perceived need to engage in sexual acts that exist in our social discourses. Compulsory sexuality includes this expectation of sexual norms that can be challenging to both asexuals and allosexuals. The messages are that people *need* sex, *should* desire sex, and *should* have these needs met. These messages lead to a rape culture that is especially dominating of marginalized identities (as things that must be conquered sexually—as power and control become part of getting these socially constructed needs met).

This hypersexualization falls under some of these allonormative expectations. One study considers the images of sex. Iraklis (2023) explores the "taboo" language around asexuality and the movement toward de-stigmatizing asexuality. They argue that Western societies have set up a culture of "compulsory sexuality" (p. 1433), which sees attraction and sexual experiences as a requirement of all people. Even more importantly, this climate creates only one way to view healthy adults—as sexually active and driven by sexual attraction. The message is, if you are meeting the compulsive sexual scripts presented by Western society, then you are ok. If you are not, there is something wrong with you (Hart-Brinson et al., 2024). Iraklis (2023) explains "this social presumption that everyone should desire sexual activity or intimacy negatively influences the asexual population. Asexuality challenges the widely held belief that sexual behavior is necessary for humans" (p. 1433). If sexual attraction is a normal variable of humans, what is it like for asexuals who live daily without this piece (Hart-Brinson et al., 2024)? Social research, medical communities, even mental health professionals are often rooted in this idea that there is a sexual normality that exists and if people are not engaging sex in a particular way, there must be something wrong with them (Iraklis, 2023; Scherrer, 2008). In one study, over half of asexuals reported feeling pathologized by the medical community (Gupta, 2017). Iraklis (2023) argues for a revisiting of normality and a breaking down of this one way of looking at sexual desire.

Brandley and Dehnert (2024) expand on the discussion of allonormativity. They define allonormativity as, "a combination of macro- and micro-level messages that cement expectations for human beings to experiences sexual and/or romantic attraction, around which societal goals and privileges are built" (p. 1563). They continue to describe allornormativity in a way that is constantly recertified by dialogs that occur in families, in peer settings, in professional circles, and other social settings. Russell (2023) shared that language around relationships clearly indicates that one form of relationship is put above all others. They shared the language of how people may ask about a person "oh are you dating?" and the reply "oh, they are just a friend"—with emphasis on the "just"—which automatically places the importance of that relationship as "less than." Our social structures are set up in ways that embrace allonormative messages.

Interestingly, in one study of asexual comments in social media, frequently asexuals depicted themselves as outside the allonormative spectrum of experiences (Brandley & Dehnert, 2024). Researchers found that in social media communities sometimes asexuals were defining themselves as "monster, alien, or robot" (p. 1573), suggesting a sense of falling outside of the expected or human norm of behavior or experience.

Imagine if asexuality was the norm and allosexuality were viewed as the pathology? How would relationships look different? Would those with a very pronounced sense of sexual attraction have to dive into themselves to understand why they are different than the norm? If we, as a society, were able to just embrace the spectrum of desire and behavior, this would be positively impactful for asexuals and allosexuals; as not all allosexuals experience the world exactly the same either.

A Note about Sex Positivity Anyone reading this section, you might be thinking that I am presenting a negative view of sexuality or even an argument that sexual experience should be underplayed. I want to make it clear that this is not my stance at all. Additionally, most asexuals I spoke with presented very sex-positive viewpoints for those around them or even for themselves and their partner(s). When I think about sex-positivity, I think this is a philosophical value that people should be able to enjoy their bodies, experience sexual desire and satisfaction, understand their physical and emotional selves, and embrace feeling good and having sexual gratification if it fits for them. It is inclusive of all kinds of experiences (e.g., from penis-in-vagina sex—to kinks and fetishes—to masturbation—to never engaging in sexual experiences). Sex-positivity is an awareness of how our bodies work and education around safe sexual practices. Most importantly, sex-positivity is about consent—both understanding what that means internally and how to make sure any sexual partners are also providing consent. ***And,*** sex-positivity is also about creating a safe place for those who have no desire or little desire to have sexual experiences—this is embracing of *their* bodies.

I just want to stress that my own feelings and many feelings of asexuals it is not at all against the fact that sex exists in the media and advertising, it is the way that it is presented in only one way (hyper-sexualized), negating the plethora of possible experiences that are present among all (but most notably, for this book, asexuals). At times, sex in the media can represent body positivity, sex education, ways to communicate about one's sexual desires, can decrease shame around desires, and can really open the door for many to even better understand their own bodies (Tarver et al., 2025; White et al., 2023). I think being sex-positive allows for embracing sexual images and representations while also critiquing a hyper-sexualized culture.

The dilemma that comes to mind is that sexual experiences should always be based on consent. If you are consuming a sexually explicit video because you want to—awesome! If you are consuming a sexually explicit video and do not really want to, but it is part of everything out there and you do not have a choice—not awesome!

Broken

A term that I hear a lot from asexuals is ***broken***. In fact, 28 of the 35 interviews I did with asexuals in my 2022 study (Glass, 2022) mentioned the term broken distinctively at some point in the interview. I find it interesting that so many asexuals I have spoken with use this term in a way to describe their sense of self before they located language around asexuality and identity. Once this identity element is discovered as part of who they are, broken is talked about in the past tense. It is such relevant language in asexual communities, I wanted to give it space here.

Conner, a demisexual participant I spoke with, shared feeling, "broken around the whole sexual attraction thing" in his adolescence. This sense of brokenness impacted his early life dating experiences. He shared that he didn't start dating when his friends started dating, stating that his sense of brokenness "stacked up overtime in a war on my confidence." Over time, learning to understand himself better, allowed him to see how his approach is unique, but not broken, and he feels confident in relationships now.

Bri used the term broken to describe their process, they stated:

> Throughout my teen years, it was definitely the hardest because I didn't have a label yet and I just felt like I was broken or something must have happened to me even though I had no memory of anything happening to me. Everybody else seemed to feel something that I did not and seemed to want things that I did not want, so a lot of it was just fear based and once I found that label (asexuality) it was very freeing for me to finally like start to understand myself better understand like what I actually wanted in life and that may be stuff didn't have to look the way that everybody else told me it had to look.

Anita, another asexual participant, reflected on locating asexuality as a sexual orientation, she stated,

> I'm no longer feeling broken, I no longer feel like I'm missing something or like I feel like this I've been searching for this for so long and now that I feel like I found it I can move forward.

We will explore asexual identity processes in the next chapter, which embraces this "ah-ha" moment that many asexuals experience, and how the construct of broken can be part of those journeys.

When I personally think about this construct of broken, it resonates with me. I visualize the symbol of a broken hyperlink. You know when you click on a hyperlink and wait and wait and wait for something to happen and then eventually you come up with an error message of sorts. This is how I experience the world at times—people may say "look at that hot person" and I look and wait and wait for some brain synapses to connect to feel and experience it like they do, but I always end up with an error message; "does not compute." But, using my example, once I realized I was demisexual, I realized I could go to another link and that one worked! I didn't have to use the same hyperlinks as everyone else.

I really appreciated the comment made by one allosexual partner I spoke with, Rowan, they reflected on this category of broken:

> Respect them (asexuals), validate them and how they are feeling, and make sure because I have heard a lot of ace people being told and feeling like they are broken in some way and that makes me feel sad because, you know, they are not, they're just, I mean everyone is different. Everyone functions differently. I just don't understand why people kind of freak out about it.

I think there is value in realizing that broken links lead to new ways of seeing things.

Queerness

There is actually some debate regarding where asexuality fits in when it comes to queerness. If a cisgender male and cisgender female connect and get married and maybe one of them starts to realize they are demisexual, does this identity really change the external perspective of their sexual orientation? In fact, some of the asexuals that I interviewed are pretty comfortable stating that their asexuality is something that others do not even need to be aware of because it only impacts them and their partner(s) or potential partner(s), but all of my participants found language around sexual orientation and asexuality to be useful in their identity process. Asexuality clearly does not fit into the socially labeled sexual majority of experiences, so considering asexuality a minority sexual orientation makes sense. Vares (2022) stated, "I locate asexuality within queer, that is as anti-normative rather than anti-heteronormative" (p. 770).

Brown (2022) shares some of their experiences as an asexual; they stated that they felt their "queerness" as an asexual was "invalidated" (p. 27). They shared that oftentimes queer identities are focused on sex and that renders asexuality invisible in some queer communities (or even by straight people who do not see asexuality as fitting into their idea of queerness). Think for a moment how you might define a "gay man"—likely you would say "oh, that is a man who has sex with a man." Or, maybe, that would be one of your thoughts about defining gay men. Queerness, attraction, and identity are so much more than sexual acts. For some queer people, sex and/or sexual attraction are very big parts of who they are and how they identify, but that does not translate across the board to all queer people.

So, what is queer anyway? Queer identities are identities that sit on the outside of what society considers normal, regular, and typical (Brown, 2022). Individuals within queer communities sometimes feel a sense of shame or internal judgment around sexual intimacy (Frey et al., 2021). Being othered often comes with a sense of self that does not fit the social expectations. As asexuality and the language around asexuality become more part of Western communities—the expectation is twofold, first, many asexuals will be able to identify their uniquenesses sooner and understand this part of themselves, which seems to be empowering for asexuals. On the other hand, there is the sense of being open to ridicule and a deepened sense of othering. I can't help but consider, for example, that the author of the Harry Potter series recently shared an acephobic comment on Twitter during asexuality awareness day. She stated, "Happy International Fake Oppression day to everyone who wants complete strangers to know that they don't fancy a shag" (Winer, blog post, Apr. 8th, 2025). Not only was she misinformed about the experiences of asexuals, but she is putting hate language out there that other and delegitimizes. Queerness, or the re-centering of heteronormativity, recognizes the impacts of discrimination and marginalization. These words by J.K. Rowling are dehumanizing and delegitimizing and were felt hard by asexual communities (and others), many of whom, at some point, idolized this author's works.

Perspectives on Labeling

In my own research with asexuals, language and tying in labels were very validating to the participants' experiences. In addition, I personally feel connected to the importance of languaging, storying, and putting words to who we are, what we feel, and why we do what we do. I think it leaves space for understanding and articulating who we are. Much of my discussion in this book reflects this assumption of the importance of language deconstruction and the reconstruction of new language that can empower, describe, and redefine things that do not fit into the norm. I do want to take a moment here to share that labels and language are confining to some people and may not feel as empowering (Adams et al., 2014). I want to present here those voices as well. Many people do feel a sense of pride and validation through an identity or a label; other people have chosen to forgo any labeling because of the confining nature of labels (Holmes & Ghaziani, 2025). Some research has considered ways that labels can create an even greater sense of *othering* by creating binaries of experience (Holmes & Ghaziani, 2025). Labels can look at gender identities and sexual orientations in terms that look at how they are different from the norm, rather than how they are the same, which is limiting to the complexity of human experience (Galupo et al., 2016). Labeling can limit the fluidity that people experience when it comes to attraction and identity (Holmes & Ghaziani, 2025). At times, labels (even asexuality as a label) can be presented from one cultural or linguistic background or from a perspective that limits intersectional components of identity (Holmes & Ghaziani, 2025; Russell et al., 2023). Language and labeling in queer communities have led to some discussions and differences in perspectives about the pros and cons with regard to categorizing (Devonport et al., 2023). I value these discussions and embrace these different perspectives and the impact on language overall.

Summary

Asexuality is often described using language that represents a void of, different than, or at odds with the allosexual language used around them (Fine, 2023). Rather than being able to say "here is my identity" and describe this from an internal space, asexuality is often described from this allonormative language—opposite than or different than. Stating "a person that does not experience sexual attraction" is a widely used definition and is couched within the idea that "sexual attraction" is the "norm" and asexuality is NOT part of this. Even most of the research presented in this book is—how asexuals are different than the norm (than allosexuals), not embracing an identity from the core of what people experience. I envision a day where our identity as asexuals can build on the language of what we do feel, not what we do not feel. Much like queer theory has worked to centralize queerness in the center or how feminist theory has moved language in ways to embrace a wide range of perspectives and understandings (not just a male-centered/androcentric way of looking at things), my hope is that asexuality can be viewed in the mix of things rather than outside of things.

It is worth a mention that when we think about language, we often consider our primary language and not how things translate in other parts of the world. It is interesting that *asexual* as a term has been used to describe organisms that reproduce without a mate. Where the reproduced living thing is more like an exact copy, genetically. I remember this word from sixth-grade physical science. I can only imagine that asexuality may be oddly translated in other languages. In South Korea, for example, asexuality is not exactly translatable (An & Kim, 2024). The use of the split attraction model and differences in considering sexual and romantic love are not as easily presented translations in Korean language. Ruiqi Lu (personal communication, July 27, 2025) is an asexual researcher in China and shared that there has been discussion in Chinese asexual communities about language and locating a different word to better represent what asexuality means to them. Considering the roots of the terminology and the linguistic challenges, there can be quite a bit of misunderstanding around terminology. Again, to say, asexuality is so much more than sex and certainly has nothing to do with replicating oneself genetically.

As you continue to build on queer and asexual language, one thing that I find important about language and asexuality is the multiple ways and multiple continuums there are around asexuality that language attempts to describe. When I think about a heterosexual, cisgender couple, there is not a lot of language around what they feel sexually or romantically and maybe there should be. But, asexuality contains all these "axes" (Dawson et al., 2018, p. 375) that help asexual people consider what their identity means to them. There is a spectrum of attraction where a person could not experience any attraction at all (asexual) or can experience variability in that (e.g., demisexual, graysexual). There is an axis for sexual interests (from sex averse to sex favorable). There is an axis for romantic attraction (e.g., biromantic, heteroromantic). The evolution of language in asexual communities has benefitted asexuals as they navigate who they are and what it means to them. I feel this evolution of language can help everyone outside of asexual spectrums as well. What if that heterosexual, cisgender couple were to start breaking down their own experience with sex. Maybe one partner is more "sex indifferent"? Maybe one partner experiences occasional homoromantic feelings? Exploring uniquenesses and differences in all people allows that space to learn and grow. Gupta (2017) had a participant share that many allosexual people just accept the social norms around dating and sexual relationships, but asexuals are "forced to reevaluate" (p. 1001) these messages, which "opens a lot of doors to new things that you would never have considered otherwise" (p. 1001).

References

Adams, J., Braun, V., & McCreanor, T. (2014). "Aren't labels for pickle jars, not people?" Negotiating identity and community in talk about 'being gay'. *American Journal of Men's Health, 8*(6), 457–469. https://doi.org/10.1177/1557988313518800

An, H., & Kim, E. (2024). Unveiling the stressful experiences faced by asexual individuals in South Korea: A consensual qualitative study. *Psychology & Sexuality*, 1–16. https://doi.org/10.1080/19419899.2024.2408018

Bogaert, A. F. (2004). Asexuality: Prevalence and associated factors in a national probability sample. *The Journal of Sex Research, 41*(3), 279–287. https://doi.org/10.1080/00224490409552234

Brake, E. (2012). *Minimizing marriage: Marriage, morality, and the law*. Oxford University Press.

Brandley, B., & Dehnert, M. (2024). "I am not a robot, I am asexual": A qualitative critique of allonormative discourses of ace and aro folks as robots, aliens, monsters. *Journal of Homosexuality, 71*(6), 1560–1583. https://doi.org/10.1080/00918369.2023.2185092

Brandley, B., & LeMaster, L. (2025). The violence of allonormativity in communication studies: Notes on asexual injury, healing, and worldmaking. *Women's Studies in Communication, 48*(2), 283–305. https://doi.org/10.1080/07491409.2025.2488021

Brown, S. (2022). *Refusing compulsory sexuality: A Black asexual lens on our sex-obsessed culture*. North Atlantic Books.

Brunning, L., & McKeever, N. (2021). Asexuality. *Journal of Applied Philosophy, 38*(3), 497–517. https://doi.org/10.1111/japp.12472

Burge, A. (2018). The rough guide to love: Romance, history and sexualization in gendered relationship advice. *Journal of Gender Studies, 27*(6), 649–660. https://doi.org/10.1080/09589236.2017.1287065

Carlson, U. *The gay alphabet*. Youtube. https://www.youtube.com/watch?v=9j7HNFao4ds

Castillo, K., Reynolds, T. C. J. D., & Elliot, J. (2024). A qualitative study on biracial Black East Asian American women and their experiences of hypersexualization. *Qualitative Psychology*. https://doi.org/10.1037/qup0000312

Ciuvat, R. M., Furnham, A., & McClelland, A. (2023). Sex does not sell: The effect of sexual content on advertisement effectiveness and interference with memory for program information. *Perception and Motor Skills, 130*(1), 149–169. https://doi.org/10.1177/00315125221138395

Cowan, T., & LeBlanc, A. (2018). Feelings under dynamic description: The asexual spectrum and new ways of being. *Journal of Theoretical and Philosophical Psychology, 38*(1), 29–41. https://doi.org/10.1037/teo0000076

Cuthbert, K. (2022). Asexuality and epistemic injustice: A gendered perspective. *Journal of Gender Studies, 31*(7), 840–851. https://doi.org/10.1080/09589236.2021.1966399

D'Emilio, J., & Freedman, E. B. (1997). *Intimate matters: A history of sexuality in America* (2nd ed.). University of Chicago Press.

Dawson, M., Scott, S., & McDonnell, L. (2018). '"Asexual" isn't who I am': The politics of asexuality. *Sociological Research Online, 23*(2), 374–391. https://doi.org/10.1177/1360780418757540

Devonport, T. J., Leflay, K., Biscomb, K., Richardson-Walsh, H., Richardson-Walsh, K., & Thelwall, M. (2023). "Nobody needs a label": Responses on Facebook to a Team GB equity, diversity and inclusion initiative. *Sport in Society, 26*(6), 1113–1132. https://doi.org/10.1080/17430437.2022.2115365

Dewitt, J. (2023, June 1). Asexual and aromantic people are often forgotten, but god sees us. *Sojouner's Magazine.* https://sojo.net/articles/joy-being-queer-and-christian/asexual-and-aromantic-people-are-often-forgotten-god-sees-us

Fine, J. (2023). From crushes to squishes: Affect and agency on r/AskReddit and r/asexual. *Journal of Language and Sexuality, 12*, 145–172. https://doi.org/10.1075/jls.22004.fin

Flanagan, R. (2024). 'Nobody ever told you, "actually, this feels great"': Religion informed sexual health education and barriers to developing sexual literacy. *International Journal of Educational Research, 7.* https://doi.org/10.1016/j.ijedro.2024.100343

Frey, J. J., Half, W. J., Goldbach, J. T., & Lanier, P. (2021). "Here in the Bible Belt, it's predominantly negative": Sexual identity stigma in the American south, 50 years after Stonewall. *Frontiers in Psychology, 12*(1). https://doi.org/10.3389/fpsyg.2021.804064

Galupo, M. P., Henise, S. B., & Mercer, N. L. (2016). "The labels don't work very well": Transgender individuals' conceptualizations of sexual orientation and sexual identity. *International Journal of Transgenderism, 17*(2), 93–104. https://doi.org/10.1080/15532739.2016.1189373

Glass, V. Q. (2022). Queering relationships: Exploring phenomena of asexual identified persons in relationships. *Contemporary Family Therapy: An International Journal, 44*, 344–359. https://doi.org/10.1007/s10591-022-09650-9

Goodwill, J. R., Anyiwo, N., Williams, E.-D. G., Johnson, N. C., Mattis, J. S., & Watkins, D. C. (2019). Media representations of popular culture figures and the construction of Black masculinities. *Psychology of Men & Masculinities, 20*(3), 288–298. https://doi.org/10.1037/men0000164

Gupta, K. (2017). "And now I'm just different, but there's nothing actually wrong with me": Asexual marginalization and resistance. *Journal of Homosexuality, 64*, 991–1013. https://doi.org/10.1080/00918369.2016.1236590

Hart-Brinson, P., Tlachac, M. L., & Lepien, E. (2024). Contradictions in experiences of compulsory sexuality and pathways to asexual citizenship. *Sexuality & Culture: An Interdisciplinary Journal, 28*(1), 187–213. https://doi.org/10.1007/s12119-023-10110-1

Hertel, M., Palla, L., & Wolff, H.-G. (2025). Sex(ism) doesn't sell: Disentangling the effects of nudity and sexism in advertising. *Acta Psychologica, 255*, 1–12. https://doi.org/10.1016/j.actpsy.2025.104909

Higginbottom, B. (2024). The nuances of intimacy: Asexual perspectives and experiences with dating and relationships. *Archives of Sexual Behavior: The Official Publication of the International Academy of Sex Research, 53*(5), 1899–1914. https://doi.org/10.1007/s10508-024-02846-0

Holmes, A., & Ghaziani, A. (2025). Situational fluidity and the use of identity labels in interactions. *Socius: Sociological Research for a Dynamic World, 11.* https://doi.org/10.1177/23780231241306466

Hosen, N., Demsar, V., Ferraro, C., & Wheeler, M. A. (2025). Consumer reactions to the use of sex appeals in influencer vs brand social media marketing. *Journal of Business Research, 199*, 1–17. https://doi.org/10.1016/j.jbusres.2025.115511

Hugues, J. C., & Rouse, S. V. (2023). Everyone belongs here: How affirming and non-affirming church messages and imagery cause different feelings of acceptance in LGBTQ+Christians. *Journal of Psychology and Theology, 51*(4), 523–536. https://doi.org/10.1177/00916471231185811

Iraklis, G. (2023). Examining the social tabooisation of asexuality: The underpinnings of antiasexual bias. *Sexuality Research and Social Policy, 21*, 1432–1445. https://doi.org/10.1007/s13178-02300884-2

Lamont, E. (2021). The persistence of gendered dating. *Sociology Compass, 15*(11), 1–15. https://doi.org/10.1111/soc4.12933

Lawrence v. Texas, 539 U.S. 558 (2003).

Leath, S., Jerald, M. C., Perkins, T., & Jones, M. K. (2021). A qualitative exploration of jezebel stereotype endorsement and sexual behaviors among Black college women. *Journal of Black Psychology, 47*(4–5), 244–283. https://doi.org/10.1177/0095798421997215

Leonhardt, N. D., Busby, D. M., & Willoughby, B. J. (2020). Sex guilt or satisfaction: The indirect role of religiousity on sexual satisfaction. *Psychology of Religion and Spirituality, 12*, 213–222. 10/1037/re100000245.

Mandigo, D. M., & Kavar, L. (2022). The experience of male asexuality: A phenomenological inquiry. *Qualitative Report, 27*(2), 488–508. https://doi.org/10.46743/2160-3715/2022.5213

Matsick, J. L., Kruk, M., Palmer, L., Layland, E. K., & Salomaa, A. C. (2022). Extending the social category label effect to stigmatized groups: Lesbian and gay people's reactions to "homosexual" as a label. *Journal of Social and Political Psychology, 10*(1), 369–390. https://doi.org/10.5964/jspp.6823

Mollet, A. L., & Lackman, B. R. (2018). Asexual borderlands: Asexual collegians' reflections on inclusion under the LGBTQ umbrella. *Journal of College Student Development, 59*(5), 623–628. https://doi.org/10.1353/csd.2018.0058

Oluwayomi, A. (2022). The fear of Black men? A fanonian cartography of anti-Black misandry as psycho-sexual pathology. *Journal of Black Sexuality and Relationships, 8*(4), 55–76. https://doi.org/10.1353/bsr.2022.0005

Rothblum, E. D., Heimann, K., & Carpenter, K. (2019). The lives of asexual individuals outside of sexual and romantic relationships: Education, occupation, religion and community. *Psychology & Sexuality, 10*(1), 83–93. https://doi.org/10.1080/19419899.2018.1552186

Russell, J. (2023). The sex lives of asexuals. In *Erotically queer: A pink therapy guide for practitioners* (pp. 59–74). https://doi.org/10.4324/9781003260608-5

Russell, S. T., Bishop, M. D., & Fish, J. N. (2023). Expanding notions of LGBTQ. *Annual Review of Sociology, 49*, 281–296. https://doi.org/10.1146/annurev-soc-030320-032256

Scappini, A., & Fioravanti, G. (2022). Gender scripts and female sexual functioning: The role of sexual pressure and sexual subjectivity. *Journal of Sex Research, 59*(9), 1110–1121. https://doi.org/10.1080/00224499.2022.2012477

Scherrer, K. S. (2008). Coming to an asexual identity: Negotiating identity, negotiating desire. *Sexualities, 11*(5), 621–641. https://doi.org/10.1177/1363460708094269

Smith, K. (2025, June 27). Growing up as an asexual Christian. *Believe Out Loud*. https://www.believeoutloud.com/voices/article/growing-up-as-an-asexual-christian/

Stevenson, R., & Hiebert, D. (2021). Silenced desire: Personal effects of the evangelical construction of female sexuality. *Journal of Sociology and Christianity, 11*(2), 59–83.

Stewart, K., Dalakas, V., & Eells, D. (2023). Does sex sell? Examining the effect of sex appeals in social media ads on engagement with the ad and actual purchase. *Journal of Marketing Communications, 29*(7), 701–714. https://doi.org/10.1080/13527266.2022.2072367

Tarver, M. L., Seshadri, G., Gutierrez, N., Fontus, F., & Boykins, B. (2025). No shame, all gain: The influence of sex positive learning on the sexual health of Black women, a feminist study. *Journal of Feminist Family Therapy, 37*(1/2), 23–41. https://doi.org/10.1080/08952833.2025.2472524

Tessler, H., & Winer, C. (2023). Sexuality, romantic orientation, and masculinity: Men as underrepresented in asexual and aromantic communities. *Sociology Compass, 17*(11), 13141. https://doi.org/10.1111/soc4.13141

Thurmond, J., & Levin, S. (2023, November). Is 'no sex' okay? *Sojourners Magazine, 52*(9), 26–29.

Vares, T. (2022). Asexuals negotiate the "onslaught of the heteronormative". *Sexualities, 25*(5/6), 767–784. https://doi.org/10.1177/1363460721993389

Ward, L. M., Reed, L., Trinh, S. L., & Foust, M. (2014). Sexuality and entertainment media. In D. L. Tolman, L. M. Diamond, J. A. Bauermeister, W. H. George, J. G. Pfaus, & L. M. Ward

(Eds.), *APA handbook of sexuality and psychology, Vol. 2. Contextual approaches* (pp. 373–423). American Psychological Association. https://doi.org/10.1037/14194-012

Weitz, P. (Director). (1999). *American pie* [Film]. Universal Studios.

White, A., Boehm, M., Glackin, E., & Bleakley, A. (2023). How sexual information sources are related to emerging adults' sex-positive scripts and sexual communication. *Sexuality and Culture, 7*, 1–22. https://doi.org/10.1007/s12119-022-10061-z

Winer, C. (2025, April 8). And then JK came for the asexuals. *The Sociologist Speaks.* https://cantonwiner.substack.com/p/and-then-jk-rowling-came-for-the

Wirtz, J. G., Sparks, J. V., & Zimbres, T. M. (2018). The effect of exposure to sexual appeals in advertisements on memory, attitude, and purchase intention: A meta-analytic review. *International Journal of Advertising, 37*(2), 168–198. https://doi.org/10.1080/02650487.2017.1334996

Wu, H., Luo, S., Klettner, A., White, T., & Albritton, K. (2021). Gender roles in the millennium: Who pays and is expected to pay for romantic dates? *Psychological Reports, 126*(2), 791–811. https://doi.org/10.1177/00332941211057144

Zehra, F., Nur, A., & Melike, Z. E. (2023). Religion and attitudes towards sexual orientation and gender identity. *Journal of Religious and Religious Dynamics, 2*(1), 27–42. https://doi.org/10.58425/jrcd.v2il.210

Chapter 4
Identity Process

A 29-year-old client walks into your room for the first session; we will call her Jenna. All you know about her is that she stated she was depressed at the intake call. Upon meeting, she is cautious and closed off. You work to build a sense of safety and trust. Then, Jenna states, "I think something is wrong with me, you know, sexually." You let her know that this is a safe space and you are not there to judge her, but if she feels like sharing more about this, you will provide the space to process what she is going through and that you may even know ways to help her get through what she is experiencing. She states, "I am just not interested in dating anyone, like I never have been." Jenna is physically shaking as she shares this information. She continues to share that she went to a therapist when she was in college who told her she just hadn't met the right person and that it would happen. She said her doctor ran some blood tests to make sure she didn't have any hormone deficiencies. Her doctor referred her back to therapy to figure out if there was trauma or something in her background that might be causing this issue. Jenna says, "I don't think I have any sexual trauma." She is so lost and perplexed. She continues to describe a lifetime of feeling different than her peers. She states that her friend group was constantly talking about sex, and it made her uncomfortable. She said, "I know, like, if everyone else is ok, there must be something wrong with me! Even my family won't get off my back—telling me I have to date and starting to refer to me as an 'old maid' or tell me I am gonna be an old lady with a bunch of cats. They might be right, I just don't understand, did something happen to me to make me this way?"

How would you know, as a practitioner or a medical provider, how to move forward with Jenna? Does putting the language of asexuality out there for every patient who may suggest a variation or odd feeling around sex or romance make sense? Throughout this chapter, and moving forward in the book, I hope to give you a little more understanding of identity formation and identity processes for many asexuals that might help guide you a little in what questions you may ask Jenna or how you might collaborate with her as she uncovers language that builds on her individual experiences.

V. Q. Glass, *Asexuality, Relationships, and Identity Formation*, https://doi.org/10.1007/978-3-032-22857-4_4

As a practitioner, queer identity process models can be useful ways of visualizing client experiences and may help identify places where you could offer support and guidance. Having a patient, like Jenna, come in distraught and sharing that they feel *broken* because they do not feel connected to sexual desire or sexual attraction in the ways that others do, could be very different from a patient who proudly shares, "I am an asexual, aromantic, and love my life and everything about my identity!" Considering where individuals are in the process of understanding their sexual orientation identity or identities can lead to different clinical goals or approaches.

When a person experiences the world in a similar way to most others in their environment, identity formation can often feel like the world is validating what you know to be true about yourself, it can feel seamless and a nonissue. If a heterosexual, cisgender male wants a romantic and sexual relationship with a cisgender female partner and they are both drawn to this dynamic—likely the identity process is very quick, because heterosexual identities are largely supported and represented as the norm (like there is no "coming out process" internally or externally, it just *is*). Heterosexual identities are typically assumed from birth, making *coming out* as a heterosexual more of just recognizing that this part of you fits in with the majority, the expectations of those around you. Cisgender heterosexuals do not *have* to adjust language or ritualistic expectations of marriage. Wedding magazines and websites often portray other heterosexual couples; there are legal and publicly supported aspects to these relationships (e.g., tax breaks, medical forms), and these relationships are validated in all areas of public Western worlds. Cisgender heterosexual identities, who they are on the inside, is not something that is different from what you see in most others (peers, co-workers, schoolmates, family, media, etc.). When a person may feel like something is different in the way they view, experience, and approach relationships and sex, the understanding of that identity often requires additional steps or, at the very least, a bit more thought and internal processing.

Identity processes are human developmental processes (Kelleher et al., 2024). If you are a cisgender woman and find yourself attracted to women, you might go through a process where you wonder why you are not fitting into the norm of what you see around you (e.g., "why am I not attracted to boys like my other female friends?"). This person may go through an internal process of identity and research the world around them for language or commonalities to what they are feeling ("ok, lesbian, that fits me"). Additionally, others in this person's world may assume that she is heterosexual, which requires another part of the process—coming out to others. These steps in understanding self and presenting who you are can be difficult for some because there might not be the support or representation to ease the process. For others, they are fearful of their family perspectives, their peer responses, or even internalized homophobia. Maybe this person decides to marry her same-sex partner at some point. Even though she might have developed a strong sense of internal identity around her lesbian identity and even maybe most of her immediate friends and family have welcomed her identity to varying degrees—she is now navigating a ritual of marriage that was constructed to be between cisgender males and cisgender females. This public ritual may require another layer of self-awareness and self-advocacy that heterosexual couples have no need to do because these rituals and the language around them have been set up to support them already.

In this chapter, I will present a history of some of the queer identity process models and present my own asexual identity process model that adds asexual identity processes to previous queer identity process models. This chapter also integrates qualitative data from 35 asexual participants that served as the backbone to the creation of this identity process model for asexuality.

Historically, *coming out models* or *identity formation models* have highlighted identity processes for individuals who identify outside of sexual and gender norms (e.g., Cass, 1979; Coleman, 1982; Diamond, 2003; Robbins et al., 2016; Troiden, 1979). Identity formation is defined as the internal process of recognizing language that explains one's experience, acceptance of their identity, and the presentation of one's identity in a more public way (Pitcher et al., 2024; Robbins et al., 2016). Kelleher et al. (2024) states,

> Sexuality is considered an aspect of one's identity that can shape their entire character and is believed to be affected by both internal and external factors. Sexual identity can be conceptualized as involving the cognitive and emotional understanding of an individual's sexuality, including sexual attractions, desires, behaviors, values, and relationships (p. 47).

Research indicates that being *out* to oneself and one's community is known to benefit a person's mental and emotional health (Pitcher et al., 2024). The process of understanding oneself can be part of a therapeutic journey for some.

Queer Identity Process Models

The oldest and most well-known identity formation model was established by Vivienne Cass in 1979. Cass' (1979) model considered sexual orientation (e.g., homosexuality or same-sex attraction). Her model outlined six stages of identity formation:

1. Identity confusion—when a person starts to consider that their sexual orientation may not be matching what they see other people experiencing.
2. Identity comparison—a person started to explore and may come across differences in language and how people identify their sexual orientation. They compare their own experiences to these identities.
3. Identity tolerance—when a person starts to make more sense of their own identity and feel more confident in describing themselves in a certain way.
4. Identity acceptance—a person accepts who they are and likely is using language (e.g., gay, lesbian) to describe themselves. Often at this stage, they are also sharing this part of their identity with others.
5. Identity pride—when a person takes acceptance a step farther and becomes a notable part of a community of others that might share similar experiences. They develop a sense of internal pride around their identity.
6. Identity synthesis—a final step in the process, a person integrates who they are in all aspects of their life. Often in this stage there is a self-acceptance, an awareness, and a desire to support others in their journeys.

Cass (1979, 1984) had an expressed goal of learning about identity formation from individuals who had the shared experience of same-sex attraction. Her results reflect some of the nuances in how people with same-sex attraction understand this part of their identity.

A few years after Cass's model, Fassinger and Miller (1996) identified a slightly different process of identity formation for sexual minorities, specifically lesbian-identified persons. They argued that earlier identity formation models did not recognize racial differences in sexual minority identity development. Fassinger and McCann state that prior models of identity formation fail "to account for the social realities of diverse groups of lesbians and gay men" (p. 520). They continue to explain, "such factors as occupational environment, geographical location, racial/ethnic group membership, family situation, legal and economic realities, and support systems determine the extent to which disclosure and politicalization are even possible for many lesbians and gay men" (p. 520). Their research led to a four-stage model of identity formation.

1. Awareness—recognizing that there is something internally that feels different than the norm and also becoming more aware of other sexual minorities.
2. Exploration—putting oneself in environments that allow them to try on and better understand their feelings and differences (e.g., attending events specific to lesbians after considering that one might identify this way).
3. Deepening/Commitment—taking more of an ownership of one's identity and feeling more closely attached to that identity. This can include the recognition of social messages and/or oppressions.
4. Internalization/Synthesis—a deeper connection to a person's sexual minority identity and a sense of fulfillment in that identity.

With Cass (1979) and Fassinger and Miller (1996) being early contributors to the understanding of queer identity formation, their theories and findings are rooted in their era. Awareness, visibility, and language have shifted a great deal since their theories originated. Despite the changes over time, many researchers have built on these models to better understand queer identities throughout decades (Aglipay, 2014; Coleman, 1982; Degges-White et al., 2000; Diamond, 2003; Robbins et al., 2016; Troiden, 1979). Coleman (1982) introduced an identity formation process model similar to Cass'; however, Colmen stressed the importance of considering social messages and social pressures and how impactful they can be on a person's experience developing a strong sense of identity as a sexual minority. Both Chapman and Brannock (1987) and Degges-White et al. (2000) considered the Cass model in looking at a sample of lesbians and yielded similar identity formation processes. Aglipay (2014) introduced the idea of fluidity of sexual orientation and that shifts in identity should be a consideration in identity formation. Diamond (2003) explored identity formation and considered differences in sexual attraction and romantic attraction in how people view their sexual orientation. Morales (1989) considered racial differences in the identity formation processes of sexual minorities, noting that most of the research on identity formation prior to the late 1980s was on primarily White sexual minorities.

Identity formation models have been applied to gender identity processes as well. Both Devor (2004) and Bockting and Coleman (2016) present identity process models for transgender individuals. Bockting and Coleman (2016) identify that transgender individual experiences replicate sexual minority stages of identity development. They identify five stages in their identity formation model of transgender identities (pre-coming out, coming out, exploration, intimacy, and identity integration). Devor's (2004) extensive research with transgender individuals led to their 14-stage model that integrates distinctions of gender diverse experiences that might include medication interventions and social transitions.

As you can see, there has been extensive research on identity formation; many researchers have increased awareness of the impacts of identity formation with sexual minorities and gender minorities. These theoretical models and the research that has contributed to and supported these models have laid a foundation for understanding the complexities of how people come to understand themselves, particularly when they are of a minority sexual or gender identity that does not feel like it fits what they are seeing around them. Asexuality, as a sexual orientation, is almost a minority within a minority. Asexuality is under the queer umbrella; however, it is a lesser known and understood identity overall. That being said, there have been shifts in research to understand asexual identity processes.

Asexual Identity Development

Researchers and theorists have addressed some uniquenesses within asexual identity processes. Identifying asexual labels and locating information on asexuality is often pivotal to identity processes for asexual individuals (Bogaert, 2015; Brotto et al., 2010; Mitchell & Hunnicutt, 2019). Language is often a means to how people envision the world and their place within it. A formidable part of the identity process includes the identification of language that represents a person's experiences, and this seems to be especially important for less visible sexual and gender minorities.

In 2016, Robbins et al. presented their research, which highlighted asexual participants' process of disclosing their asexual identities to others. Robbins et al. (2016) found that asexual participants' coming out and identity process experiences are similar in some ways to how others of different sexual orientations experience identity formation (e.g., Cass, 1979). Robbins et al.'s (2016) model highlighted the following:

Stage 1: Identity confusion
Stage 2: Discovery of language
Stage 3: Exploration and education
Stage 4: Identity acceptance and salience negotiation
Stage 5: Coming out
Stage 6: Identity integration

As discussed in previous queer identity process models, asexual people, in Robbins et al.'s (2016) study, had similar experiences of knowing they are different. The researchers point out that for asexuals, terminology for asexuality is not as widely known and, as a result, asexuals may experience a period of time in their life where they feel like something is wrong with them. Stage 2 of the model identifies this "discovery of language" where asexuals may encounter the vast terminology under the asexual umbrella. For many asexuals, this can be an ah-ha moment and certainly has been replicated in my own research (which I will discuss more below). This experience of locating language is unique to asexuals in some ways; however, with language and visibility increasing, this uniqueness may shift with time.

More recently, Kelleher and Murphy (2022) also considered asexual identity development. These researchers highlighted the impact of social expectations in both heteronormative and queer communities that sexual attraction is what is *normal* and anything diverting from that is often seen as unhealthy or a cause for concern. These social expectations contribute to some asexuals repressing their feelings or working to mask their lack of sexual attraction and desire. Their findings suggest that, prior to identifying terms that fit for them, many asexuals experience a sense of "feeling different" (p. 872) around sexual attraction and just not feeling like they "get the hype" (p.872) around sex. Often, asexual participants, in their study, reported avoiding being in situations where dating or sexual activities were primary conversations (Gupta, 2017). This feeling of being different or avoiding things often leads asexuals to seek out answers (which sometimes can start with therapists or physicians). Once the terminology around asexuality is located—sometimes in social media, internet searches, queer communities, or even practitioners—there is often a connection. It is after language has been located that many asexuals begin to feel validated. At this point, they often start to explore what this means for them in terms of community, relationships, and a better understanding of self.

Mandigo and Kavar's (2022) research looked at the identity process of male asexuals and noted a similar process of identity formation that includes an initial emotional response, a feeling of "otherness" (p. 498), a process of learning about asexuality, a feeling of connecting to the community, and a sense of connection to the split attraction model. Their research suggests some ways that masculinity may impact the process differently. In initial identity formation stages, asexual male participants seem to struggle differently in peer groups because of the over-emphasis and sexual expectations of male peers. There is a real feeling of being excluded from conversations and experiences that may not fit for asexual male participants in mostly allosexual peer groups.

Another research study on asexual identity development identified intersections of identity. Foster et al. (2019) conducted a research study that explored identity formation and identity recognition processes for non-White asexual women. Non-White asexual participants in Foster's study suggested that they struggled finding a community that embraced their intersections. The participants expressed a clear sense that their asexual identity intersected with their gender and racial identities, one participant saying, "face it, people are always going to be a lot more accepting of a White asexual than they are of a Black asexual" (p. 133). There was a clear feeling among participants that they were underrepresented in the asexual community (which is often assumed to be mostly White). Additionally, from the data reports presented in Foster et al.'s study, participants seemed to share experiencing microaggressive comments and fears of rejection more notably than by (mostly White) participants. It would be interesting, in future research, to see if this is in fact the case. Despite these distinctions, Black asexual women participants did seem to have similar identity processes around feeling a sense of difference, working to understand that difference, and finding a label that helped them better embrace that difference.

Disclosure

I think of many queer identity processes as having two components: the internal awareness of one's queer identity and the external awareness (sometimes this one is called *coming out*—where people inform others of their identities). Disclosure for asexuals takes on a lot of different forms. Some asexuals feel it is part of their identity that no one, except possible partners, should have to know about. Some asexuals wear the identity pridefully and openly, others may decide to share with others as a way of supporting other asexuals through visibility. MacNeela and Murphy (2015) explored how asexual participants experienced disclosure of identity to others. Participants would often experience internal relief with the recognition of language and community; however, this often felt at odds with external expectations of desire and relationships. Interestingly, in one study that looked at demisexual adolescents and compared them to non-demisexual asexuals, demisexuals were more likely to disclose their demisexual identity with their peers and communities (Pitcher et al., 2024). This may have something to do with the fact that many demisexuals do feel sexual attraction at some point and maybe this is more understandable and even acceptable to others.

Initial research on identity process and asexuals often looks at parts of the stages of previous queer identity process models (Kelleher & Murphy, 2022; MacNeela & Murphy, 2015; Mandigo & Kavar, 2022; Robbins et al., 2016). To summarize, I collapse some of the major themes of identity formation and consider how each stage could be different for asexuals (see Table 4.1).

Split Attraction Model

I keep coming back to the split attraction model! The split attraction model is often a vital part of the identity process. The language around the split attraction model is helpful to a lot of asexuals—in their internal and external identity processes

Table 4.1 Comparing asexual experiences with queer identity formation stages

Stage	Defined for queer identities as a whole	Possible uniquenesses for asexuals
Stage 1: Identity confusion	In this stage, queer individuals reported knowing something was different (Mandigo & Kavar, 2022; Robbins et al., 2016). For some, there can be an awareness of language that might describe their difference and/or knowing others or being aware of others are "like them" (Cass, 1979)	For asexual individuals, there is often a lack of knowledge that this identity even exists (Robbins et al., 2016). There is little representation in the media or in communities of asexuality as a sexual orientation.
Stage 2: Discovery of terminology	In this stage, queer populations start to explore terminology that might fit their experiences (Cass, 1979; Coleman, 1982; Macneela & Murphy, 2015; Mandigo & Kavar, 2022; Robbins et al., 2016). For example, a teenage cisgender male finds himself attracted to other males and recognizes language around the term "gay" might fit his experience.	Because asexuality is not a widely known construct, asexual people may stumble upon the asexual language and representation in varying ways (Robbins et al., 2016). Additionally, locating language may not happen (or at all) because language around asexual terminology is not part of the mainstream.
Stage 3: Exploration and education	The Cass (1979) model identifies an "identity comparison" stage for gay and lesbian persons where they may start to examine what these identities mean for other people and how their experiences fit.	In this stage, asexual people are in the learning stage of "coming out." They are seeking out more information on asexuality and considering how this language might fit for them (Robbins et al., 2016).
Stage 4: Identity acceptance and salience negotiation	The Cass (1979) model indicates that gay and lesbian people start to accept that this identity is something that fits for them.	Asexual experiences involve a more "precise articulation" (Robbins et al., 2016, p. 758) because of the variations with the spectrum and the language (e.g., microlabels) around these variations. For example, an aromantic, sex-averse, asexual individual may see themselves as not interested in relationships at all (or in varying degrees); whereas a graysexual, sex positive, biromantic individuals may experience sexual attraction and romance in varying ways.
Stage 5: Coming out	Coming out models (e.g., Cass, 1979; Coleman, 1982) identify a stage of disclosure. Cass (1979) identifies this as pride and feeling integrated into a community.	For asexual individuals, this can look different because of the lack of social knowledge on these identities and because some asexuals may not really find the need to share with larger groups. Other asexuals may want to be out to their communities as a way of representing their identity and their differences.

(continued)

Table 4.1 (continued)

Stage	Defined for queer identities as a whole	Possible uniquenesses for asexuals
Stage 6: Identity integration	Cass (1979) identified a final stage in gay and lesbian identity development that involved "identity synthesis." In this stage, gay and lesbian people develop a sense of peace and acceptance. Robbins et al. (2016) suggested a sense of pride in self (despite external coming out or not).	MacNeela and Murphy (2015) and Mandigo and Kavar (2022) both discussed how external social messages and reactions to asexual identity disclosure is mixed and not always understanding or supportive. At the same time, all of the asexuals I interviewed seemed to have embraced this part of themselves and learned to appreciate and understand their identity.

(Antonsen et al., 2020; Mandigo & Kavar, 2022). The split attraction model provides language to explain some microlabels or distinctions. This model splits up the ideas of *sexual attraction* and *romantic attraction* into microlabels (Asexuality and Visibility Education Network [AVEN], 2022). An example of how a person would view themselves within the split attraction model could be—a person feels sexual attraction to male individuals but may feel romantic attraction to people of all genders, or another person may not feel sexual attraction to anyone; however, they are romantically attracted to women. The split attraction model has not been commonly researched; however, the language is common in many asexual and queer communities (AVEN). Research on asexuals identifies that asexual persons often use language that contributes to a better understanding of the distinctions within the asexual spectrum (Elgie, 2020; Haefner, 2011; Mandigo & Kavar, 2022). This model allows asexuals to see how their variances in experience can be described, the split attraction model can validate those nuances for many asexuals. The split attraction model plays an important role in the three-stage asexual identity development model.

Introducing the Three-Stage Asexual Identity Process Model

In my own research, I have uncovered some distinctions in the identity formation of asexual individuals and how this identity formation process seems to exist in a direct response to relationships and dating (Glass, 2022). This direct response is partly because relationships, dating, and the scripts around them are ingrained into the narratives of society. My exploration within participant responses identified an asexual identity process model. I will present this research and the model the data supported.

I am proposing a three-stage asexual identity process model based on phenomenological data from asexual participants. These stages include:

Stage 1: Juxtaposing Identity
Stage 2: Interpreting Identity
Stage 3: Integrating Identity

In comparing this model with earlier queer identity models, the thing that I have found unique about asexual identity experiences is that there is a major *ah-ha* moment when language is located. I feel that many other queer identities are part of mainstream culture currently and this *ah-ha* moment for other sexual orientations is a longer mulling over process because the language and representation are out there. But, there is often a lack of awareness of asexuality, the identity of asexuality, and what asexuality means as a sexual orientation—so once people are aware of the terminology, it can be quickly validating. Asexuals may not have heard of the terminology, and once they do, it seems they quickly resonate with the identity and feeling a sense of self-awareness, peace, and ultimately pride in that identity. To explore asexual identity process experiences, I constructed a research study with asexual adults. One of the main purposes of this research was to explore asexual experiences within the context of relationships, and I reported on that part of my analysis in 2022 (Glass, 2022). I will present some of those results and participant data throughout other chapters in this book. However, in this chapter, I will take a detailed look into one of the four themes that arose from the original research, "evolving asexual identity development" (Glass, 2022, p. 344). The following section of this book will describe the data, the analysis, and journey into the asexual identity processes that participants experienced. This research informed the evolution of the three-step asexual identity process model presented.

Research Introduction

The three-stage asexual identity process model was developed from the voices and stories of 35 asexual participants who participated in interviews with me. Phenomenology (Willig et al., 2017) and queer phenomenology (Ahmed, 2006) guided the research process and data analysis. Loosely using Giorgi's process of analysis, my analysis included (a) a thorough and detailed reading of transcripts, (b) an initial coding of emerging themes from the transcripts, (c) a collapsing of themes into more meaningful units, and (d) intuitively identifying larger thematic units (Willig et al., 2017). Note that internal review board permission was granted, and I sought participants through asexual groups on social media.

Background of Participants

An overview of the 35 participants includes varying geographical locations across the United States ($n = 31$), the United Kingdom ($n = 3$), and Mexico (n = 1). Age ranges of participants were: 25 and under ($n = 4$), 26–35 ($n = 21$), 36–45 ($n = 6$), and over 45 ($n = 4$). Education levels included some college or college degree ($n = 15$), some graduate school or graduate degree, advanced degree, or other beyond undergraduate degree ($n = 20$). Participants identified varying professional backgrounds, some included: counselor, law enforcement officer, fuel clerk, web developer, veterinarian, nurse, and student. All participants defined themselves on the asexual spectrum, 18 also mentioned they were demisexual, and 10 shared that they were graysexual. Participants also often disclosed micro-identities. These included romantic microlabels, about half of participants ($n = 16$) expressed romantic identities that included: aromantic ($n = 3$), biromantic ($n = 6$), panromantic ($n = 7$), grayromantic ($n = 2$), or demiromantic ($n = 1$) (note: some identified more than one romantic microlabel, for example, panromantic and demiromantic). Some participants used microlabels that described their reactions to sexual activity, which included sex-favorable ($n = 16$), sex-indifferent ($n = 9$), or sex-averse ($n = 2$). Sexual orientations outside of the participant's asexual identity were also mentioned by 21 participants. These included heterosexual, gay, lesbian, bisexual, or queer or a combination of some of these sexual orientation identities. Participants described their gender identity as cisgender ($n = 26$), nonbinary ($n = 6$), transgender ($n = 1$), agender ($n = 1$), or gender fluid ($n = 1$). Nine participants self-disclosed identifying as polyamorous.

Phenomenological Results and Asexual Identity Process

To introduce the theme of identity process, I want to begin with a reflection on Ellis' journey. Ellis' reflections here would likely resonate with most asexual individuals and highlight much of the identity searching and understanding that asexuals experience.

Ellis defines themselves as nonbinary, sex-indifferent, aromantic, and asexual. Ellis shared,

> So, finding out I was ace, I didn't really stumble into that right away, it was more something I realized…I always just thought, oh love will happen, when it gets here an attraction will just happen, so it is fine, it is not a problem that I am not feeling like this is a Disney movie. As I grew older, I realized that my experience wasn't matching up with other people.

Ellis discussed a running joke they have with their friends that they call "the barista and the tree." Once, Ellis and their friends were at a coffee shop. Ellis' friends were "talking to a cute barista" while Ellis was admiring the beauty of the "pretty tree outside the window." After the barista walked away, the friend group began a conversation: "that barista was super cute and said hi to you" and Ellis' response was "huh?" Ellis was totally unaware of the sexual energy the barista was putting out there. Ellis had been admiring a tree and literally was missing what all the others had picked up on. They shared they were paying attention to the tree, which brought out laughter among the friends who were baffled that Ellis did not pick up on the sexual, flirty energy. This was a huge recognition for Ellis and their friends of how different asexuality and allosexuality could be. Ellis had shared their asexual identity with their friends prior to this, but this one event put it in perspective for everyone at that table. Ellis and their friends have developed a long-standing inside joke as a result of these experiences (asking each other—“are you paying attention to the barista or the tree?”). This one experience allowed both Ellis and their friends to apply language to some of the differences in asexuality and allosexuality. Ellis' story highlights a similar experience many other participants shared during their interviews, which they gleaned from their social context that they experience the world differently. Ellis shared their friends were more understanding of their sexual orientation after that moment. Symbolic language and awareness provided both internal and external support, through the recognition of uniquenesses that were not aligned with the friends' understanding of the world.

The interview data uncovered an identity process as asexual participants consider the world around them and their different ways of engaging with it. The prevalence of symbolic messages in social communities that embrace allosexual identities made locating and understanding identity a bit challenging for asexual spectrum participants. Dominant language that often favors flirting, visual sexual appeal, sexual energy, and sexual actions presents a constant reminder that the inner experiences of asexuals are different and that they do not meet social expectations. I will break down this model and present some of the data from the interviews to highlight each stage.

Juxtaposing Identities Participants shared their identity process, which often included comparing their ways of looking at relationships with the way their peers did. Often, participants reported moments of feeling like there was something wrong with them because they did not seem to have the same feelings as others. Many times, participants used the term *broken* when they started to look at themselves and how they did not feel like they were the same as their peers. They felt they lacked the ability to fit in when it came to sexual attraction and/or romantic attraction and the conversations and feelings that arose from that.

Participants expressed common experiences of not finding others initially physically attractive. Alex shared:

> Growing up Christian, you were always taught you're not supposed to have sex before you get married, so I figured disinterest in sex was normal…it is normal to not think about sex and to not have urges and to not be attracted to people. When I was in high school and everyone's hormones are going crazy…I honestly thought they were faking it. I thought they were pretending to be attracted to each other to appear more mature…I realized ‘oh wait, they are serious, they do think sexual attraction is a real thing.’ I had this question of what's wrong with me that this thing that comes so natural for everyone is completely foreign to me.

Alex's discussion reflected the sense that something was not quite right.

Another common discussion among participants and in asexual circles is a lack of connection to crushes on celebrities as a teen. Often heart throbs are a major part of many allosexual experiences. Participants often noted that, in adolescence, conversations around celebrity crushes were common and this was an area where many participants recognized differences in their reality. Emmaline shared, “everyone else (in high school) would have posters on their wall of celebrity crushes and I didn't have any of that, I didn't really understand it.” Kym, who identifies as demisexual, summed up how she felt about celebrities,

> I could recognize celebrities as attractive…but I would feel no sense of personal attraction, like if (celebrity) magically appeared in front of me, I wouldn't have sex with him, that sounds revolting to me because I would have no relationship with him.

Participants reflected that friends and peers were sexualizing their celebrity crushes, and this was just something that was not clicking for them.

Participants often mentioned that visual attraction was commonly discussed in social settings, and this was also not fitting into the reality they felt. Amy stated:

> Growing up in high school, when all the other girls would start talking about 'oh my gosh, that guy is so hot' or 'he is sexy' and it is like, I can recognize that he is aesthetically pleasing. I like his features and they align with the sociocultural standards of attractiveness…that person looks good in my eyeballs, but it has nothing to do with romance or sexuality.

Amy's comments suggest that there are two things going on related to attraction. One, there are the social standards of what is attractive that evoke a kind of arousal in her friends, and two, that people around her are actually feeling physical attraction that she does not have. Amy identified that a person looks visually nice, but there was no connection for her to physical feelings. E shared a similar disconnection to sexual attraction stating,

> From a young age, I was like, I understand that this person is making a comment about this body part and that has to do with sexual attraction, but it does not compute…it was an experience that was very foreign to me.

Similarly, when sexual conversations were going on with peers, participants felt a little on the outside, not connecting to reactions that seemed to be common with peers. Joni stated,

> If there is sex in a movie or people are telling jokes about being attracted to people, I was always like 'huh'…clearly I was the only person who (didn't get it), I don't see someone from across the room and be like 'oh yeah, I'll tap that,' I never have those thoughts about people.

Parker said, "I remember, as a teenager, experimenting with sex and just thinking 'oh, that's it, that is kind of boring.'"

These interactions with peers brought participants' internal feelings into question. They perceived that their allosexual peers were experiencing things in a way that they were not. This comparison led them to question themselves. Blair shared, "you spend your whole life either being outright told, or in my case, just internally believing that this is the right way and anything that isn't that means there is something wrong with you." Kai shared,

> When I was in middle school, when people started talking more about sex, when it was more part of our little society, I thought it was gross. I never understood it and my friends would always talk about who the hot guys were, and I didn't understand it.

Asexuals often adapt to create space for themselves in allosexual worlds (Hampson, 2020). For example, asexuals may opt out of the big college party, seek out queer groups of people, or ease their way out of social conversations of sex and attraction. These early experiences, for some, pushed them into considering that something could be wrong and they went on a journey to fix this thing they felt was wrong.

Participants recognized that this difference was incongruent with the social messages of normality around how people should experience relationships and attraction. Bri stated, "I felt like I was missing something, but it was society convincing me that who I was, was not the way to be human."

Matilda shared difficulties she had navigating cultural messages,

> I was considered undesirable or unfuckable, I never talked about boys or did anything to draw them to me…I was bullied a lot…in my culture, sex and dating and being sexy is encouraged and, in my society, virgin equals being a loser and I was treated as such.

Participants were faced with exclusive language; they frequently mentioned the word *broken*. Others mentioned being perceived as a "prude," "frigid," or externally viewed as having something wrong with them. Some participants internalized language around these constructs. Some sought medical and/or mental health expertise. Claire stated, "I just assumed I was broken and I tried sex therapists and I tried other therapists and we tried all kinds of wacko ideas and nothing ever worked." Raven shared, "I thought there was something wrong…I was generally seen as 'frigid,' I started talking to doctors because I thought maybe there was a hormonal imbalance, there is something that seems to be missing." Sally shared,

> I never really got what the big deal is about sex…we did premarital counseling…it was this is something that people need and they have to have it, like food and water and shelter…and it just doesn't happen for me…I generally don't notice sexual attraction and it isn't something I experience very often.

Sally was being told by professionals and others in her life that she was not doing things right and this represents a larger societal message that there is only one way.

> At times, participants would try to fit in. Claudia shared,
>
> For a long time, I was trying to fit in. I know that enjoying your sexual life is something that should be positive and empowering and I just rather not. I thought I had to try more things and ended up doing a lot that I didn't enjoy.

This sense of pressure to conform sexually was mentioned by a couple participants. Jessica stated,

> I was dancing with a guy I met, he was a nice guy and we were sort of kissing, but then I was like 'I have to get out of here before you ask me to go home with you,' I was having a good time and wasn't afraid of him or anything, but I was like 'I don't want to do that.'

Some participants mentioned this experience, where they gave their consent; however, they did not, internally, feel like they were wanting to engage in sexual experiences way they felt they should. (I will talk more about this consent process for asexuals in the next chapter). This is a powerful recognition that social messages of normality are so strong that people are pushing themselves into spaces that are not comfortable. It is important to note that some participants did occasionally feel sexual attraction, as asexuality is a spectrum of experiences. Additionally, some participants enjoyed sexual experiences; however, there still existed this common experience of not feeling exactly like their peers when it came to attraction and desire.

Interpreting Identity Participants shared experiences that mirror other sexual and gender minorities when it came to learning about their identity for the first time. Cass' (1979) coming out model presented 6 states: (a) identity confusion, (b) identity comparison, (c) identity tolerance, (d) identity acceptance, (e) identity pride, and (f) identity synthesis. In the first stage (identity confusion), there is a sense of difference, which the participants seemed to note in their discussion above under the *juxtaposing identities* theme. In the next three Cass stages (identity comparison, identity tolerance, and identity acceptance), queer persons go through stages where they are looking at others who might be similar and seeing if these labels or experiences fit for them. These three middle stages seem quicker and more definitive with asexual participants, kind of like they do not know what they are looking for until suddenly it is there. Often asexual spectrum persons do not have people in their communities that are role models or others to help them compare some of their own feelings with. So, understanding and acceptance feel more like an *ah-ha* moment; they locate language around how they are feeling and there can be almost an immediate sense of recognition and acceptance. Alex stated,

> I saw the word asexual and thought 'oh, what's that mean?" And, I looked it up and it was like a light bulb moment, like, oh my gosh, there is a word for this, there is nothing wrong with me, I am not broken, I am just this. And, there is a word for it which means other people experience it too. I was just excited knowing there is a word for how I feel and there is nothing wrong with me. This is just a different way of being.

Kai shared a similar moment,

> When I was 17 years old, I discovered the word asexual and what it means and then I had this big moment where the light bulb went off in my head and I realized that is me and why I have been feeling this way all along.

Claire stated, "If you understood what it was like to not understand who you are and to get it, that is just mind blowing, I live in a completely different world now." Claudia had a similar sentiment, "It was liberating, I felt like I was taking off a weight that I didn't even know I had." Cora shared her relief upon understanding her identity: "it makes a lot of things that I thought were deeply wrong with me or were associated with my trauma make sense. It basically meant that I was not as fucked up as I thought I was." Miranda stated,

> It has all been very liberating to figure out what is going on, I don't feel attraction to people in the normative way, I don't have to try and force it or keep trying all the time. Just having that understanding of self makes a big difference.

Language and labels were often important to participants. Locating labels helped them better understand themselves, better communicate with others about their experiences, and rendered them visible. Bri stated, "I think that the fact that most of society doesn't know this (asexuality) exists and doesn't really accept us as valid or happy…a lot of people think we are sad or something…we are happy and do find happiness." Kym stated, "I finally had a label to be able to shorthand talk to other people about it…I finally had a label and realized I am not alone." Parker shared, "I started reading about what asexuality meant and I realized there is a word for that and there is not anything wrong with me." Amy shared:

> I was so happy being single, I was vibrant and active, and you know, I took myself out on dates, I bought myself things, I loved me…I was never lonely and never regretted anything. I found the terminology for a romantic asexual and, I was like, 'yeah, I've felt this was for a long time and now to know there is a whole community of people who feel the same way.'

This *ah-ha* moment allowed participants to explore, educate themselves, and place language on these parts of their identity. It was liberating and allowed them to move into a stage of embracing what this all meant to them. Many participants shared that this *ah-ha* moment came from internet searches or connections to online communities.

A Note about the Split Attraction Model Participants in this research frequently talked about the split attraction model and how impactful this model was to their own understanding of self. The split attraction model was something many participants mentioned as a piece of language that helped them better define who they were. Megan reflected on how she started to understand herself better after knowing about the split attraction model. She stated,

> I have learned the difference between your sexual identity and your romantic identity. I love hugging and kissing and cuddling and all that romantic stuff, but the sex stuff doesn't mean anything. It isn't that it repulses me, I just don't care about it, and it doesn't come to my mind at all. The realization that I could be asexual and still have romantic feelings…I do love all those things (Glass, 2022, p. 352).

Phoebe shared relief in learning about the split attraction model, she stated "I didn't know that sexual and romantic attraction were two very different things." Matilda touched on her journey to understanding the split attraction model, "I was feeling confused in adolescence because I knew I liked men romantically, but I didn't know if I liked them sexually."

The split attraction model was a critical piece of *interpreting identity* that opened up language in a way that represented participants' experiences. The recognition of the split attraction model (Diamond, 2003) was game changing for participants who could embrace being able to articulate their sense of identity in terms of romantic and sexual attraction. Some asexual people, even if they have previously heard of asexuality, dismissed it as a part of their identity because they wanted relationships and love the idea of romance (and to a degree maybe even sex). Recognizing that romantic attraction can be a different feeling from sexual attraction was impactful for participants overall. It provided a whole new way to look at identity through language. Terminology, such as heteroromantic, panromantic, homoromantic, etc., has evolved in ways that allow asexual people (and even allosexual people) to embrace different ways that they form attraction and what it means.

The split attraction model can be applied to all people. After describing the split attraction model to a cisgender, allosexual, bisexual, male friend of mine, he stated that he felt so seen. He stated, "oh, I just realized I am romantically and sexually attracted to women and only sexually attracted to men!" He shared that he never wanted a long-term, romantic relationship with a male, but did find sex with men to a significant part of his identity. So, this made sense to him. Anyway, as you can see, language continues to impact identity. This language can be validating and can lead to a sense of pride and honor in self (as it did for participants in this study).

Integrating Identity Participants often shared that they live fulfilling and happy lives, especially after understanding asexuality and that part of their identity. Research suggests that when a person becomes more aware of their asexual identity, "individuals must reconcile their developing asexuality identity with prevailing heteronormative and allonormative social pressures" (Hille, 2023, p. 1). I do feel like the *integrating identity* stage does represent both internal and external coming out types of experiences. Some participants experience this integration as a more internal identity awareness, while others express this part of their identity externally to those around them. A great deal of participants shared how positive their openness around their asexuality was to their romantic, sexual, or QPR partner(s).

Alex shared how they felt about being open regarding their asexual identity in their intimate partnership, "I feel completely fulfilled, even though we are not romantic or sexual with each other, there is still something really strong that I can't imagine being without him" (Glass, 2022, p. 354). AP shared some reflections on integrating their identity:

> Now that I fully realize who I am, that has made me a lot more confident because before I assumed that there was something wrong with me, that I had some kind of like hormonal thing, and I should be more into sex. I think just discovering who I am has made me a lot more confident in my relationship and in the way I interact with the world (Glass, 2022, p. 351).

Identifying as an asexual individual can play a role in how a person creates and maintains intimate relationships. With participants, intimate relationships fed back into their understanding of self because they noticed differences in how they experience the world compared to their partner(s). Keep in mind that my research specifically addressed asexual spectrum people in relationships; there are many asexual persons that do not seek out intimate relationships, and their experience around this integration component may vary. Defining identity helped participants communicate and interact with partners in a way that they have not been able to prior to putting a label on their identity. AP stated, "I think discovering who I am has made me a lot more confident in my relationships and the way I interact with the world" (Glass, 2022, p. 351). Claire discussed the importance of language within her current relationship. She explained,

> Having hard conversations with my husband and it was difficult for him. It started a brand-new journey of trying to figure out what is going on and it was really hard for him to digest. For me, it was this weight off my shoulders and it was an absolute relief to finally say I get it and know who I am now. It is just something we have to coalesce and what we decided on was to work on compromising and we do see a sex therapist and that is mostly to understand how to frame our wants and needs. We communicate better (Glass, 2022, p. 352).

Cass's (1979) last two stages in her identity process model involved identity pride and identity synthesis. Identity pride is a sense of ownership and even excitement around a person's identity. In the identity pride space, many queer people disclosed their identities more frequently to the outside world and developed a clear sense of self that they feel prideful of. *Identity synthesis* is feeling at peace with one's identities. Blake, an asexual participant, shared a little about his journey, "it (asexual identity) has become something that I am really proud of, something that makes me special. My asexuality makes me more in-tune with nonsexual ways of giving and receiving pleasure and I think that is super neat."

Overall, asexual participants reported very welcoming partners who worked to better understand participants' identities. Anita stated:

> Once I realized I was asexual, we explored more…like sensual touch, we both enjoy massage, so that is something we found we can do more of and have that intimacy. I am definitely a cuddler. I very much enjoy that and kissing and hugging.

She cited "communication" as the main factor in how she connects with her partner.

Outside of these significant relationships, participants varied in their decisions to share their asexual identities with the outside world. Bogaert (2015) explored some nuances in the coming-out experiences of some asexuals compared to those of other sexual orientations. They noted that there is an invisibility that exists for asexual identities, often making disclosure a process that requires extensive explanation or clarification due to widespread misunderstanding. In addition, outing oneself as asexual can be context oriented—like with people who may want to be part of sexual or romantic relationships. Some participants were involved in asexual pride groups or worked to vocalize or represent asexual voices in queer communities. Other participants shared that they had not disclosed their identities outside of their relationships. Despite these differences in disclosure to larger communities, I certainly felt a sense of identity pride radiating from participants in their eagerness to jump in, schedule an interview, and share their journeys. Often, participants mentioned the importance of this research to help others better understand their own asexual identities.

Identity disclosure to others can be a unique process for asexuals and can have both positive and negative implications (Brozowski et al., 2025). On one hand, being out to one's community can connect asexuals to other asexuals who may better understand their experiences. On the other hand, there could be negative effects of discrimination that could be impactful. Biancofiore and Hughes (2025) found that asexuals are sometimes questioned about the legitimacy of their identity, and this can carry a sense of loneliness or feelings of a lack of self-worth. At times, asexuals feel they do not even need to share their identities with others, for example, a heterosexual passing couple may not feel the need to correct social assumptions (Hampson, 2020). Some asexuals may just use the terminology *queer* (Mollet, 2023). Overall, when thinking about identity process, for some minority sexual orientations, there is an internal and external coming out process. It is possible that for many asexuals, identity formation does feel more internal than external (Mollet, 2023). The external coming out for asexuals can be impacted by the lack of language and understanding in their communities. Some asexuals suggest that being open with larger communities about their asexuality is often met with a sense of denial (Gupta, 2017). People will state "you can't be asexual" or even outright deny that it is an identity. This denial is hurtful and marginalizing. I have heard asexual participants say that sharing their identity can be like sharing a whole paragraph of information and getting weird glances and feeling a lack of understanding. That also resonates with my experience. In queer groups, sometimes I will out myself as demisexual; however, in general groups if identity comes up, normally, I just say *queer*—it makes my life so much easier.

Conclusions

Language can propel asexuals into a whole new way of looking at the world. I discussed, at the end of the last chapter, that language is constantly shifting and meaning-making is being re-centered all the time. This philosophical underpinning of social construction seems to resonate with this model—like—no language causes confusion ➔ finding language causes an *ah-ha* ➔ integrating language creates new, welcoming social constructs. Language can be a critical component to better understanding oneself and can have some profound meaning to the invisibility that asexual persons may feel prior to locating language (Mitchell & Hunnicutt, 2019). The integration of language and the meaning of language was life-altering for participants. Participants shared that their journey started with the recognition that they felt different and processed relationships, romance, and sex in ways that they felt did not fit with the world around them. Much like other models of identity formation (e.g., Cass, 1979), participants sought a better understanding of their differences and felt an *ah-ha* moment once they connected to a common language. Once their uniquenesses were given labels, they felt relieved and even liberated. This labeling process allowed them to better understand themselves, relate to others, and communicate with others about their uniquenesses.

The participants in this research study seemed prideful and embracing of their asexual identity. Participants also self-selected to be part of this study. Analysis of the data recognized this open and willing group of individuals. It is not clear how participants who might be struggling with their asexual identities would present. The jump that these participants made to accepting and owning the language around self might not fit for some asexual individuals in other stages of the identity process. We might assume that not self-selecting could be a sign that others might be struggling and that those that self-selected represent a different phase in the languaging process. Participants, in this study, seemed to lean on language as part of their own identity and how they related to others; however, some people find labels too stringent or confining. Further research could consider the role of labels or language for larger groups of asexual individuals. This three-stage asexual identity process model nicely informs practitioners and others who work with and provide affirmative care to all.

Do you remember Jenna from the start of the chapter? Jenna is feeling overwhelmed because she is not fitting in with social expectations and feels she does not connect to the world like those around her; she is comparing herself to others and might be in the juxtaposing identity stage of this model. She may not ever have heard the term asexual and certainly does not seem to consider how it might apply to her. If we consider this three-stage asexual identity process model, just bringing possible language to Jenna's experience could be profound to her. Right now, she feels broken, and people have been telling her what she is feeling is wrong. It is quite possible that finding a label that fits, knowing others experience this, learning more about asexuality, and finding community may allow her the liberating feeling that many of the participants I have interviewed describe. What would be our role in this process as practitioners? I think suggesting "have you ever heard of asexuality?" or even "there is a sexual orientation called asexuality and many asexuals share similar experiences that you have shared with me" are completely appropriate directions. I have had heard other practitioners ask, "what if you bring up asexuality and the person is not asexual." And, I reply back, "well, then it won't resonate with them and you can continue other methods of helping them identify their situation." It is much like having a client who is in a heterosexual relationship share they have kissed someone of the same gender. Many practitioners will just ask "have you ever considered you might be bisexual or lesbian?" If the client does not resonate with those words, they will normally tell you, "I wondered that a couple times, but, no, I am totally not a lesbian, I love being with men romantically and sexually and don't have desires for women."

Jumping forward in time, let's say Jenna has already embraced an asexual identity and is in the integrating identity stage. She has done her own research on asexuality and, internally, feels quite at peace with who she is. Maybe she is coming to therapy because she has found herself in a relationship that she wants to grow and is curious more about navigating that as an asexual. Maybe she is entering therapy with a personal challenge that really does not have to do with her identity; however, your awareness as a practitioner of the possible shifts she has experienced may allow you to connect with her and understand her better. In the next couple of chapters, we will consider the application of this model as we discuss relationships and affirmative care.

References

Aglipay, F. A. (2014). The Cass' theory of sexual identity formation: Complexities of queer identity. *Psychology Research, 4*(6), 411–418. https://doi.org/10.17265/2159-5542/2014.06.001

Ahmed, S. (2006). *Queer phenomenology: Orientations, objects, others*. Duke University Press.

Antonsen, A. N., Zdaniuk, B., Yule, M., & Brotto, L. A. (2020). Ace and aro: Understanding differences in romantic attractions among persons identifying as asexual. *Archives of Sexual Behavior, 49*(5), 1615–1630. https://doi.org/10.1007/s10508-019-01600-1

Asexual Visibility and Education Network. (2022, February 1). https://www.asexuality.org/

Biancofiore, S. E., & Hughes, I. M. (2025). Asking about me: The impact of identity-related questions from others on asexual peoples' well-being and functioning. *Psychology & Sexuality*, 1–19. https://doi.org/10.1080/19419899.2025.2465989

Bockting, W., & Coleman, E. (2016). Developmental stages of the transgender coming-out process: Toward an integrated identity. In R. Ettner, S. Monstrey, & E. Coleman (Eds.), *Principles of transgender medicine and surgery* (2nd ed., pp. 137–158). Routledge/Taylor & Francis Group.

Bogaert, A. F. (2015). Asexuality: What is it and why it matters. *Journal of Sex Research, 52*(4), 362–379. https://doi.org/10.1080/00224499.2015.1015713

Brotto, L. A., Knudson, G., Inskip, J., Rhodes, K., & Erskine, Y. (2010). Asexuality: A mixed-methods approach. *Archives of Sexual Behavior, 39*, 599–618. https://doi.org/10.1007/s10508-008-9434

Brozowski, A., Chopik, W. J., Weidmann, R., Oh, J., & Weaver, J. R. (2025). Demographic and experiential characteristics of asexual individuals and associations with well-being. *Archives of Sexual Behavior: The Official Publication of the International Academy of Sex Research, 54*(2), 575–588. https://doi.org/10.1007/s10508-024-03068-0

Cass, V. (1979). Homosexual identity formation: A theoretical model. *Journal of Homosexuality, 4*, 219–235. https://doi.org/10.1300/J082v04n03_01

Cass, V. (1984). Homosexual identity formation: Testing a theoretical model. *The Journal of Sex Research, 20*(2), 143–167. https://research.ebsco.com/linkprocessor/plink?id=992340ff-5fb1-3fba-96bd-2fefd3b010f9

Chapman, B. E., & Brannock, J. C. (1987). Proposed model of lesbian identity: An empirical examination. *Journal of Homosexuality, 14*, 69–80. https://doi.org/10.1300/J082v14n03_05

Coleman, E. (1982). Developmental stages of the coming-out process. *Journal of Homosexuality, 7*(2–3), 31–43. https://doi.org/10.1300/j082v07n02_06

Degges-White, S., Rice, B., & Myers, J. E. (2000). Revisiting Cass' theory of sexual identity formation: A study of lesbian development. *Journal of Mental Health Counseling, 22*(4), 318–333. https://link.gale.com/apps/doc/A66961150/AONE?u=anon~a0aa014&sid=googleScholar&xid=da99860f

Devor, A. H. (2004). Witnessing and mirroring: A fourteen stage model of transsexual identity formation. *Journal of Gay & Lesbian Psychotherapy, 8*(1–2), 41–67. https://doi.org/10.1300/J236v08n01_05

Diamond, L. M. (2003). What does sexual orientation orient? A biobehavioral model distinguishing romantic love and sexual desire. *Psychological Review, 110*(1), 173–192. https://doi.org/10.1037/0033-295X.110.1.173

Elgie, E. (2020). *Being and doing: Interrogating dominant narratives of asexual kinship in an amatonormative culture*. Master's thesis, University of British Columbia. UBC Theses and Dissertations.

Fassinger, R. E., & Miller, B. A. (1996). Validation of an inclusive model of sexual minority identity formation on a sample of gay men. *Journal of Homosexuality, 32*(2), 53. https://doi.org/10.1300/j082v32n02_04

Foster, A. B., Eklund, A., Brewster, M. E., Walker, A. D., & Candon, E. (2019). Personal agency disavowed: Identity construction in asexual women of color. *Psychology of Sexual Orientation and Gender Diversity, 6*(2), 127–137. https://doi.org/10.1037/sgd0000310

Glass, V. Q. (2022). Queering relationships: Exploring phenomena of asexual identified persons in relationships. *Contemporary Family Therapy: An International Journal, 44*, 344–359. https://doi.org/10.1007/s10591-022-09650-9

Gupta, K. (2017). "And now I'm just different, but there's nothing actually wrong with me": Asexual marginalization and resistance. *Journal of Homosexuality, 64*, 991–1013. https://doi.org/10.1080/00918369.2016.1236590

Haefner, C. (2011). *Asexual scripts: A grounded theory inquiry into the intrapsychic scripts asexuals use to negotiate romantic relationships*. [Unpublished doctoral dissertation]. Institute of Transpersonal Psychology. https://www.proquest.com/openview/43af8997930280430aedef74a340816f/1?pq-origsite=gscholar&cbl=18750

Hampson, E. (2020). Negotiating (in)visibility: A phenomenological analysis of asexual students' experiences of university. *Psychology of Sexualities Review, 11*(1), 26–41. https://doi.org/10.53841/bpssex.2020.11.1.26

Hille, J. J. (2023). Beyond sex: A review of recent literature on asexuality. *Current Opinion in Psychology, 49*, 1–4. https://doi.org/10.1016/j.copsyc.2022.101516

Kelleher, S., & Murphy, M. (2022). Asexual identity development and internalisation: A thematic analysis. *Sexual and Relationship Therapy, 3*, 865–893. https://doi.org/10.1080/14681994.2022.2091127

Kelleher, S., Murphy, M., & Murphy, R. (2024). Variations in sexual identity milestones among asexual people. *Archives of Sexual Behavior, 54*, 561–573. https://doi.org/10.1007/s10508-024-03031-z

MacNeela, P., & Murphy, A. (2015). Freedom, invisibility, and community: A qualitative study of self-identification with asexuality. *Archives of Sexual Behavior, 44*, 799–812. https://doi.org/10.1007/s10508-014-0458-0

Mandigo, D. M., & Kavar, L. (2022). The experience of male asexuality: A phenomenological inquiry. *The Qualitative Report, 27*(2), 488–508. https://doi.org/10.46743/2160-3715/2022.5213

Mitchell, H., & Hunnicutt, G. (2019). Challenging accepted scripts of sexual "normality": Asexual narratives of nonnormative identity and experience. *Sexuality & Culture, 23*, 507–524. https://doi.org/10.1007/s12119-018-9567-6

Mollet, A. L. (2023). "It's easier just to say I'm queer": Asexual college students' strategic identity management. *Journal of Diversity in Higher Education, 16*(1), 13–25. https://doi.org/10.1037/dhe0000210

Morales, E. S. (1989). Ethnic minority families and minority gays and lesbians. *Journal of Homosexuality, 17*, 217–239. https://doi.org/10.1300/j002v14n03_11

Pitcher, K. J., Smith, R. L., & Watson, R. J. (2024). Outness and social-emotional adjustment among asexual and demisexual adolescents. *Journal of LGBT Youth, 21*(3), 507–525. https://doi.org/10.1080/19361653.2023.2200385

Robbins, N. K., Low, K. G., & Query, A. N. (2016). A qualitative exploration of the "coming out" process for asexual individuals. *Archives of Sexual Behavior, 45*(3), 751–760. https://doi.org/10.1007/s10508-015-0561-x

Troiden, R. R. (1979). Becoming homosexual: A model of gay identity acquisition. *Psychiatry: Journal for the Study of Interpersonal Processes, 42*(4), 362–373. https://doi.org/10.1080/00332747.1979.11024039

Willig, C., Rogers, W., Giorgi, A., Giorgi, B., & Morley, J. (2017). The descriptive phenomenological psychological method. In *The descriptive phenomenological psychological method* (Vol. 0, pp. 176–192). SAGE Publications Ltd. https://doi.org/10.4135/9781526405555.n11

Chapter 5
Asexuality, Intimate Relationships, and Family

> Asexuals can "let their relationship be whatever they want it to be rather than what society prescribes relationships to be" (Asexual interview participant).

As a family therapist, I really enjoy working with couples! There is a banter, a connection, and often a true genuine love unique to the couple that I feel humbled to be part of. I think watching two or more people who have grown to support each other, challenge each other, be vulnerable with each other, and admire each other is an insight into human nature that I never get tired of. I am a systemic therapist deep down, and view the world through connections and interactions, couples can be a microcosm of this professional identity.

This chapter will explore some of the uniquenesses that asexuals in relationships might experience. On the one hand, you may have a cisgender (male and female), monogamous couple, where one partner identifies as demisexual. This couple might present some similar experiences as allosexual heterosexual couples. In fact, the external world may not ever know about the demisexual queer identity. As a couple's therapist, even with my expertise in queer communities and asexuality, I may not even know, in fact, the couple may not even have labeled their relationship in this way. Another example might be an identified aromantic asexual that is part of a polycule (polyamorous community) and describes fulfilling connection needs through various nonsexual partners. There might be a couple where one partner identifies as a sex-indifferent, homoromantic, asexual, and the other partner as allosexual. This couple may have adapted in some ways to meet their varying identities. All these differences in asexuality and asexuality in relationships are varied in experiences and needs, yet are all valid. A married cisgender male/female couple is equally as valid and important as an asexual who is in partnerships or QPR and reports no sexual activity or romantic elements of their relationship. Again, those that are not in socially labeled relationships are also equally as valid.

I found that libido and sexual desire were incredibly varied among asexuals I interviewed, in ways that challenge some asexual stereotypes. One participant shared, "I have an extremely high libido," other participants shared little interest or

V. Q. Glass, *Asexuality, Relationships, and Identity Formation*,
https://doi.org/10.1007/978-3-032-22857-4_5

connection to sexual pleasure. There are asexuals who are involved in kink communities (and may or may not have penis/vagina sex as part of these experiences). There are asexuals who are in polyamorous relationships (which may or may not include sex, romance, and/or affection). There are asexuals who have no interest in any kind of relationship—romantic or sexual—and may have never had one. There are asexuals who report very high libidos and frequently engage in sexual activities with partners and/or self-pleasuring. And… everything in-between!

Let's start with some percentages. Clark and Zimmerman (2022) reported that 23% of asexuals in their study reported being in romantic and/or sexual relationships and 54% reported that they have been in romantic and/or sexual relationships. In comparison, an earlier study noted that 67% of asexuals reported being in a relationship (Van Houdenhove et al., 2014). I think the discrepancy here is more about defining coupling and the variability of what this might look like in asexual (and queer) communities. Another study noted that, of alloromantic asexuals, more than half reported desires to get married (60%) and/or live with a partner (50%) (Tessler, 2025). Even some aromantic asexuals may seek relationships, with only 76% in Tessler's study stating they never want a romantic relationship.

If you have been in a romantic relationship in your lifetime or if you are currently in one, consider all the parts of that relationship that make it feel genuine, real, important, etc. You may put passion or intimacy into the equation, but other factors also exist. Maybe you think about affection, mutual support, respect, companionship, humor, building a family, care, concern, fun, romance, communication…you get the point. If you consider all these parts of relationships, and break it down, it doesn't feel out of the way to think that a person might be able to have a very satisfying relationship even if sexual intimacy looks a little different from what is expected by normative social standards. In this section, I will consider asexual people in relationships and their partners. I would say this is limited to asexuals that experience attraction, but even aromantic and sex-averse asexuals are sometimes partnered or date. I will also discuss queer platonic relationships, which is a new idea to many individuals. What is it like to be asexual in a relationship? I will break down different relationship experiences that asexuals report being part of, I will discuss some notable relationship themes that have been uncovered through existing research and my own engagement with asexual participants, and finally, I will explore key points for relationship therapists.

Queer Platonic Relationships (QPR)s

I want to start the discussion of relationships with QPRs (Queer Platonic Relationships) because awareness around QPRs (especially outside asexual and other queer communities) is lacking. Additionally, I think QPRs can represent a major shift in thinking from allosexual and amatonormative expectations of relationships. Language around QPRs is a little difficult, because so much of our common language related to relationships focuses on romantic or sexual language. A definition of QPRs is "a relationship that is not romantic, but emotionally closer than what we generally think of as a friendship" (Birdsong, 2020). A queer platonic relationship is flipping the ideas and expectations of relationships that exist in society and allowing new meanings in relationships to emerge. Young (2023) says "queerplatonic is a term to describe the indescribable" (p. 163). Those in QPRs report intense connections, support, and intimacies that many with romantic partners may express in similar ways or those with deep friendships may express in similar ways (Young, 2023). Some might describe QPRs as similar to romantic relationships without the romance—QPRs might live together, support one another in daily life, have a bit of physical and/or emotional intimacy—but their relationship just may not fit that standard definition of a romantic relationship. In one research study, asexual participants who reported being in QPRs described them as "intense family friendships, family-like bonds, or romantic relationships without the romance" (Higginbottom, 2024, p. 1910). At times, QPRs can include sexual or romantic activity, but the expectation around sex and romance is sometimes different than social norms regarding sex and romance.

QPRs are influencing different ways of being in relationships that do not fit the social normative expectations. Tessler (2025) states,

> The concept of love and expressions of love are also intertwined with sex and romance. Love does not have to be sexual or romantic, and can instead be platonic or a form of intimacy beyond the boundaries of these labels (p. 526).

In social media comments and in social circles, I often hear people ask, "how is a QPR different than friendship?" I think the answer is—isn't that up to the people in the relationship? For example, I remember a heterosexual couple in my extended family who has been together for years. People sometimes referred to this couple as "living like friends," sometimes this was a joke, I think because the couple was not openly intimate and had different bedrooms. These comments were also judgmental—they were not fitting the social discourse of a real relationship. How a person grows and defines relationships is so incredibly varied, and the defining characteristics are really left up to the people involved in that relationship. What is important is that those external to that relationship (especially relationship therapists) are not part of the equation; it is about embracing and affirming the value the individuals give to their relationship. In one study, researchers examined content from asexual social media conversations (Caruso & Celardi, 2025). Many asexuals who described their QPRs responded with frustration that they were even expected to define their relationship within the confines of social romantic and sexual definitions of relationships, feeling these relationships defy current language and expectations.

To highlight QPR experiences, I want to share a little bit of Alex's journey. Alex is an aromantic, asexual participant from one of my research studies. Alex described their relationship this way:

> I am actually in a queerplatonic relationship with this guy I met like 14, about 15 years ago…we had this whole friend group that would chat and at some point I started to notice the way I feel about him is different than everyone else, it is not romantic, but there is something here that is different…he is my closest and most important relationship…I am com-

> pletely fulfilled even though we are not romantic or sexual with each other, there is still something really strong and I can't imagine being without him (Glass, 2022, p. 353).

Alex's description of their relationship reflects an intense bond that defies conventional descriptions of relationships. Later on, in the discussion, Alex shares that they occasionally cuddle with their QPR. The two often hold hands and sleep in the same bed together. They stated, "sometimes we have done things that some other people consider romantically coded." Alex is faced with having to defend their relationship, they shared that they have been asked by others "are you sure you aren't secretly in love with him and oblivious to your own feelings?" and they correct them "I have to tell them, ok, I am incapable of romantic and sexual attraction and I can guarantee you it is not like that because I never feel that way for anyone."

The external social world seeks romantic and sexual language to define something that, for Alex and their queer platonic partner, does not fit. On the one hand, this relationship is deep and meaningful (and "completely fulfilling") to Alex; at the same time, Alex's experience reflects the external messages that discount relationships when they do not meet the amatonormative expectations.

Another asexual participant, Miranda, also identifies as polyamorous. She shared a description of one of her relationships, which she defines as a QPR. "Another important relationship in my life is a platonic relationship, we've decided we want to be platonic life partners. We enjoy living together and we want to buy a house together. She is a super important foundation in my life." Miranda's discussion of her QPR differs slightly from Alex's; however, each embraces this relationship as a critical and valued part of their lives.

Like Alex and Miranda, some asexuals may be drawn toward queer platonic relationships because the expectations do not necessarily bring in sexual and/or romantic components (Higginbottom, 2024). There can be a comfort in this lack of social pressure to define a relationship in a way that may not feel congruent to the person. The less welcoming part of QPRs is that there is a lack of recognition of the importance by external persons and external systems (e.g., family, community, medical care, mental health care, etc.). If Miranda were in therapy and you were the practitioner, how might you respond to her if she shared she wanted to do couples therapy with her QPR? How might this look different? What if there was an emergency and the QPR had no legal rights to information, yet you knew the significance of their relationship? How might you do an assessment or a family genogram differently given the possibility of QPRs and other significant relationships that are not legally recognized?

When we think about amatonormativity, the social expectations of marriage and partnering, and that being the one and only most important and significant relationship, we discount the many types of critical relationships out there. QPRs are as legitimate as any other relationship dynamic. As an instructor of marriage and family therapy, I feel quite stuck and constrained by the way the MFT field and other fields legitimize married, biological, or legal relationships as the ones we consider important. Yes, as a field, MFT has moved more into the language of "coupling," rather than legal terms of "marriage," but this still leaves out a lot of relationships that are of particular importance to clients.

Polyamorous Relationships

Perhaps one of the findings in my own work (Glass, 2022) that surprises people is the frequency with which asexual participants, in that study, reported being involved in polyamorous/consensual non-monogamous (CNM) relationships. In my personal experience as a therapist and in asexual groups on social media, it seems asexuals in CNM communities are more common than one might expect. Some participants that I spoke with noted that CNM relationships were a nice way to meet partners' different sexual needs. Some participants noted that external relationships were ways they felt connected or supported in many ways. Others noted they appreciated that their partners were being appreciated by others (see also: Copulsky, 2015; Copulsky, 2019; Hille et al., 2024). Additionally, some polyamorous participants mentioned a sense of compersion, where they experienced joy or happiness knowing their partner was being sexually satisfied (Flicker et al., 2021).

Hille et al. (2024) noted several reasons that some asexuals felt most comfortable in CNM relationships. These CNM relationships included, meeting needs (sexual and/or romantic), exploring options and differences in a variety of people, as a way to help partner meet needs, because it was a part of who they felt they were, as a way to grow, because they rejected the traditional notions of monogamy, or maybe a partner introduced them to polyamory. It might be that polyamorous relationships feel a bit safer for some asexuals. Copulsky and Hammack (2025) reported that some asexuals noted that there can be a space between friendship and romance that is different for some asexuals who could make CNM relationships ideal for them without the pressure to be everything for one partner.

Asexuals report being in polyamorous relationships for some of the same reasons as allosexuals do, to some degree (e.g., attraction, varying physical and/or intimacy needs, romantic desires, independence in relationships, a recognition that traditional expectations of relationships do not fit them) (Copulsky, 2015). That being said, I think that when people who are partnering start to look at the intricacies of sex, attraction, romance, and partnership (e.g., like the split attraction model) they may start to process these needs and desires as not fitting into one way of doing things—opening the door to less common ways of being in relationships.

Clinically, there are some biases in mental health communities when it comes to CNM (Herbitter et al., 2024). Continuing to open awareness of the multiple ways that relationships look and embracing clients in all forms of relationships (or not having relationships) and normalizing a person's desires and experiences is critical to affirming care. One asexual participant, Joni, described her experiences,

> I am polyamorous… My journey into polyamory happened at the same time as I discovered this asexuality term. Some of my partners I have sex with and some I don't, for various reasons. I just make sure I don't have any pressure to have sex if I don't want to, which is really what everyone should do. Most people (partners) want to more often than I do, some of my relationships are entirely non-physical and some of them are pretty snuggly, but not sexual.

Joni's responses represent her personal experiences as an asexual and how she navigates the world around her in ways that make sense for her. She identifies both physical and nonphysical needs in her relationships and how CNM plays a role in how she is able to meet these connection and intimacy needs.

Kink

Similar to other misconceptions of asexuals, many people are unlikely to equate asexuality with kink, fetish, and/or fantasy. Some asexuals report being part of both sexual and nonsexual kink communities. I heard several of my participants share experiences they have had as part of kink communities. In general, *kink* can be either sexual or nonsexual activities that differ from normative sexual scripts or standards—they can be "physical, sensory, or psychological" (Caruso & Celardi, 2025, p. 6). Kinks can create a space that allows for intimacy or physical connection where a sexual desire or sexual attraction may not be necessary. A fetish is the act of desiring something that can create a sense of stimulation (Sprott, 2020). Fantasy is a creative world that explores intimacy, sex, and nonsexual connections and experiences. Sometimes kinks can establish connections (friendships, sexual partners, or community).

Winter-Gray and Hayfield (2021) researched the interplay between fantasy, fetishes, and kinks among 48 asexuals who also identified having a kink or fetish. Their research highlighted several themes: (a) that asexuals with a kink or fetish may go through an inner process of considering how these two parts of their identity fit together, (b) that kinks, fantasy, and fetish can be solo activities and not even involve sexual attraction/partners, and (c) that kink can include other ways of thinking about physical bodies (e.g., play, touch, power, trust, etc.) and/or can be different ways to experience touch or pleasure that may be nonsexual with partners. In essence, for some asexual individuals, kink, fantasy, and/or fetish can provide a space for thinking, desire, even stimulation that may not fit normative sexual scripts.

Let's Talk About Sex

What does sex look like for asexuals? Well, the answer is probably starting to look more obvious—it could look like anything. Some asexuals report very active sexual lives, and others report never having had sexual experiences and never desiring to. Everyone does sex and intimacy differently no matter what their sexual orientation. Oftentimes, what is healthy for one person or works for a partnership sexually, may not work for another (Higginbottom, 2024). It is about locating that space (that may or may not include varying degrees of physical intimacy) that meets the needs and desires of the people in the relationship.

Hille et al. (2020) explored a sample of asexual participants in order to better understand what sexual intimacy might look like for asexuals. Of their 1093 participants, over 98% reported they had engaged in sex during their lifetime. Note that most participants did define sex as penile/vaginal intercourse; however, this was not the case for all participants, as sex is subjective. When asked about desires, participants in Hille et al.'s study reported less interest in future sexual intercourse (less than allosexual counterparts); however, they did report favorable attitudes toward other sexual behaviors (e.g., toy use). In this particular study, most asexual participants (76.6%) noted favorable reactions to cuddling types of intimacies in their future, and many (45.4%) were favorable to kissing in their future. Also, of note in this study, many participants reported they were totally open to sexual intimacies if their partner wanted it (30.6%). This study supports the varying nature of sexual microlabels and the different ways that asexuals experience and engage in sexual intimacies.

Research highlights the biggest common misconception about asexuality—this idea that asexuals never have sex, never want to, and/or that there are medical, emotional, physical, or mental health reasons they cannot have sex. One research study explored the differences in desires to engage in sex between asexual and allosexual participants (Clark et al., 2025). Their research found that among asexuals who were not engaging in sex, it often came down to "apathy" (p. 447), this sense that they were either averse to sex overall or just did not really think much about it. In contrast, most of the allosexual participants shared their reasons for not being sexually active—these more often included moral or religious (e.g., saving oneself for marriage) reasons or just lack of feeling ready to have sex. In this same study, both allosexual and asexual participants mentioned a lack of interest contributing to their not engaging in sex. The uniquenesses that many asexuals may experience (particularly sex-averse or sex-indifferent asexuals) is that these lack of interest feelings are more about their innate identity, something they feel most of their life that is different. It is likely that allosexuals with a lack of interest may find sexual interest feelings to be fluctuating throughout their lives and not so much an innate feeling, rather a period of time where they just don't want to eat those chocolate chip cookies, despite almost always having had the craving.

One possible clinical challenge that practitioners might see with asexual clients is lack of sexual experiences. Again, I hesitate to make this jump because sexual experiences are so variable among asexuals. However, it is possible that an asexual person may not have a great deal of sexual experience and maybe they are more curious about how to add more sexual experiences to their lives. They could be dating an allosexual or just wanting to learn a bit more about their own bodies and responses.

When considering relationships overall, it is possible that asexual people who want to date or be part of romantic relationships might be struggling or even feel distrustful of allosexual people (Higginbottom, 2024). One asexual participant that I spoke with, Luca, was reflecting on past relationships with allosexuals, they stated, "there is a little dislike in how sexual the world is, that can feel uncomfortable, uncomfortable is not the right word, but more intense than that, more like jarring or it is almost invasive." Luca is currently in a relationship with an allosexual individual, but also seems to reflect on challenges they have experienced navigating the dating world that consists mostly of allosexuals. Asexuals may have experienced a dating culture that moves quickly toward sexual expectations that might not have felt comfortable to them. So, it is possible some have avoided sexual or intimate relationships for this reason.

Russell (2023) noted that some asexual individuals may struggle navigating sex and sexual relationships. A possible lack of experience may challenge asexuals' language around their body and their understanding of how to communicate their own needs, desires, and the sexual experiences they do not want. Consider you may have an asexual/allosexual partnership, and there is a clear difference in sexual pasts and sexual history of experimentation. Granted, this could also happen in allosexual/allosexual couples, but when you build in the not feeling sexual attraction piece of asexuality, there might be different ways to uncover and explore sexual relationships. As a practitioner, it might be about sex education in some moments, being open to dialogues around what they desire and what they do not desire and also working with partners to learn more about each other and how they may experience intimacy.

I have found that asexuals sometimes experience sexual arousal in different ways than allosexuals. Those who want to have sexual contact may have to clearly articulate to partners what this might look like or how they might get to the point of feeling sexually aroused. Many demisexuals that I have interviewed discuss a "slow warming up" period when it comes to sexual activity. The nature of demisexuality as feeling attraction after a connection is made makes this feeling congruent. Perhaps many demisexuals do desire a connection feeling even in a moment of intimacy before sexual activity can happen more naturally. This possibility could be something to discuss with couples and figuring out ways for the non-demisexual partner to be aware of and/or adapt to those differences. Many graysexuals feel sexual attraction variably or under certain conditions. This sense of sexual attraction and fleshing out what these conditions are could help couples navigate sexual experiences.

Sexual desires among asexuals can vary like sexual experiences. Clark et al. (2024) explored couples that reported experiencing different desires in their relationships and some of the ways that these couples worked to meet these differences and differing needs in their relationship. Couples, in their study, identified that masturbation and/or mutual masturbation was one way they adapted. Clark et al. also discussed taking penetration out of the picture was helpful for some couples. Another noted theme was the use of verbal or nonsexual touch as a way to connect.

Despite my own musings and some of the existent research that asexuals may need help with communicating around sexual needs and desires (Russell, 2023), I found participants in my own research contradicted this message; they seemed to have figured this part out! I interviewed 35 individual asexual spectrum participants who report being in a relationship (Glass, 2022) and nine couples (18 people) where at least one partner identifies as asexual. Communication of needs, desires, sexual interest or disinterest, and ways to adapt were very much part of the lives of almost all, if not all the asexual participants I interviewed. Participants I spoke with seemed to have spent time **de-constructing** expectations and norms around sex together with partners and then **re-creating new sex narratives** as a way to understand themselves in relation to wherever they fit in terms of desiring sexual experiences.

De-Constructing Sex

Asexual participants and their partners created language around sex in a way that embraces a plethora of experiences beyond the goals of penis and vagina sex and orgasm. One allosexual participant (Patrick) who is partnered with an asexual shared:

> I am hypersexual, but one of the things that worked out between us is that my definition of sex is very loose. A lot of people are—if it is not penis and vagina, it is not sex. I think if there is energy and intention, that is it sexual, it is sex. Regardless of the outcome, whether or not anyone has an orgasm, if your intent is to have that feeling, then it is sexual and it can be whatever you want it to be. I think when people adopt a wider frame of sex they tend to enjoy themselves more and find more pleasure.

Many couples that I interviewed redefined needs and intimacy. Aspen (asexual) and Jess (allosexual with demisexual/sapiosexual tendencies) shared the importance of vulnerability and how that looks in their relationship. They describe a sense of togetherness where there is a felt sense of safety between the two of them where they can say things they may not normally share. They also share that being flirty is another way they engage in intimacy. Jess says,

> It is like very flirtatious and sweet and sometimes spicy, like just knowing that their motivation is a little different, but really appreciating that you (Aspen) do take the energy to be like, I am going to ping this and see if you pick it up…rather than being hormonal, it is more of an invitation to play.

Social standards of sex somewhat dictate a specific process—flirt → kiss → hormones start to take over → foreplay → penis and vagina (PIV) sex → both orgasm → resolution. There are no spoken rules behind this process, and it obviously does not always happen this way; however, a lot of asexuals and their partners deconstruct this expectation. Aspen and their partner Jess shared their perspectives on their sexual experiences that differ from the traditional expectations. They used food as an analogy (steak = intercourse).

> Aspen: It isn't like, here is the steak…we are going to do this.
> Jess: It is like we are going to do a little tasting menu.
> Aspen: Yeah, it is not foreplay as a lead into PIV sex, no, what if we actually just get eight appetizers today, or four and order another plate.

The couple considers how the standard script (steak) does not always make sense for them; however, they can break that down into parts (appetizers) that do work for them.

Sage (asexual) and Rowan (allosexual) break down how they are different from social standards when it comes to sex. They are talking about moments when they are sexual,

> Sage: We are really opposite in the actual moment (of sexual experiences)…you (Rowan) get really caught up in it and are like focused, but not focused, because you are listening to your body and experiencing the experience, whereas I am thinking really hard…basically it is just more mechanical for me. I enjoy doing it, depending on what we are doing, but it is like I have to be in a certain headspace to enjoy it.
> Rowan: It is to a level of compromise when we do stuff, we meet somewhere in the middle.
> Sage: I sort of remove myself from my own body and try to have fun, like focus on them and not worry about what I am (feeling).
> Rowan: Because I know it is largely a thing that you do for me because I am your partner…
> Sage: Like, it can be fun in a non-sexual way (for me) even though it is sex. It is like I can find ways to make it fun because it is like there is an emotionally intimate part that I enjoy.

In this conversation, Sage and Rowan break down sexual needs and sexual desires and how they each experience this differently. Sage adapts by finding the part that they do enjoy and need (the emotional intimacy and the fun). They see sex outside of social scripts and expectations.

Often, in my discussions with asexuals and their allosexual partners, there is a sense that the relationship is better than purely allosexual relationships, because, essentially, the desire and the sex are not "getting in the way" of other ways to connect. Sage and Rowan also comment on this. Rowan (allosexual partner) stated:

> I think about how many different ways that we get to connect…I feel like some allo couples just focus too much on sex, just put so much into that and do not explore other avenues of connection enough. I feel like we have a really good basis of our relationship just because we're focused on our emotional connection, and being on the same page, and talking about what we want, because I have also seen allo couples get married without talking about serious things…about what they want from each other on a deeply emotional level…I feel like we have just explored more forms of attraction and connection than maybe the typical allo couple.

Sage and Rowan tap into this sense of relief and openness that exists where they can explore more than sex, and this is what intimacy is for them.

In my research on asexuals and partners, there was one couple I interviewed where both individuals identified under the asexual umbrella, Ruby and Noah. Ruby defined herself as sex-repulsed, which means she feels physically averse to thinking about sexual experiences. She stated that when she experiences any sexual sensations, "I have always felt like complete panic." Noah shared being indifferent about sex overall and had no desire to shift what they experience as an intimate relationship to a sexual relationship. The couple has been together for over 7 years and shared that they met and fell in love before even knowing about their asexual identities. The couple describes a sense of emotional intimacy that they experience. Ruby stated,

> I think one thing that blew both of our minds is that a lot of allosexual people pretty much only have those (deep, vulnerable conversations) like pillow talk, like after having sex. Like, we have that just cooking dinner on a Tuesday, like why aren't you talking about that stuff, you don't need sex to be like I am going to talk.

The deconstruction Ruby discussed here is about vulnerability and closeness that doesn't need sex as a precursor. They processed how their relationship differs and what intimacy means to them separate from a social perception of sexual experiences. Later Noah followed up with,

> You know, if having a sexual relationship was important to me and something that I thought that we should either pursue or look at options…I would have that conversation with her, it just isn't something I pursue, it is not something of interest to me…you know I am not like obligated to do stuff with her and we are both coming from it from the same place, it is just that we have had so many ideas from the media of that a relationship should have a sexual component.

The couple continues to deconstruct the expectations put on them by society that part of happiness for them is a sexual component. Both Ruby and Noah were "completely satisfied", "happy", and "secure" in their relationship and found their connection differs from allosexual conventions, but is just as strong (even, according to them, stronger in some ways).

Many asexuals I spoke with felt that a preoccupation with sex, sexual attraction, and/or romance takes away from other things in their relationship or in their life. E, an asexual, stated,

> I save so much time not worrying about or thinking about sex…I have so much time to read books, to watch movies, I can go hang out with my dog and my friends and not be trying to balance the thinking about sex or the urges to connect with someone sexually.

Joni, another asexual participant, shared,

> If I think about it (sexual attraction) as compared to what everyone else deals with on a daily basis, it just eliminates this huge distraction, like I don't have to worry about that. I don't even think about it when I am meeting people, it doesn't cloud anything. Being sexually attracted to people I would think clouds all kinds of judgments and opportunities that I think are important and I don't have to worry about that.

Sometimes, the de-constructing of sexual expectations is a challenge for asexuals living in a mostly allosexual world. Asexuals may struggle at times to grasp where allosexual peers and partners might be coming from. One participant, Blake, shared their experiences with a past relationship,

> It was hard to watch someone I loved and cared for so deeply decide that the infinite amount of love I had to offer wasn't good enough. It was hard to wrap my head around the idea that sex was something that was so important to people.

Later on in the interview, Blake shared how this narrative has shifted with their current partner, they stated,

> I like that I am able to explore my sexual desires in an environment free of external pressure. In my previous relationships, I usually did things my partner wanted me to. Now I do things because I actually want to. I realize I do actually enjoy doing some things. I realize my sexuality is just as complex as anyone else's is and that I am allowed to be sexual and explore even if I am ace. I like that my partner is open-minded and doesn't take things personally. I like that we can be silly together and we can also be vulnerable together. I like that we are both free to do our own thing.

Overall, asexuals in relationships, regardless of their own interest in sex, are cognitively aware of the years of messages that are present in society around what sex and intimacy *should* be like, and they have to break down these messages and embrace what works for them aside from these expectations. An allosexual partner (Rowan) said it best, "having a different sexual desire is not any different than having a different favorite color."

Creatively Shifting Sex Narratives

Previous research on asexuality has identified how asexuals in relationships recreate new narratives around intimacy that is outside social norms (Batchelor, 2024). One study concluded that asexual/allosexual couples in their study,

> …used allonormative and asexual discourses to make sense of their relationship, but they didn't stop there. Many of the ways that couples talked about their relationship reflected new ways of thinking and doing things, forging new paths, trying new things, and throwing out existing expectations for what a relationship should be (Batchelor, 2024 p.16).

Imagine throwing out socially prescribed dating and sexual scripts and starting over, defining who you are for yourself.

Luca (asexual) and Theo (allosexual) also talked about breaking down sexual scripts in ways that lead to a new intimacy, a new reality for them. Theo stated,

> There are so many narratives socially about how you are supposed to have sex, and what is the right way, what is the cool way, what you should bring to the alter. I have always had a bit of contempt for that concept, while simultaneously falling into so many of them. This (the relationship with an asexual) has just sort of breaking all that down and being able to see, like ok, there are all these scripts and all of the unconscious things that I thought of as intrinsic to sexuality and they are just scripts, right, and we can rebuild them however we wanted to and so that has been very liberating.

Theo's relationship with an asexual person allowed for creating a new way of looking at their own sexuality and embracing more than what has been projected.

If you think back at some of the microlabels asexuals sometimes use with regards to sex (e.g., sex-favorable, sex-neutral, sex-averse, sex-repulsed). And, you connect that with a possible partner who may identify differently, sometimes sex, intimacy, pleasure, arousal, and physical connection require clear untangling and recreating. In my research, I have found myself feeling quite in awe of those individuals that make these physical connections and needs work with these varying degrees of desires, attractions, and needs. Thinking about the previous section of deconstructing sex narratives, many asexuals (and possible intimate partners) were able to fill their intimacy buckets quite comfortably after deconstructing their expectations around the way they have been told it should be.

Sometimes, the basic understanding of what intimacy may mean for any given two people differs from social conventions. For example, physical intimacy for one couple may include connecting emotionally or maybe it includes physical connections such as holding hands or cuddling (Caruso & Celardi, 2025). A satisfying intimate relationship for another couple could be nonsexual kinks. Perhaps a couple finds they connect through late-night intimate conversations. Or, physical, sexual experiences are present but vary from intercourse. Or, a couple needs a night of passionate sex at least once a week to feel connected. Being able to open the door to look at self and satisfaction, communicate that desire or need, and figure out ways to work together to better understand each other—this is what I think of ultimate connectivity between two (or more) people.

> One couple I interviewed reflected on a growing understanding of each other. Lydia (asexual) and Patrick (allosexual) had this dialog:
> Patrick: You do like intimacy.
> Lydia: Yes, I like the connection.
> Patrick: Right, but you don't necessarily want me to be inserting myself in you, which is fine, right?
> Lydia: Right.
> Patrick: She likes being adored and she likes being objectified.
> Lydia: I like the rawness too, the energy…he doesn't have to be inside of me for that connection to happen, basically.

This couple has found a rhythm. Through communication and respect, the partners have come to understand one another's needs and together they found a way to make these differences work.

Similarly, Kai (asexual) discussed how they and their partner Jacob (allosexual) adapted their intimacy. The couple discussed a situation where they sat down to have a deep conversation because there was something amiss. Jacob stated, "I was like, I personally like having touch, I want touch in our relationship." Kai agreed that they realized it made him "feel loved" to have those physical moments in a way that Kai did not feel. Kai stated,

> We are a team and we want to find a solution together that works for both of us, so I have gone ahead and learned what the little touches look like. I will come by and I'll hug or I'll rub their shoulders for a bit while I am walking by. Like, even though it doesn't come natu ral to me it is something that makes (Jacob) feel loved and appreciated. So, I have practiced doing it so that I do it more spontaneously.

An asexual participant, Elleanor, described her relationship and intimacy and how it differs from conventional standards. She stated,

> People would be surprised if I told them, for months I might not be interested (in sex), but we figured out a way how to not let that get in the way. People feel like sex is such an important part of our relationship but like just not wanting to do it at all, would make people not want to be in a relationship, but for us there are so many different things that are more important than sex and it is just one thing we can't do to have fun, but it isn't the only thing that matters (Glass, 2022, p. 354).

There is an intentional focus in these couples' experiences that is respectful and also committed. There are boundaries set, and communication is present.

Couples generally do not feel similarly when it comes to sexual wants and desires; sometimes couple's therapists struggle not knowing where to go with this difference. I sometimes pause because I almost want to say "what is the big deal? Like just because A person wants more sex than B person—or just because A person likes X and B person doesn't like X—can't they just do something different?" Maybe this sounds a little insensitive or biased on my end. I have come to know that this is just my context and my frame of reference, and everyone has different needs. All practitioners come from a context and have to put that aside to focus on the couple in front of them. I also think because I am deep into research with asexual individuals in relationships, and frequently I am able to see these couples consider unique shifts in what they do in order to best accommodate both partners' needs and boundaries—I have grown accustomed to hearing how couples break free from expectations and make it work a different way. I could argue that we, as a society (in our own relationships or working with relationships), are just so entrenched in the message that there is one best way to be intimate that we can easily get stuck, especially if it resonates with our own intimacy needs.

One of the most common "make it work" themes that I heard asexual/allosexual couples discuss was the use of self-pleasuring as an option to differences in sexual needs. Lydia (an asexual) and her partner Patrick (allosexual) had a conversation that felt like many other participants' conversations around this topic.

> Lydia: We have created sex loopholes, so to speak, like we're big into mutual masturbation.
> Patrick: Yeah, it is like my thing, if like I want that and you don't want to do it, I am not making my problem your problem, I can do a thing (masturbation) and I am perfectly happy.

Masturbation and mutual masturbation were tools that many asexual/allosexual couples used to reframe desires and sexual needs as different from (at times) intimacy needs or connections.

Another tool that I noticed in a lot of asexual/allosexual partner participants, was viewing sex more as a gift (for allosexual partners) and that, by providing this gift to their partners, it was rewarding and even pleasurable. Megan, an asexual, stated,

> In relationships we do things for our partners that maybe aren't a big deal for us, but we do them because they (partners) enjoy them. It is like going to baseball games, I couldn't care less about a baseball game, but I go with you (partner) because it is something that you enjoy, it isn't a sacrifice for me, I go because you enjoy it and she doesn't care about the symphony…it is something she does because she knows I like it. In my brain, sex comes into that too, it is just something that I know she really likes and I can do it for her (Glass, 2022, p. 353).

The act of providing sexual intimacy for the sake of meeting a partner's sexual needs and desires came up quite a bit in talking with asexuals.

Sometimes asexual/allosexual partners voiced shifts (among them both) in libido and sex interest. Communication around this was the most helpful way to approach these shifts. Lydia (asexual) reflected on her sexual relationship with her allosexual partner, describing their intimacy as a "carefully negotiated dance between two bodies finding homeostasis together." People can experience intrinsic and extrinsic motivations when it comes to sexual activity and engaging in sex with partners (Agrawal et al., 2025; Bulmer & Izuma, 2018). Engaging in sexual activity because it is something we want for ourselves or because we want to give the experience to someone else can play a role in what sexual activities take place and where that boundary of when to stop or what not to do comes into play.

Consent ←→ No Pressure

This all leads me to this important topic and distinction. There are two areas of discussion that I feel are frequently brought up in interviews when it comes to asexuals and relationships. The terminology of ***consent*** and the importance of experiencing ***no pressure*** when it comes to romancing, sex, and all things relationships—though the sexual part will come out more loudly in this conversation. The idea of consent and the idea of not pressuring a person were discussed a lot by asexuals in relationships; these feel a bit like opposing terms, but there are some critical ways I feel they are related and important to asexuals. These constructs and the ways that asexuals spoke of them can also be important and applicable to all people who experience intimate relationships. Actively agreeing to sex is very different from passively agreeing to sex (Russell, 2023). Many asexuals do report engaging in sexual acts because of internal or external pressures (e.g., not fitting in, fearing a partner will leave because of not engaging in sexual acts). In one study, some participants reported having negative reactions at times after engaging in sex with partners, e.g., "feeling numb, blank, unsatisfied, disgusted, and dissociated" (Agrawal et al., 2025, p. 10). Some of the participants I interviewed reflected on past relationships where they engaged in sexual experiences they did not really want to engage in, but did give verbal consent.

Consent

What comes to mind when you think about consent? Likely, you have been in sexuality education or watched something on television that brings up "no means no." The idea of verbal "yes" or "no" consent to engaging in sexual contact with a partner has been simplified in this way both legally and socially (Peterson, 2025). Sexual consent is technically "an agreement to engage in a sexual act" (Kedzior et al., 2025, p. 273). This idea of consent, however, is not always easy to understand—internally and/or externally (Kedzior et al., 2025). There can be a lot of things going on inside of a person that drives consent or lack of consent—these can include hormonal messages, social messages, lack of self-awareness, peer pressure, development, etc. An individual may have doubts internally, yet they still technically give verbal or nonverbal consent to a partner. Then, how those messages are transmitted to another person is also complex. At times, a person might be very explicit "no, I do not want to do this" or "yes, I want to do this." Sometimes, less explicit consent is given (e.g., taking clothes off, continuing to kiss, not saying no) or taking away consent is implied (e.g., by a person moving away or breaking from an embrace). There are verbal and nonverbal cues of consent and non-consent between partners. What if what is going on internally is "no I don't want to, oh my gosh I want to, hum, maybe I shouldn't, goodness, yes…" and the yes is stated out loud and sexual contact moves forward? Keep in mind that *true consent* is clearly articulated *enthusiastic consent* between the people involved; however, I recognize that there is such variability in how this actually looks from person to person and situation to situation.

Unwanted consensual sex is "freely consenting to sex that is neither wanted nor desired" (Goodman et al., 2019, p. 142). Unwanted consensual sexual relationships have been explored in research on (likely mostly allosexual) sexual relationships (Barnhart et al., 2025). In one study of couples that experience differences in sexual desires, over 13% of the partners, who reportedly were less sexual, consented to sex even when they were not interested, just to resolve the differences (Clark et al., 2024). At times, participants in this study noted that the reason for this was because it made their partner feel good and that made them feel good to give that to them. Women are more likely to report these unwanted consensual experiences than men (Barnhart et al., 2025). This finding could be rooted in social messages around expectations of women or differences in communication. Other research findings include males giving consent when they did not want to, suggesting a pressure to preform that males experience (Peterson, 2025). Some research explores past sexual history of victimization that could play a role in unwanted consensual sex (Goodman et al., 2019). Personally, in my work as a therapist, I would say many people, at some point in life, have engaged in sexual experiences that they did not really want to engage in, but still gave consent.

Keep in mind, I think there is a huge difference between "eh, I wasn't into it, but did it anyway" and "I was violated" and a whole plethora of other in-between unwanted internal conversations that maybe do not come out to the other partner involved. Even as I write this, I feel uncomfortable even saying that consent can be tricky, because, in reality, communication and respect when it comes to sharing of bodies should create environments where consent should not be tricky at all. But, that is the ideal and not the reality, sexual messages are messy, confusing, and intertwined with social expectations and social constructions that interfere at times with our own understanding of self. Verbal consent (the "yes" or "no") might be oversimplifying what consent should be; building social messages that prioritize sexuality education, awareness of self, and open communication are important mechanisms that could increase one's understanding of personal consent and how to set boundaries around desires and actions (Peterson, 2025).

Asexuality and unwanted consensual consent have been discussed in research. Gupta (2017) noted a theme in their research that suggests some asexual participants do engage in sexual activities that they are not overly enthusiastic about. These moments of engaging in sexual activity are almost internally motivated—the participants who discussed this noted a desire to fit in or felt they had to engage in some activity because of this undercurrent of social expectations. Higginbottom (2024) mentions that their research found a "gray area of consent" among some asexuals and their partners. I found a similar thing in my own research (Glass, 2022). Some asexuals report engaging in sexual activity with partners even when they are not really interested in these activities; they do technically consent to these activities, and partners are not necessarily manipulating or even being coercive. Yet there is sometimes less enjoyment or a sense of obligation around doing sexual activities.

One asexual individual I interviewed, Luca, discussed past relationships and what consent looked like for them. They reflected on why they engaged in a sexual relationship when they were not feeling comfortable with it. They stated they were,

> …developing this narrative, like if I don't please her (past partner) sexually, then I will lose her. I have definitely carried that into my relationships because it wasn't outright said, but it is definitely that pressure…the pressure hasn't ever felt very external, I haven't felt it much from the outside, it is just more inferring it…it is almost like sex was implied and so it wasn't outright pressure, it was just worry about what would happen if I said no or what would happen if I didn't, if I sort of stopped the path. There have been times where we would be in the middle of this and it turns out I don't really want to be doing this, but it is just easier to just follow it to completion than it is to stop it. So, it is like this internal pressure of, am I going to please them, what is going to happen if I don't meet their needs, will they leave? Those sorts of things build up pressure.

Sophie, a demisexual, shared a similar story,

> Like, we both have needs and there is compromise that works for us, without making an asexual person have sex when they don't want to. I think there are probably a lot of asexual people in relationships that likely just go through the motions because they haven't really come to understand that part of their identity or they feel compelled to just do whatever society tells them to do and make their partner happy.

Luca and Sophie both describe an undercurrent of internal expectations around sexual experiences.

It might be that asexuals experience consent a bit differently and maybe language and communication should look a bit different to better approach intimacies and boundaries. Kai, an asexual participant, discussed their views on asexuality and consent. They stated,

> Consent can look different when you are asexual. It is a little bit different because there are a lot of people who struggle with the line between like, I am doing this because I want to do something nice for my partner and I am being pressured to do this or I feel like I have to fulfill this obligation or I am not a good partner.

Similarly, Parker shared her past experience with relationships,

> I was very desperate to keep someone in my life and I thought that if I allowed myself to have frequent sexual relationships that would keep them in my life. I have a feeling that people on the ace spectrum are maybe more prone to getting involved in sexual activities to try to keep a partner because you know that is what partners want.

Even given these perspectives and cognitively recognizing the process, there is sometimes a lack of clear-cut understanding of what consent really is. Blake, an asexual, described it this way,

> I have myself struggled to understand the difference between having sex just to make my partner happy and a lack of consent. Sometimes I have sex because it feels nice, sometimes I have sex because I enjoy watching my partner experience pleasure, sometimes I have sex because I realize it makes my partner feel loved. These are all valid. But, when I am having sex because I feel like it will upset my partner (and I don't), then I feel really awful during it, that may be an instance where my boundary was crossed and I didn't actively consent.

Some asexuals discuss a sense of satisfaction that can occur when they are pleasing their partner. Aspen stated, "the satisfaction in giving is lovely."

Like these examples, many asexual participants I spoke with touched on some reasoning behind moving forward in certain intimate relationships when they may not have completely wanted the experience themselves. Sometimes these reasons are more altruistic and/or finding satisfaction to the connection overall, at other times, these felt internally coerced to some degree based on social scripts and expectations that were difficult to decipher in the moment.

Part of the discussion of consent makes me think of the discussion around compromise in relationships and in relationship therapy. One of the most common reasons that couples enter couples therapy is feeling like their sexual desires are mismatched (Emond et al., 2024; Vowels & Mark, 2020). This discrepancy can cause difficulties in a lot of relationships and is a very real challenge for many couples. I do argue that sex therapy and relationship therapies often go a little too far in working to identify a problem for this sexual desire discrepancy and working on a *fix* that fits more into allonormative terms. A stated clinical goal for those that differ in sexual desire is to remove some of the distress that occurs around their sexual relationship (Borden & Allan, 2024); however, I think the unstated clinical goal (for the couple and the therapist) is often to have more sex.

The climate in medical and therapeutic worlds tends to favor sexual relationships as the healthiest goal for a relationship that is struggling. A recent article in the *Journal of Marital and Family Relations* stated, in the first line of the article, "a healthy sexual relationship is a key component of satisfying long-term romantic relationships" (Busby et al., 2025, p. 1). Think about the scripted meaning here behind the words "key component" and "satisfying." The message is that without sex, you are unhealthy and won't have longevity in your relationship. I mentioned earlier in the book how I get frustrated hearing conversations from relationship therapists where there is almost an expectation for couples to work out sex—if one person has a lower libido or just isn't that interested—there is this expectation that the one with less interest or libido step up to the plate and deal with it. This message is probably coming from allosexuals who, often see tremendous value of sexual relationships in their own lives and in their relationship. However, this allo-centered view of sexual relationships can be harmful to both asexuals and non-asexuals because it prioritizes one way of being, one way of creating healthy long-term relationships. Imagine telling a person who defines themselves as a lesbian and is uncomfortable or unaroused by males to just have more sex with a man. Ok, conversion therapies are still doing this! But, that is a different conversation. If you are a hyper-sexual, allo-sexual person, imagine being told you should just not have sexual pleasure and be happy about it. This feels like the message asexuals often get—you are the wrong one, so do it the allosexual way.

A Surprising Solution—"No Pressure"

In conversation after conversation that I have had with asexuals and asexual participants in my studies, one element that feels incredibly strong to the experiences of asexuals in self-defined healthy relationships is the importance of not experiencing pressure from partners (for sex or intimacy of any kind). The fact that this conversation came up so often and the fact that it truly resonates with my own experience make it feel like a valuable discussion to present to practitioners. And, again, I feel this is important for all relationships, no matter the sexual orientation.

Asexuals describe that when their partner(s) do not put pressure on them that they felt understood, welcomed, respected, and even tended to be more affectionate or even sexual. I think there is a lot I could hypothesize here, but I feel this comes down to the incredible masking that many asexuals have had to do in their lives. I think it comes down to these moments of unwanted consensual sexual relationships that may have been part of their past and taking any pressure off is a relief, a sense of safety. I think it comes down to the oversexualized world that we live in that makes it very difficult for some asexuals to feel connected or respected because of their uniquenesses. Having a partner who understands asexuality can create a bond that grows more deeply and allows for conversations around sex and intimacy to work *with* the asexual partner's identity and not against it.

Jennifer (asexual) and her partner Kyle (allosexual) shared a conversation around pressure and guilt. Jennifer had shared that she experienced a great deal of guilt and shame about her differences in sexual attraction and desire. This was their discussion:

> Jennifer: Having somebody that you feel secure enough with to take on this journey (of understanding asexual identity) with no guarantees that it is going to be successful in the end, but when I come to him and look in his eyes, he is there looking back at me, we are in this together and there is value in sticking it out and seeing where this can take us and that I really feel that sense of safety that has helped with guilt.
> Kyle: And I don't want her to have any guilt.
> Jennifer: Well, you too either, I mean I know that sometimes you feel pressure.
> Kyle: You might have some people, like a guy who is dating a woman who becomes lesbian, and there is a hit to his masculinity, this is not a hit to my masculinity, she is figuring herself out and I get that, so I am not going to feel guilty about that and I don't want her to feel guilty.

Jennifer and Kyle have located this sense of awareness of each other, a respect, which allows them not to apply pressure and to open the door to understanding one another.

One couple I interviewed, one partner identified as a sex indifferent asexual (Lydia) and the other partner as hypersexual (Patrick). Lydia stated, "We created a safe space early on and that is what drew me to him from the very beginning, it was an immediate safe space." Later on, she stated,

> Just the fact that he hears me when I am at that exhaustive point and accepts me for me, he is the first partner I have had that doesn't make me feel badly for saying I can't do that tonight. I don't feel any pressure with him and that is the difference and makes it easier to say yes to just touch me and that is cool.

Feeling like she has a voice and that her partner respects her boundaries around sex allows her more of a sense of openness toward some physical connection, because she knows there is no pressure to go beyond where she wants to go. Another couple shared a similar thought on this sense of safety and not feeling pressure. Kai (asexual) and their partner (Jacob) discussed the importance of how Jacob approaches intimacy without pressuring Kai. Kai stated,

> Whenever Jacob and I first met, I was in a relationship with someone who did not respect my boundaries and that is part of the reason why, early on, I learned to trust Jacob so deeply and right off the bat because when I said 'no' to doing something, Jacob was like 'ok, we don't have to'...Like I can say no and you aren't going to give me a bunch of shit about it.

Later Kai reflected on shifts in their sexual behavior that they noted was a direct result of Jacob not making them feel "obligated" to do anything they didn't want to do. They stated,

> Jacob has always made me feel like I can say no from the very beginning and that made me feel a lot freer to open up and do more sexual things. Before I would have said I was like sex-neutral, bordering towards sex-repulsed...and now I feeling more on the sex-positive side of the spectrum, like now I actually enjoy doing things in the bedroom with the discretion of like I control what happens with my body and I know my partner respects that.

Other asexuals I have interviewed shared similar sentiments. It is almost like the feeling of complete respect of boundaries with a partner that is willing to better understand and respect the asexuality—it made sexual relationships much easier. Another couple also brought up how important not feeling pressured was to their relationship. Mia stated her partner "isn't pushy about sex or repeatedly asking for it so that I am not feeling pressured." Jessica, an asexual participant, stated what worked well for her and her allosexual partner. She shared,

> It has been helpful like establishing time for like physical connection where there is no pressure to have sex...it is like the pressure is lifted and I am more likely to have sex, like the amount of time between the warming me up a little has been good.

Respect for boundaries was key to intimacy in asexual/allosexual couples. Aspen compliments their allosexual partner, "(we) just take it slow and communication...you are kind with me too...it is like 'is this ok?' 'are you feeling ok?' 'are you mentally in a good place for this?'" Aspen's words suggest an appreciation for this space. Another couple, Theo (allosexual) shared how they have respected their asexual partner, Luca. Theo stated,

> We start setting aside time, not necessarily like—ok this is when we are going to have sex—because that pressure feels bad, but like, ok, we are going to put ourselves in a position where we could (be sexually intimate), where everything would feel good, you know, it is like that connection aspect no matter where we end up going.

Later, Luca shared the importance of Theo creating that safe space for them and how valuable it was to the growth of their relationship. There was a strong connection between a felt sense that the partner is not pressuring intimacy, while also making space for each person in the relationship to communicate and present what works for them and what they desire.

Summary of Consent and No Pressure

Ever since I heard the words *enthusiastic consent*, I challenge almost all my clients, who discuss sexual intimacy as a part of their lives, to process what this means. Asking partners "how do you really know that is something they really want to do?" puts a whole new perspective on the dialog around sex. Sharing a body with a person requires more than "do you want to have sex?" and an "ok, I guess so." Enthusiastic consent can be wanting and desiring parts of sexual experiences… like holding a person while they experience sexual pleasure or having a back rub. But, these intricacies must be discussed in order for complete consent to be applied. Even with allosexual couples where both partners have high libidos, having partners ask each other "what are you both enthusiastic about when it comes to intimacy?" can change the conversation. I think focusing in on how to find this balance between *enthusiastic consent* and *willingness* is crucial for each person in a relationship to explore and define for themselves—and then, be able to communicate this to partners. Kai (asexual) was discussing a past partner that didn't respect their asexual boundaries. They put it this way "I think that my physical well-being and safety matters more than you getting off." Right!

Advice from Asexuals in Relationships

After researching and spending time with all sorts of people under the asexual umbrella who are part of relationships, I have come to three conclusions

1. We are all human. When it comes to relationships, we can all learn from each other on how to build healthier and stronger relationships; it does not matter our differences in attraction, desire, needs, etc.—human parts of us find connections to human parts of others. For this very reason, allosexuals may read all of this book and find that some of these experiences mirror their own relationships.
2. Everyone does relationships differently no matter what a person's sexual orientation is. We might connect on that human level, but the intimacies and vulnerabilities we show others may look different for any two people.
3. There is so much that everyone can learn from breaking apart relationship norms and putting them back in ways that fit the people involved in the relationship. All people can learn from asexuals' experiences doing this!

In light of these points, I am going to focus on what I feel like people can learn from my research on couples—if you are in a relationship, if you work with people in relationships, if you just want to understand relationships—the voices and experiences that are part of this book, the journeys of asexual participants, can contribute to an even deeper understanding of relationships. I am breaking this section down into key themes that I have found within the experiences of asexuals in relationships. I will share what participants disclose about what makes their relationships healthier, stronger, and/or better. These points might be helpful to other asexuals in relationships, practitioners working with asexuals in relationships, or even when strengthening allosexual relationships.

Communication and a Lot of It!

Learning point number one is in so many discussions on couples—communication. When we think of what makes a relationship strong, likely the first thing most people say is *communication*. Most couples that I have had in therapy will put on their intake form "better communication" as the presenting problem. Many asexuals in relationships that I interviewed focused on almost a hyper-level of communication with partners, particularly surrounding needs and intimacy. And, as someone who has worked with so many allosexual/allosexual couples—I can say first-hand that I found many asexual participants' focus and intention with regards to communication to be incredibly profound! The ways that many described their communication process with their partners can provide tools for all couples. Communication existed on a daily basis for the asexual participants I talked to. Communication often included deep, respectful clarity arounds physical needs, relationship needs, trust, safety, differences, and really, life goals and experiences. I do hypothesize that given the different focus around physical intimacy, perhaps for many asexuals, it does leave room for an emotional intimacy (as Ruby said: "talking about deep stuff").

Kai (asexual) and their partner Jacob (allosexual) discussed how important honesty was in their relationship. Kai says honesty "made our foundation for our relationship much stronger." They also share that this kind of communication can be a "learning curve" in both saying what you mean and trusting the other person to say what they mean. Lydia is an asexual partnered with an allosexual and shared some of the detailed communication that she has with her partner around intimacy. She stated,

> I think everyone, allosexual and asexual, everyone in general would be much happier if they negotiated their sexual experiences before it happened. It would alleviate 90% of the problems couples have.

Her partner, Patrick, follows up,

> We talk about it ahead of time, where is this going for me? Is this for both of us? I always ask, how do you want to feel? Because, for me that is more important right? If I succeed at getting you to feel the way you wanted then that is what I am going to feel good about, what makes me happy and brings me a lot of joy and pleasure.

Later, Patrick explains,

> Most couples don't talk about sex at home. Like, not even like the conversation around why they aren't having it (sex). But, not just that, it is never. (They don't discuss) what don't I enjoy having it (sex)? Why don't we do it more often? Like, what is stopping us from having it? It is always someone else blaming someone else for not having it. But, you (people

> in general) need to find out why you aren't having it, is it good? Maybe it is bad and if you are not communicating, you don't know. People don't like to tell people. It is awkward to say to someone, especially when it is around sex, like 'hey you know that thing you did last night? I didn't enjoy it, it felt bad, please don't do that again.' Like, that is hard to say, but if you have a safe place to talk about it. That's why we started, we started this whole document and there was like a feedback section in there to talk about overall purpose and it was designed like that.

The couple discussed their vigilance around communicating sexual experiences by crafting a document that they would share with what they liked and disliked when it came to all forms of intimacy. A couple of other couples that I spoke with had similar ways of communicating through digital organization of thoughts and following up with each other. For many couples generally, the pre-thought, the pre-communication around a possible sexual experience is not necessarily common, at least from what I have seen in my many years of working with couples.

Another couple shared a similar dynamic. Aspen (asexual) and their partner Jess talked about communication. The couple was talking about intimate moments at the start of their relationship, and Aspen stated,

> I stumbled into the—I don't have scripts here…yeah, I don't know your scripts yet, I don't know what you are looking for, if you say you would like some more of this, I don't know what that looks like.

They continued to share, "really good communication" is key, "I mean really really good, even early on…a lot of comfort and understanding that this is going to be a conversation that is complicated, but will be good and will work itself out."

There are theories, models, and techniques in helping fields that aid couples with communication challenges. Applied research on couples and communication focuses on so many possible couple directions, for example: in the moment techniques (e. g., listening before responding, grounding, reflexive listening) (Lebow & Snyder, 2022), being open and vulnerable to partner(s) (Williamson & Chen, 2025), teaching and practicing empathy (Lebow & Snyder, 2022), shift from aggressive responding to compassionate responding (Lebow & Snyder, 2022), focusing on couple cycles of emotion and attachment injuries (Johnson, 2019), attention to betrayal and trust (Gottman & Gottman, 2017), and a host of others. I feel that asexual participants and their partners would add to these theories and techniques a level of depth and intentionality. Communication, for many I spoke with, was frequent, was deep, and really dove into clear expectations and boundaries.

Make Time for ALL Kinds of Intimacy

The second point to bring in is intentionality behind making time for each other. Having busy lives is impactful to many relationships. Asexual participants and their partners shared the importance of setting aside time together, which may or may not include sex or physical intimacy (depending on the couple). Batchelor (2024) shared the importance of de-centering allonormative expectations of what intimacy should be and making room for "out of the box ideas" (p. 27). Intimacy might include quality time, talking, watching shows together, playing video games together, laying in bed ("sharing body heat"), etc. Kai (asexual) and their partner Jacob (allosexual) were talking about being busy and making time for each other. Jacob shared, "what little time we have, we can eat together and make the most of it, I appreciate those moments more than anything else." The intention that the couple puts into making the time they have something that is of quality for both of them is prevalent throughout their interview. Research on couples indicates that often in relationships, the time together tends to be more focused on life organizing, attending to children's needs, or even arguing (Hogan et al., 2021). More intentional space where couples are seeking connections outside of the daily task-focused elements of their lives can play a role in relationship satisfaction overall.

One way that asexual participants and their partners discussed making time for each other included—literally scheduling intimate and non-intimate time. Patrick, an allosexual partner to an asexual, stated,

> You have to schedule it (intimate time)…like sometimes you have to schedule time to connect, like for me physical touch is a big deal…like holding her hand…just having her around, her presence. As long as we make time for each other, physically next to one another.

Patrick and his partner Lydia discussed time periods when Lydia has gone out of town for work. The pair scheduled time to be close physically and be together in the same physical space and make it happen specifically and intentionally.

Aspen and Jess shared a similar discussion of time management and the importance of working in connecting with one another. Jess stated,

> Our time is dedicated time versus time that we are casually in each other's face. There is a degree to which, like when we are spending (focused/planned) time together that it is intimacy…even when we are watching a movie or something, there is also like a safety where I am end up saying things out loud while we are watching show that I normally say in my head, but I feel so safe that every thought comes out.

It is clear that Jess felt their connection in these planned moments is so strong that safety and vulnerability are second nature in those spaces.

Aspen and Jess also shared they are "explicit" about setting up time together to meet their sexual and nonsexual needs. Aspen stated,

> Sometimes it (organizing times) is more like an explicit conversation, like we are going to have a stay-at-home day this weekend, what are some ideas of what you might want to have? What are some things you might like to check off? There is a discussion in advance.

The couple creates space to discuss and organize what they both need from the togetherness space.

Commitment

I bring in intentionality to both the points above: communicate and have time for one another. Intentionality can fit hand-in-hand with commitment. Commitment is an obvious keyword in relationships and something that most people would agree serves as a foundational component of relationships. With asexual participants in relationships, they noted the importance of commitment to the relationship, to differences in sexual/intimacy desire differences, and to education and awareness of differences. Aspen (asexual) and Jess (allosexual) shared that they focus on commitment and make sure they each are aware that the other is committed. Jess equates a sense of safety in their relationship to this undercurrent of commitment that they feel regularly. Jess stated,

> I feel like I have been in a lot of relationships where when you have conflict, you don't really know if you are going to be ok, that is very much not the case here (in relationship with Aspen), where it is like there is a faith in it, that it is going to be ok, literally the relationship is going to be fine.

Jennifer (asexual) and Kyle (allosexual) have been married for 29 years. Kyle shared that even with the awareness of Jennifer's asexual identity, he "still has issues with it every now and then," but the couple identifies commitment as key to working through these moments. Jennifer stated, "there was a moment where I finally just came out and said, I figured it out—I am asexual, and in that moment there was a paradigm shift in our relationship. He stuck with me and we did it." The couple shared that this undercurrent that they would work through anything in their relationship facilitated this difference between the two of them. Later, Jennifer stated,

> The one thing we did very well (as a couple) was to take the labels and acknowledge them and then set them aside and say, 'ok, this is a marriage of two people, they are both complicated people, this one has these needs and these prohibitions and this one has these needs and these prohibitions, and we are going to pretend nobody else exists in the world and it is just you two, what do you need and what do you need, where are the compromise points, are there compromise points…if there are, let's break down the barriers and get to those compromise points.

The undercurrent of many couples I spoke with was this sense of commitment to knowing and understanding all of each other, which led to a feeling of safety and security that laid a foundation for difficult conversations.

Compromise and Adapting

Another common facet in relationships is understanding that there is going to be some compromise and adaptation. Sometimes asexuals and their partners talked about compromise as shifting things overall in ways that meet both people's needs. When it comes to sex and intimacy, often compromise is assumed to be that a person who is not as interested in these things should shift or do more sexual and intimate things. Compromise for asexuals and their partners was more about different ways of meeting needs and adapting. Jennifer (asexual) and her partner Kyle (allosexual) described the differences between compromise and sacrifice.

> Kyle: Not everyone is going to be able to compromise, accept, and don't take the acceptance as compromising their own values.
> Jennifer: The answer can't be one of them sacrifices themselves and that is where the line gets strong.

Kyle: What I am doing, I am pulling back my own libido, other guys may say well, you had to sacrifice…it is a reminder that not every day is going to be about you, it has got to be about you all (the couple) and, so yeah, there is compromise.

Jennifer and Kyle suggested a language difference with the terminology of compromise versus sacrifice and that there is a difference between giving up a root part of oneself and one's values and working as a team to figure out how to make things work.

Something that some asexuals brought up was a bit of a warming-up process for sex that might look different from allosexuals, "different ways of getting in the mood" as Aspen shared. One lesbian couple shared their experience of this adaptation. Sophie (demisexual) and her partner Leah (allosexual) have learned that connection can lead to Sophie feeling sexual. Sophie stated, "when we are connected, it opens me up." Leah followed up with, "it is about respecting her boundaries and almost letting her lead to a degree, I have learned that quality time leads to more intimacy." Sophie reiterates, "I have to have closeness before I can feel like sexy time stuff and she has come to recognize this." Sophie and Leah have adapted to appreciate each of their ways of doing things and experiencing things.

Sage (asexual) and their partner Rowan (allosexual) shared this story about their own adapting.

Sage: Sex freaks me out…when I was in high school, the idea of having sex made me like physically gag, which is why I felt I was definitely on the asexual spectrum because I was very averse to the idea of any kind of sexual contact. And, also, being trans, I didn't want certain body parts to be touched…now that we have gotten together, I am less grossed out by it, I think the concept is gross, but I am more ok with it now.
Rowan: It (working out differences in desire) is different depending on the day and exactly how you (Sage) are feeling about it that day…sometimes if I really like need it (sexual experience) but they are not like in the mood, I will just take care of myself and I am fine with that or there are different levels of their involvement in it…if they are not feeling it, but they are ok touching me, but I just don't touch them.
Sage: And, obviously there are a lot of moments where their (Rowan's) body is saying something and I am like, ok, we are going to take care of that, but if I am not in the mood per se, I can touch them or we have toys and we can use those.

The two of them recognize their differences but work together to make something work that they can both be on board with. Luca (asexual) and their partner Theo (allosexual) shared that they do a "slow and stop" adaptation to their sexual intimacy. Theo shared that he adapts by "slowing down" so we can "feel the moment." This allows time for Luca to better present verbal or nonverbal consent each step of the way.

Aspen (asexual) and Jess (allosexual) discussed moments when Jess may want a more sexual moment and Aspen is not quite in that headspace. Once Aspen shared that they are not interested in sex in that moment, Jess may say "ok, do we want to snuggle right now?" Jess continues to explain, "there is still a physical closeness which I think is a lot, I mean other sexy things are a lot of fun, but I am very happy with physical closeness." The couple found this to be a comfortable compromise that works well for both of them.

I think in relationship therapy, helping clients of all sexual orientations to recognize that each person is unique in their desires and needs is important. At times, the re-writing of scripts, as discussed earlier, is a possibility as the couple navigates new ways to connect that the allonormative world has not previously taught them. It is important to mention that, at times, these differences could be too overwhelming for the couple or the couple finds themselves unable to be satisfied with adaptations or collaborations to meet physical and/or romantic needs. These differences can even occur in different degrees among allosexual/allosexual couples. In my work with couples, I have realized that I am never the one who can make the choice for any couple about their future. I can guide, make suggestions, help them with past hurts, help with boundaries, help with communication, create new goals with them, bring in sexuality education or psychoeducation, etc. At times, some couples will defy more challenges and become stronger and deeper than I could have imagined, whereas other couples decide that their differences will leave at least one of them unhappy or unsatisfied. For me, this is about individual understanding and really allowing each person in the relationship to have a voice.

Education as Validation

One element of success that was described by many allosexual/asexual couples was education around asexuality. In my research, it is undeniable that the allosexual partner's complete respect for the asexual's identity was critical to the relationship. This finding follows other research (e.g., Clark, 2023). Rowan (allosexual) shared a lot of their experiences with educating themselves on asexuality and working to be a better partner for their asexual partner. They shared,

> I just want to respect them (partner) and validate how they are feeling and you know, because I have heard a lot of ace people being told and feeling like they are broken in some ways and that makes me feel sad because they are not. They are just, I mean everyone is different, everyone functions differently and views things differently.

Rowan has taken on learning and understanding, and this has positively impacted their relationship with their partner.

It seems that, during some interviews, it was obvious that couples were educating each other. Allosexual partners were learning more details about asexual partners and vice versa. In one conversation. Sophie (asexual) and her partner Leah (allosexual) were talking about their differences.

> Sophie: I realized allosexual people have this instant kind of sexual attraction thing, like they have an instant feeling of sexual attraction, like they get aroused when they see a person, is that right? (she turns to ask Leah).
> Leah: I mean kind of, I can see an attractive woman and it can sort of take me a minute to re-group.
> Sophie: And, I don't have that like you, like I know she is attractive, I admire her style, but don't drool over her or even think about body parts or sex.
> Leah: It is where we are different. I do drool sometimes…we went to a bridal party with my friend and someone set up a stripper for the party, we joked…
> Sophie: Right, the whole time, I was thinking 'her nipples are and interesting color and go well with her eyes,' but no lust or attraction, we laughed…

> Leah: I couldn't tell you the color of her eyes.

The pair seemed to laugh over this revelation in their relationship and the education they both got about their differences in sexual attraction. Both were open to learning and appreciated each other's differences. Education, for couples, included both exploring language and asexuality overall, but also being in-tune with their partner's needs and how they describe their identity.

Exploring Other Intimacies

Discussions with asexuals and their partners suggested a focus on exploring all kinds of intimacies outside of sexual intimacy. Asexual participants frequently mentioned differing intimacy needs and desires that did not always fit under the umbrella of sexual contact. Jennifer (asexual) shared,

> To me, intimacy is moments of connection with no walls up, you've got deep communication, affectionate touching, you have a sense of safety that is remarkable. You could reach that moment doing anything, you could be holding hands in the park, you could be sitting together at somebody's wedding…when you have an overwhelming sense of the two of you as a unit, that's kind of unbreakable and vulnerable and safe together. It can happen during sex, but it doesn't have to.

Jennifer's partner, Kyle (allosexual), shared that he has shifted and appreciates this focus on other intimacies, sharing, "The foundation of intimacy doesn't have to be any sexual contact whatsoever or even the thought of it."

Sage (asexual) and Rowan (allosexual) had a discussion on what intimacy looks like for them that they make intentional space for. They were reflecting on a friend who had recently come over when their favorite band released an album at midnight. The couple reflected on how intimate that moment was and how important those moments are to them.

> Sage: Our friend the other day, we were talking about music and albums and new bands coming out with new music and she said 'do you guys want to stay up until midnight and listen to the new album with me when it comes out' and she described it as a very emotionally intimate experience for her.
> Rowan: I was like yeah, I get that!
> Sage: Like listening to an album at midnight with someone is like the most emotionally intimate thing I can think of, and I was like 'yes!'
> Rowan: Sometimes it is things that you don't even think about until you are doing it and you are like this is just an intimate experience and I am really connected to this person.
> Sage: I kind of struggle with intimacy as an autistic person as a whole, but sometimes it is like parallel play, like in the room, doing two different things and some people would be like 'how is it intimate to be in a room doing two different things and not talking?' and I am like, because I don't mind their presence, like most people I would be annoyed if they were there.
> Rowan: I think it is really special that you are autistic and authentically 'don't touch me' but you like touch from me and you like being around me. You can be alone with me.

The two of them have found this space of intimacy that really connects them and allows them to grow as a couple. I think that the idea of new forms of intimacy can just be uncovered as people break down sexual expectations and relationship scripts. I think opening up new intimacies, for couples I interviewed, but also in viewing clients' experiences overall, can only make the relationship stronger.

Overall, participants—both asexual and allosexual participants—provided such substance for considering what relationships can look like outside the allonormative box. Communication, compromise, validation, education, and exploring intimacy are common variables of most relationships; however, when a relationship does not fit allonormative expectations, these key relationship elements can look at little different. For all people in relationships, challenging the social scripts by taking these key elements into account in ways that embrace unique individual differences can increase relationship growth and strength.

Challenges

Changing directions just a bit, I have spent a lot of time sharing how open and connected asexual participants and their partners can be. That does not mean there were not, at times, discussions on challenges asexuals and their partners faced. Previous research has highlighted some possible challenges that could exist for asexuals who are part of romantic and/or sexual relationships.

Compared to allosexuals, asexuals typically report having had less sexual and romantic experiences (controlling for other demographics) (Clark, 2023). Similarly, asexuals, in this same study, perceived they would engage in less future sexual or romantic experiences compared to allosexuals. Asexuals also report less interest in sexual activity than their allosexual counterparts (Clark & Zimmerman, 2022). Of course, these differences could be minimal if an asexual person partners with another asexual person; however, these differences could play a role in asexual/allosexual relationships. Perhaps asexual partners are learning to navigate some of the nuances of being in a relationship in ways that look different than allosexual partners.

Earlier, I discussed moments when there can be a mismatch in sexual attraction, desire, and stated physical needs between two people. All participants I spoke with had figured these differences out to some degree and worked to communicate and adapt in ways that both partners felt satisfied. Note that in my research, being in a committed relationship was the requirement for participation. So, I have not necessarily tapped into a participant pool of asexuals where their relationships did not work. That being said, many of the participants I spoke with discussed previous relationships and alluded to this mismatch as part of the reason for the relationship ending. For example, Kai (asexual) shared a story about a past relationship that didn't work, they stated,

> He (ex-partner) didn't respect my boundaries and made me feel like I was lacking. It kind of made me feel more obligated to give him physical affection or sexual affection…so like, yeah, that was part of why we broke up, I was eventually like, I can't do this anymore.

Other participants reflected on past relationships where their partners were not comfortable or respectful when it came to their asexual identity.

In addition, quite a few of the asexual/allosexual couples I spoke with said something along the line of "I don't know if the relationship would have worked if I was sex averse." Some asexuals and their allosexual partners considered the challenges that they might experience if the asexual partner identified as *sex repulsed* or *sex averse* and the other partner was allosexual and/or hypersexual. They would mention that they did not know if a relationship like this could work for them.

Asexuals partnered with allosexuals sometimes shared that the asexual partner's leaning toward either *sex favorable* or *sex indifferent* allowed for more flexibility in these adaptations and meeting of physical desires. The key factor is the different ways that each person in the relationship approached intimacy needs and the comfort each has in exploring a variety of physical and intimacy options. One couple, Mia (asexual) and Mason (allosexual), shared that they still struggle with sexual intimacy and figuring out the fit for both of them. Mia stated, "it (sex) is still a work in progress, still something we are trying to navigate." The couple is working on this and shared that they plan a "weekly check in" where they discuss "intimacy and sex." These check-ins are an opportunity for them both to discuss what is working and what is not working.

Allosexual partners respected and embraced their asexual partners, however, that did not always come without some confusion, some moments of feeling unattractive or undesired, or just not understanding. Even when allosexual partners threw themselves into working to understand and respect asexual partners, at times, there were some lingering questions. Rowan, an allosexual partner of Sage (an asexual) shared they have moments where they struggle because Sage does not desire them sexually. They share,

> It is like, logically I know that (lack of desire) is not necessarily what is happening and I know they love and care for me and they just want me to be happy, but I think there is just some chemical thing about my brain sometimes, like earlier on when I was still trying to fully understand it (asexuality), I would have moments where I was like 'oh, I like you more than you like me.' But, then I logically think about it and I am like, no, I know they care, it is just that we might express it or feel it in slightly different ways.

Kyle (an allosexual partner) discussed moments where he would still feel a little confused about his partner and understanding her. He was talking about times when the couple was intimate and shared,

> we engage in sex and there are times she separates herself and where she doesn't, those are the times things can be more intense and it seems like she is more engaged or maybe it is those times when she is more disengaged…I think of a person who is disengaged as more robotic, automatic…so it is very confusing.

Kyle and his partner shared a deep commitment to working to understand each other; however, in Kyle's words here, there are still moments when he still struggles.

One thing that I have noticed is that many asexuals discuss when it comes to relationships is a fear that they may not meet partner needs and this could impact their relationships. Kai (asexual) reflected on some fears they had at the start of their relationship. They stated,

> Growing up feeling like I was wrong or broken somehow…if this is a thing I am going to have to deal with the rest of my life, anytime I am dating someone who is not asexual, are they going to be like 'well this isn't good, because you aren't sexually attracted to me.'

They continued to discuss this later, stating, an asexual person…

> …might feel the need to put out, so to speak, in order to make sure they don't leave you for somebody that isn't asexual, that is definitely a fear I struggled with on and off throughout life, am I ever going to be good enough for somebody else even if I feel good enough for me?

Sage, an asexual, shared a similar concern,

> I was worried that nobody would want me because I grew up hearing people talk about—oh sex makes your relationship so much better and you feel so much closer to your partner—and I was like, if I don't have that attraction, am I not going to feel as close to my partner as they feel to me?

Some asexuals put a lot of pressure on themselves despite reassurance from their partners. I heard a lot of asexual participants mention a sense of guilt or feeling like they are not meeting sexual standards or pleasing their partners. Ruby (asexual) stated

> I'll sometimes panic because I am like 'I am a bad wife', I am like a bad wife because we are not having sex…I am not giving him what he wants, I am so sorry that I didn't want that.

She shared that she "defaults to allosexual relationships" because that is what she sees and hears and even if her partner does not even care or want a sexual relationship, she still feels that guilt because it is the way society expects her to be. Mia (asexual) shared that they experience a lot of guilt, stating that sometimes "I feel bad internally, we both can't be mutually happy in that and like every aspect of enjoying sex together all the time."

Conclusion

A person's decision to enter a relationship (romantic and/or sexual and/or queer platonic) is a complex interplay of internal messages, identity, personal desire, and social constructs (Ang, 2024; Barros & Doyle, 2025). In many ways, asexuals are helping to re-write the scripts that there is only one way to do this; however, at the same time, asexuals exist within the contexts of these largely unquestioned beliefs that romance and sex are the only ways to happiness. Breaking down these expectations can create space to build whatever fits for the individual and allows them to define for themselves what is important to them when it comes to human connections and the building of family—this in itself can be empowering for asexuals (Ang, 2024). Allosexual partners of asexuals can also find a sense of liberation from adapting to understanding the multiple layers of intimacy that can be part of relationships.

References

Agrawal, N., Shainy, M. R., Sebastian, J., Srivastava, A., & Scoats, R. (2025). Sex without sexual attraction?: Perceived sexual experiences of Indian sex-favourable asexuals. *Psychology & Sexuality, 16*(4), 1–21. https://doi.org/10.1080/19419899.2025.2518977

Ang, M. W. (2024). Dynamisms of romantic family imaginaries and asexual identity-making. *Journal of Family Studies, 32*(1), 1–16. https://doi.org/10.1080/13229400.2024.2396440

Barnhart, K. J., Leahy, K. E., & Wildey, M. N. (2025). Unwanted consensual sex among college students: What makes an individual more likely to consent to sex they do not want? *Behavioral Sciences, 15*(7), 981. https://doi.org/10.3390/bs15070981

Barros, S. P., & Doyle, E. M. (2025). Trans-cending the mononormativity of relationship therapy: An intersectional framework for increasing competency. *Journal of Marital & Family Therapy, 51*(3), 1–10. https://doi.org/10.1111/jmft.70025

Batchelor, C. (2024). *Beyond 'the whole sex thing': Co-constructing fulfilling asexual/allosexual relationships* [Doctoral dissertation: University of Memphis]. Electronic Theses and Dissertations. https://digitalcommons.memphis.edu/etd/3684

Birdsong, J. (2020, June 20). *The queering of friendship: Rethinking platonic relationships guided by LGBTQ models.* Salon. https://www.salon.com/2020/06/20/the-queering-of-friendship-rethinking-platonic-relationships-guided-by-lgbtq-models/

Borden, L., & Allan, R. (2024). Integrating sex therapy with emotionally focused therapy to treat sexual desire discrepancy. *Family Journal, 32*(4), 522–530. https://doi.org/10.1177/10664807241264813

Bulmer, M., & Izuma, K. (2018). Implicit and explicit attitudes toward sex and romance in asexuals. *The Journal of Sex Research, 55*(8), 962–974. https://doi.org/10.1080/00224499.2017.1303438

Busby, D. M., Allen, C. Z., Leavitt, C. E., & Jensen, A. C. (2025). Physical aspects of sexuality, attachment, and sexual satisfaction. *Journal of Marital and Family Therapy, 51*, 1–15. https://doi.org/10.1111/jmft.12760

Caruso, G., & Celardi, E. (2025). Intimacy and identity negotiation in online asexual communities: Beyond normative assumptions. *Culture, Health & Sexuality, 28*(3), 1–13. https://doi.org/10.1080/13691058.2025.2542842

Clark, A. N. (2023). Using social exchange theory to examine relationship processes in asexual-allosexual couples. *Journal of Family Theory & Review, 15*(2), 352–372. https://doi.org/10.1111/jftr.12495

Clark, A. N., Walters, T. L., & Hanna-Walker, V. (2025). "Much like skydiving, I would really rather avoid it if I can": Asexual and allosexual adults' motives for not having sexual experiences. *Psychology & Sexuality, 16*(2), 438–453. https://doi.org/10.1080/19419899.2024.2446774

Clark, A. N., Walters, T. L., & Lefkowitz, E. S. (2024). "It's an ongoing discussion about desire": Adults' strategies for managing sexual and affectionate desire discrepancies in romantic relationships. *Journal of Marital and Family Therapy, 50*, 669–686. https://doi.org/10.1111/jmft.12709

Clark, A. N., & Zimmerman, C. (2022). Concordance between romantic orientations and sexual attitudes: Comparing allosexual and asexual adults. *Archives of Sexual Behavior: The Official Publication of the International Academy of Sex Research, 51*(4), 2147–2157. https://doi.org/10.1007/s10508-021-02194-3

Copulsky, D. (2015). Asexual polyamory: Potential challenges and benefits. *Journal of Positive Sexuality, 2*, 11–15. https://doi.org/10.51681/1.213

Copulsky, D., & Hammack, P. L. (2025). Consensual nonmonogamous relationships during the COVID-19 pandemic. Sexualities, 28(1-2), 699–723. https://doi.org/10.1177/13634607231212809

Copulsky, D. (2019). At the intersection of polyamory and asexuality. In B. L. Simula, J. E. Summerau, & A. Miller (Eds.), *Expanding the Rainbow: Exploring the relationships of Bi+, Polyamorous, Kinky, Ace, Intersex, and Trans People* (pp. 199–208). Brill.

Emond, M., Byers, E. S., Brassard, A., Tremblay, N., & Péloquin, K. (2024). Addressing sexual issues in couples seeking relationship therapy. *Sexual & Relationship Therapy, 39*(1), 115–130. https://doi.org/10.1080/14681994.2021.1969546

Flicker, S. M., Vaughan, M. D., & Meyers, L. S. (2021). Feeling good about your partners' relationships: Compersion in consensually non-monogamous relationships. *Archives of Sexual Behavior: The Official Publication of the International Academy of Sex Research, 50*(4), 1569–1585. https://doi.org/10.1007/s10508-021-01985-y

Glass, V. Q. (2022). Queering relationships: Exploring phenomena of asexual identified persons in relationships. *Contemporary Family Therapy: An International Journal, 44*, 344–359. https://doi.org/10.1007/s10591-022-09650-9

Goodman, L. C., Hamilton, L., Koerten, H. R., Mattei, G. M., Froemming, M. W., & Dubow, E. F. (2019). Childhood victimization, cognitive schemas, and unwanted consensual sex among college students. *International Journal of Sexual Health, 31*(2), 142–153. https://doi.org/10.1080/19317611.2019.1595258

Gottman, J., & Gottman, J. (2017). The natural principles of love. *Journal of Family Theory and Review, 9*, 7–26. https://doi.org/10.1111/jftr.12182

Gupta, K. (2017). "And now I'm just different, but there's nothing actually wrong with me": Asexual marginalization and resistance. *Journal of Homosexuality, 64*, 991–1013. https://doi.org/10.1080/00918369.2016.1236590

Herbitter, C., Vaughan, M. D., & Pantalone, D. W. (2024). Mental health provider bias and clinical competence in addressing asexuality, consensual non-monogamy, and BDSM: A narrative review. *Sexual & Relationship Therapy, 39*(1), 131–154. https://doi.org/10.1080/14681994.2021.1969547

Higginbottom, B. (2024). The nuances of intimacy: Asexual perspectives and experiences with dating and relationships. *Archives of Sexual Behavior: The Official Publication of the International Academy of Sex Research, 53*(5), 1899–1914. https://doi.org/10.1007/s10508-024-02846-0

Hille, J. J., Bhuyan, L., & Tillewein, H. (2024). Ace and poly: The motivations and experiences of people on the ace spectrum in polyamorous relationships. *Sexes, 5*(2), 111–119. https://doi.org/10.3390/sexes5020009

Hille, J. J., Simmons, M. K., & Sanders, S. A. (2020). "Sex" and the ace spectrum: Definitions of sex, behavioral histories, and future interest for individuals who identify as asexual, graysexual, or demisexual. *Journal of Sex Research, 57*(7), 813–823. https://doi.org/10.1080/00224499.2019.1689378

Hogan, J. N., Crenshaw, A. O., Baucom, K. J. W., & Baucom, B. R. W. (2021). Time spent together in intimate relationships: Implications for relationship functioning. *Contemporary Family Therapy: An International Journal, 43*(3), 226–233. https://doi.org/10.1007/s10591-020-09562-6

Johnson, S. (2019). Attachment in action—Changing face of 21st century couple therapy. *Current Opinion in Psychology, 25*, 101–104. https://doi.org/10.1016/j.copsyc.2018.03.007

Kedzior, S. G. E., Rumbold, A. R., Manning, N., Calabretto, H., Lassi, Z. S., & Moore, V. M. (2025). "It's complicated": Young people's views on the complexity of asking for consent and the role for sex and relationships education. *Sex Education: Sexuality, Society and Learning, 25*(2), 273–289. https://doi.org/10.1080/14681811.2024.2317330

Lebow, J., & Snyder, D. K. (2022). Couple therapy in the 2020s: Current status and emerging developments. *Family Process, 61*(4), 1359–1385. https://doi.org/10.1111/famp.12824

Peterson, D. (2025). Healthy sex, moving beyond legal consent framing in sex education: A call to action in US colleges and universities. *Sex Education, 25*(2), 171–183. https://doi.org/10.1080/14681811.2023.2296469

Russell, J. (2023). The sex lives of asexuals. In S. Neves & D. Davies (Eds.), *Erotically queer: A pink therapy guide for practitioners* (pp. 59–74). Routledge. https://doi.org/10.4324/9781003260608-5

Sprott, R. A. (2020). Reimagining "kink": Transformation, growth, and healing through BDSM. *Journal of Humanistic Psychology, 64*(6), 987–992. https://doi.org/10.1177/0022167819900036

Tessler, H. (2025). Aromanticism, asexuality, and relationship (non-) formation: How a-spec singles challenge romantic norms and reimagine family life. *Sexualities, 28*(1/2), 514–535. https://doi.org/10.1177/13634607231197061

Van Houdenhove, E., Gijs, L., T'Sjoen, G., & Enzlin, P. (2014). Asexuality: Few facts, many questions. *Journal of Sex & Marital Therapy, 40*(3), 175–192. https://doi.org/10.1080/0092623X.2012.751073

Vowels, L. M., & Mark, K. P. (2020). Strategies for mitigating sexual desire discrepancy in relationships. *Archives of Sexual Behavior: The Official Publication of the International Academy of Sex Research, 49*(3), 1017–1028. https://doi.org/10.1007/s10508-020-01640-y

Williamson, H. C., & Chen, P.-H. (2025). Current theories and epistemologies of couple communication center white American modes of interaction. *Social and Personality Psychological Compass, 19*, 1–10. https://doi.org/10.1111/spc3.70040

Winter-Gray, T., & Hayfield, N. (2021). 'Can I be a kinky ace?': How asexual people negotiate their experiences of kinks and fetishes. *Psychology & Sexuality, 12*(3), 163–179. https://doi.org/10.1080/19419899.2019.1679866

Young, E. (2023). *Ace voices: What it means to be asexual, aromantic, demi or grey-ace*. Jessica Kingsley Publishers.

Chapter 6
Asexual Affirmative Care

Queer affirmative models rose out of pathologizing stigmas of queerness that are rooted in mental health care (Harvey et al., 2022). Consider my field, marriage and family therapy, the name, marriage and family therapy, is founded in heteronormative assumptions of marriage. My training included learning about key founders of the field in the 1950s and 1960s who frequently identified healthy family dynamics under a heteronormative umbrella. Of course, in this field, the conversation has shifted a great deal; however, that does not always preclude the founding messages of the importance of heterosexual marriage and family and the vision of one expected way to be in relationships. I appreciate Russell's (2023) summary of this point, "All clients, not just asexual clients, need to be supported in developing the breadth in relationships, but asexuality brings our attention to how significant those relationships can be without sexual contact" (p. 98–99). Queer affirmative care recognizes this historical past while concurrently validating and affirming identities and experiences that do not fall into these heteronormative experiences. By amplifying queer affirmative care to the many helping disciplines, a focused effort to provide inclusive awareness of all queer people evolves as an ethical standard.

Queer affirmative care models are designed to identify ways for practitioners to create a safe and welcoming space for individuals of all sexual orientations and gender identities (e.g., Giammattei & Green, 2012; McGeorge et al., 2015; McKinney et al., 2020; Rock et al., 2010; Thacker Darrow et al., 2025). Adopting an affirming lens builds in a comprehensive view of how clinicians can integrate queer cultural competency into their practice (inclusive of social, cultural, and historical impacts on queer communities). Additionally, affirmative care challenges practitioners to tackle internalized messages of homophobia and transphobia.

Social justice and activism are part of queer affirmative models—creating larger safe spaces in our communities for gender and sexual minorities. It is undeniable that a lack of queer-affirming care in mental health can be detrimental to gender and sexual minorities, notably higher risks of depression, anxiety, and suicide are trends among gender and sexual minorities who do not receive affirming care (e.g., Amos

V. Q. Glass, *Asexuality, Relationships, and Identity Formation*,
https://doi.org/10.1007/978-3-032-22857-4_6

et al., 2025; Bhatt et al., 2022; Budge et al., 2024; Burger & Pachankis, 2024; Mondave et al., 2025). Additionally, affirming care allows for a more open and specific professional discourse around queer experiences, clinician self-awareness, guidelines, and policy.

What Encompasses Queer Affirmative Care?

Queer affirmative care provides a mind-set, an awareness of internal messages and social scripts, and an understanding of the impacts of social discourses on queer persons. It is a deep respect and celebration of sexual and gender minorities, and it is a solid understanding of challenges and strengths of queer persons. Queer affirmative care is about un-learning heteronormative messages and expectations (Harvey et al., 2022). Queer affirmative care is about focused self-awareness as a clinician and a recognition of the impacts of social messages, discrimination, and violence that can be part of the lives of sexual and gender minorities. Queer individuals often face impactful stressors from society inclusive of heteronormative messages, microaggressions, and violence (Burger & Pachankis, 2024). Queer affirmative care acknowledges these social stressors and the impacts on queer individuals overall.

Intersectionality is a key component to queer affirmative care (Bowleg et al., 2023; Freeman-Coppadge & Langroudi, 2021; Kahn et al., 2018; Singh et al., 2025). Building on queer affirmative care is the recognition of the multiple ways people experience queerness and how other identities, contexts, and backgrounds can impact queer persons, particularly when taking into account multiple minority identities. A queer person's religion, race, culture, background, income, education, immigration status, gender, disability status, the list is continuous—can impact how a person experiences, perceives, and/or identifies their strengths and challenges with regards to their gender identity and sexual orientation. Intersections of identity open an expansive and almost undefinable spectrum of unique ways people experience sexual orientation and gender identity.

On the outside, queer affirmative care can look like creating a welcoming physical environment for people of all sexual orientations and gender identities (Thacker Darrow et al., 2025). In a therapy office, this would include inclusive paperwork that reflects different identities and relationships. It might include pictures or books in the area that are inclusive of all types of people, identities, and relationships. An office might have pamphlets, stickers, or representations of queer-affirming symbols. A welcoming space is aware of embracing language and checks in with all clients when it comes to their descriptions of their identities.

Overall, queer affirmative care is a place for people to feel welcomed and celebrated. It is a place where individuals can feel safety and support. It is a place where people can explore their own identities without risk of judgment or discrimination. This involves embracing all of a person's background and identities and includes embracing asexuality.

Asexual Experiences with Healthcare and Mental Health Care

What goes into providing appropriate, supportive, and affirming care for asexual individuals? Because many practitioners are unfamiliar with asexuality or how to embrace asexuality, asexuals can experience negative reactions when seeking medical or mental health care (Flanagan & Peters, 2020; Lu & Chui, 2025). In a study done in 2020, almost half of asexual participants, who disclosed their lack of sexual attraction or lack of desire to engage in sex to medical providers, were given an inaccurate diagnosis (e.g., mental or physical diagnosis) when likely they did not need any diagnosis at all (Flanagan & Peters, 2020). Asexuality is not part of mental health and medical health learning curriculums (Schneckenburger et al., 2024). Many medical and mental health practitioners seek out a cause for things that asexuals can report (e.g., not feeling sexual attraction and/or maybe not feeling interested in sexual relationships) instead of looking at the possibility of asexuality as a sexual orientation. This lack of awareness and education can lead to change efforts (sex therapy, medication, etc.) for something that is innate to a person, further pathologizing or stigmatizing asexuals.

Sometimes practitioners question if an asexual person is not being forthcoming about their situation (Flanagan & Peters, 2020). For example, a college-aged participant in Flanagan and Peter's study shared a story of a physician inferring that she was lying about the fact that she was not having sex or interested in having sex. There are experiences in asexual communities around being dismissed by professionals, being told there is something wrong, or stating that they are lying about their experiences.

Asexual participants I spoke with had a lot of thoughts on this topic. Some participants would discuss difficult experiences with medical professionals or therapists who just did not understand or would take them down a path that made them feel more *broken* and less validated. According to participants, practitioners seem to think, at times, that the feelings asexuals are having are "not real," "rooted in trauma," or have "some medical reason." Blake, an asexual participant, discussed the assumptions many practitioners have about asexuality being rooted in trauma; they stated that practitioners should,

> Never try to convince them (asexuals) that they need therapy to 'fix their asexuality.' And, unless they have told you they want to heal from prior trauma…don't assume this…and don't assume they will stop being ace once their trauma is healed.

A couple participants even stated that some practitioners will question a person's happiness in their relationship if they are not having sex. These initial messages that some participants got from medical and mental health communities challenged their own identity process.

Some participants stated they felt they had to educate therapists, even supportive therapists. There was a sense that therapists lacked awareness, self-reflection, and education on asexuality. One asexual participant shared a situation with a therapist where the therapist "challenged" her sexual orientation "rather aggressively." She stated that the therapist "questioned me on that (sexual orientation) and didn't believe it." Another participant, Miranda, discussed that many practitioners feel that a lack of sexual attraction is "a result of trauma." She stated, "not a whole lot of therapists are aware of or trained to handle (different kinds of relationships)…" and therapists "still discount those (different relationships) as unhealthy relationships." Blair stated their advice to therapists, "One of the first things is, they (therapists) always want to confirm that you (asexual) have seen a doctor, don't have a medical condition or mental health condition…maybe don't jump to that first, let them explain themselves first." She added, "you (asexuals) spend your whole life either being outright told or in my case, internally, believing there is something wrong with you…we all get told one way or another that we are wrong for how we feel." I will say that a couple of participants shared experiences with physicians or therapists where asexuality was brought up, and this terminology allowed them to start to understand their own identity more. These couple of participants appreciated this step in their identity journey; however, it seems to be a rare occurrence overall that practitioners will present asexuality as a possibility.

Supportive and Non-Supportive Therapy

It is not uncommon for asexuals to enter into medical or therapeutic relationships and experience microaggressions or a lack of understanding by the practitioner. One study identified themes that highlighted some of the supportive and non-supportive experiences that asexual participants reported during therapeutic encounters (Lu & Chui, 2025). The researchers put their participants' responses into two categories: those who felt they had a good therapy experience and those who did not feel good about their therapy experience. Some of the highlights of this research include the following positive counseling experiences that some of the participants noted:

1. When practitioners were aware of and knowledgeable of asexuality.
2. When practitioners were open to learning about asexuality.
3. When practitioners were affirming in other ways (e.g., using gender-neutral language).
4. When the asexual client felt that the practitioner was not judging their identity
5. When the practitioner provided a safe space to allow the client to fully explore their asexual (or other queer) identities.

Participants who had a negative experience in therapy noted the following things that were part of their therapy:

1. The practitioner was not aware of asexuality, did not have a solid understanding, or had a misunderstanding.
2. The practitioner did not seem interested in learning more about asexuality or the client's identity.

3. The asexual client felt microaggressions from the practitioner (e.g., when the practitioner seemed to be searching for something wrong with the client when the asexual identity was disclosed).

It is not uncommon for asexuals to enter into medical or therapeutic relationships and experience microaggressions, lack of understanding, allonormativity, or dismissiveness (Boot-Haury, 2023; Schneckenburger et al., 2024). Practitioners or medical professionals often jump to asking about medical issues that *cause* a lack of sexual attraction, stressing bloodwork, gynecological exams, hormone replacement, etc. (Flanagan & Peters, 2020). These experiences can contribute to what could already be a negative self-worth, an internal struggle, a feeling of brokenness, or any variety of emotional or mental health challenges. Asexuals may be coming to practitioners to heal and to seek understanding, and they may leave feeling more broken because of a lack of awareness or because of practitioner bias.

Evolving Asexual Affirmative Care Research

A handful of researchers have begun expanding on queer affirmative care with regard to asexuals, in mental health and medical care (Boot-Haury, 2023; Flanagan & Peters, 2020; Foster & Scherrer, 2014; Jones et al., 2017; Pavanello Decaro et al., 2025; Schneckenburger et al., 2024). Schneckenburger et al. (2024) explain asexual affirmative health care this way,

> Providers can create a welcoming environment by affirming asexuality when disclosed, approaching clients non-judgmentally, using inclusive language, demonstrating empathy for challenges faced, listening to asexual experiences without assumptions or dismissal, normalizing little or no sexual activity, and being comfortable talking about sex and sexuality (p. 325-326).

The importance of education on asexuality is noted as a critical step for providers, particularly given the lack of education in training programs (Boot-Haury, 2023; Flanagan & Peters, 2020; Pavanello Decaro et al., 2025; Schneckenburger et al., 2024). One of the most critical steps in creating mental and physical health care that is affirming to asexuals is to not view lack of sexual attraction from a medical model lens, rather consider asexuality as a sexual orientation (Schneckenburger et al., 2024). Another critical element for asexual affirmative care is believing asexuals' experiences and journeys as real and valid without pathologizing.

In addition, asexual affirmative care includes elements of practitioner self-reflection (Boot-Haury, 2023). Asexuality is a less commonly known sexual orientation, and most practitioners are viewing aspects of asexual experiences from their own point of reference. Self-reflection can include how the practitioner experiences their own sexual attraction or the value they place on sexual relationships. Additionally, personal allonormative or amatonormative belief systems can come into play that do not allow space for other ways of being.

Finally, some research has stressed the importance of recognizing the possible external stressors that asexuals might be experiencing (Boot-Haury, 2023). Affirming care includes creating a safe space for asexuals to process minority stress, microaggressions, and relationship challenges (Foster & Scherrer, 2014). Maybe even more importantly, affirmative care can embrace the pride and sense of meaning that many asexuals do feel with regard to their identity (Jones et al., 2017).

Asexual Affirmative Care Model

I have created an expansion to queer affirmative care models that encompasses asexual identity development and the existent research on asexual affirming practices (Boot-Haury, 2023; Flanagan & Peters, 2020; Foster & Scherrer, 2014; Jones et al., 2017; Pavanello Decaro et al., 2025; Schneckenburger et al., 2024). This asexual affirmative care model builds on both the research laid out before on queer affirmative care, asexual affirmative care, and the voices of the asexual participants I have encountered. In Chap. 4, I presented a view of identity development that evolved from phenomenological research data. This identity development data serves as the backdrop for considering asexual affirmative care and the emergence of the model that I will present here. As a reminder, the identity development process included: (a) juxtaposing identity, (b) interpreting identity, and (c) integrating identity.

The asexual affirmative care model is presented in Fig. 6.1. The asexual identity process is in the center of the graphic, and the elements around the graphic are the parts of the asexual affirmative care model that I will define and describe

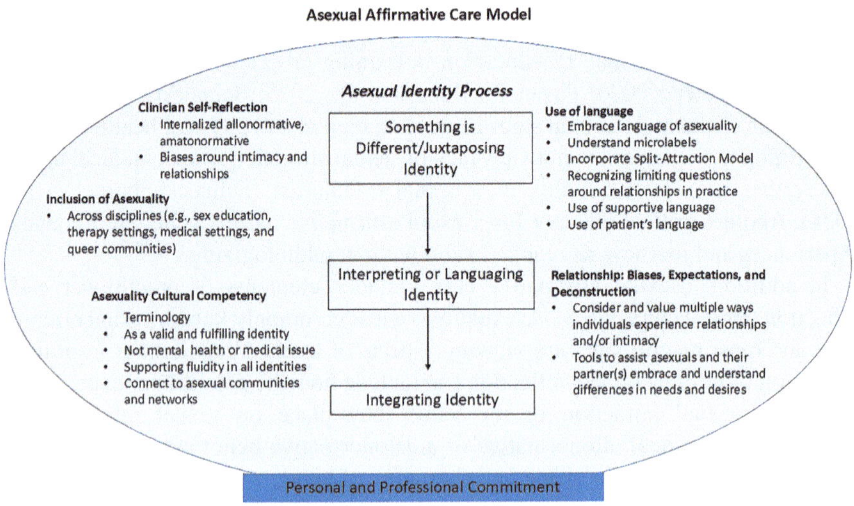

Fig. 6.1 Asexual affirmative care model

individually. This model is tied together by *personal and professional commitment* or intentionality, bringing an intentional awareness and focus to affirming asexuality.

A. *Clinician Self-Reflection*

Queer affirmative therapy stresses self-reflecting on internalized homophobia, transphobia, and heteronormativity (Carlson & McGeorge, 2012; McGeorge et al., 2015; Rock et al., 2010). Asexual affirmative self-reflection should also consider how the practitioner views relationships, sexual experiences, and desire (Glass, 2022). Western cultures highlight that romance, love, and satisfying sexual relationships are the keys to happiness (Brunning & McKeever, 2021; Glass, 2022). Frequently, practitioners internalize these messages and may (even sub-consciously) identify that there is one best way to build relationships that are typically heterosexual and allosexual. These biases could negatively influence work with asexual populations. Asexual individuals might be completely fulfilled without a sexual relationship or a romantic relationship. Some asexual persons do seek out relationships and sexual intimacy and find these fulfilling. It is crucial to recognize these variations and not make assumptions about needs, desires, and paths to happiness and satisfaction.

Having an open mind and embracing difference is a major element of self-reflection. Lindsey, an asexual participant, shared a story of going to an older therapist and educating her on asexuality. She told the therapist about asexuality, described it to the therapist, and then also shared that she was part of the kink community. Lindsey reflected, "oh my gosh, when I explained I was kinky, her mind was just blown…poor woman, I changed her for life." Asexual participants often comment on therapist's need to self-reflect on their own biases. Bri shared that therapists need to recognize their possible false bias that "sex is required for a relationship to succeed" (Glass, 2022, p. 355). Anita shared many therapists force people to consider that they "need sex to be happy," her advice to therapists, "if someone is sex averse, leave them the fuck alone." E, an asexual, who is also a counselor, shared,

> I think the biggest advice I would give to a therapist is exploring their own biases…maybe it is going into your family of origin and thinking about how sex was presented and what its' purpose was…why is it your gut impulse to say 'ok, let's figure out a way for you to have sex' and why is that your impulse…interrogate that and also some self of the therapist work around that (Glass, 2022, p. 355).

Another asexual participant I interviewed, Megan, equated a lack of clinician self-awareness to asexuals feeling unsafe in the therapy setting. She shared that when clinicians are not self-reflecting, this can lead to a sense of "stigma" for asexual patients and feeling "judged" by the clinician.

As an MFT supervisor and educator, I am frequently meeting therapists in their early training who say something along the lines of "I don't really agree with same-sex relationships, but I know I will be open to all clients." Some may say this because they have seen in the AAMFT ethical discussions that there is an expectation of queer affirmative care and maybe are hearing similar messages from courses, colleagues, and supervisors. However, they have not done the work—the self-reflection work that would allow them to be genuinely embracing of all queer people. I challenge clinicians with this perspective to think about what they are saying and to dive deep into the impacts of these thoughts. Do they really feel like they can side-swipe the work of acceptance, and the queer client in their office will believe they are supportive? Maybe in some cases this is true, but, having lived as a queer person for over 50 years, I can say that the undercurrent emotion, judgment, and unacceptance of a person in front of me can often be felt. If a therapist is saying "I welcome your lesbian identity" but is feeling "hm, this is uncomfortable or I don't understand this," it may cross into a disruptive discomfort. On a larger scale, what if a client has been working with a therapist for a year and has been vulnerable about their identity as a transman, and the therapist expresses they have an affirmative approach. After a year in, the client comes across a picture on social media of the therapist with their arm around a notable anti-trans activist. The impact on that client could be devastating—trust, safety, sense of self, could all be ruptured. I think that if we have not done the self-work, it ***will*** impact our clients, subliminally or otherwise. I will add to this that I do not feel we have to be in a space where we know all the answers or even understand all of our clients' perspectives or contexts; it is about an openness, a commitment, and an honesty with yourself as the clinician to better understand those parts of self.

How does one do this? It is a constant, intentional focus on self and understanding one's own context. In all my years of being part of queer communities, I am shocked when an occasional heteronormative idea pops in my head. I am committed, heck, I am queer, but I am also part of my context. Being as aware of these messages as I can be when they flow into my headspace is critical for my work with clients and queer communities. For me, this can include a conversation with a supervisor or colleague (if the thought came during a clinical experience). It can include journaling or just sitting with my thoughts. For those of you who identify as allosexual and are hearing a lot about asexual perspectives for the first time in this book, it might take some time to de-center these ingrained expectations of relationships.

B. ***Inclusion of Asexuality Information and Resources***

Asexual affirmative therapy includes an awareness of what is out there in the community to support asexuals, are there asexual social groups or support groups (An & Kim, 2024)? Some larger cities have asexual social groups or asexual support groups. There are tons of virtual groups on various social media platforms. There is an increasing number of books and resources (in fact, you might be reading a good book at this moment that would be a nice addition to your office décor).

Another way to think about information and resources is to think about how you can contribute to your profession's awareness of asexuality. Some ways to educate larger professional helping communities on asexuality include: building in community education (e.g., sexuality education, health centers), presenting education in therapeutic settings to individuals, couples, and families on asexuality, and making sure resources are available within queer communities that also encompass asexual experiences. Practitioners can speak out against language or messages that view sex and attraction in one way (Schneckenburger et al., 2024) or speak up at the conference when a colleague discusses relationships in biased ways. You can remind colleagues and patients of the varying ways that sexual attraction presents itself and the unlimited ways that people experience intimacy, connection, and physical needs. And, make sure schools, clinical settings, medical settings, and training programs have solid information on asexuality. If you are an educator, consider how to integrate more information about asexuality into your course curriculum and clinical programs.

C. ***Developing Asexual Cultural Competency***

Queer affirmative care includes cultural competency and building on one's knowledge of queer experiences, queer identities, and social challenges that queer individuals face (McGeorge et al., 2015; Rock et al., 2010). Keep in mind, my own view of cultural competency differs from historical ways this term has been used. I think of cultural competency as more like developing some understanding of a uniqueness or difference. It is a springboard of understanding, a place to have some foundation of where a person is coming from without the expectation or bias that all people fit under some category. Competency can start with training programs. Often asexual identities and experiences are left out of training programs and research (Hartwell et al., 2017). One participant, E, is a therapist and an asexual, and described, "there is no training I ever went to…I even went to an LGBTQ affirmative program…there was no mention of ace (asexuality)." This is also my experience, I have a doctorate in MFT, I have attended countless trainings, conferences, and continuing education programs (many focused on queer populations) and I find asexuality is not discussed, it isn't even mentioned. Developing cultural competency with asexual populations might include independent research and education or immersing oneself in communities that embrace asexual experiences. Competency includes an awareness of the stigmas and social pressure that asexual individuals might face (An & Kim, 2024; Boot-Haury, 2023; Flanagan & Peters, 2020).

Claire, an asexual participant, discussed her therapist's lack of cultural competency related to asexuality. She shared that her therapist, "would have wanted to kind of talk me out of it (asexuality), except that it said in a book not to do so," she continued, "there was really no chance I was going to get any real help from her based on her level of familiarity." Claire was immediately distrustful of this therapist because of their lack of knowledge. Amy shared,

> A lot of therapists could do good by reminding people that other types of relationships exist, platonic friendships, or romantic relationships without sex, or sexual relationships without romance—that those all exist and can all be fulfilling in different ways.

Creating education around all kinds of relationships can support and validate asexual clients.

With a lack of cultural competency, there can be a microaggressive undercurrent in the therapy room. Emmaline, an asexual participant, shared their experience:

> The biggest thing I have heard as a major issue we feel as an (asexual) community is not being recognized as being real and also the fact that a lot of people assume that if you are ace, you must have had some kind of trauma in your past, I get that is part of some people's

> history, but that is a specific sub-set of aces. The biggest complaint I hear is people being told they need to seek out therapy for an underlying trauma that they are suppressing…it just feels very negative to how you feel and you question yourself…it is just not about making assumptions about us (asexuals) and our motives or our past, it is about being open to listening and being receptive to our stories (Glass, 2022, p. 355).

Cultural competence with asexual patients can include recognizing what asexuality is not (An & Kim, 2024; Flanagan & Peters, 2020). One participant, Blair, shared that therapists should not "assume" that lack of desire is "a medical condition" or "trauma." Joni shared that there is judgment and questioning if people are asexual "because they have experienced trauma or were abused," and continued, "that is not part of my life and that did not happen to me."

Asexuals report hearing others' beliefs that trauma influences asexuality, a notion that is echoed in research on asexuality (Bogaert, 2015; MacNeela & Murphy, 2015; Mitchell & Hunnicutt, 2019). Blair continued "you spend your whole life either being told outright that this way (e.g., allosexual) is the right way and anything that isn't that means there is something wrong with you." For practitioners, recognizing the legitimacy of asexuality as a sexual orientation is one major step in cultural competency. One participant, Conner, summed this up nicely: "being ace (asexual) and demi(sexual) isn't being broken, it is just relat(ing) to the world in a different way." Asexuality is a healthy sexual orientation and should be accepted as such (Foster & Scherrer, 2014).

D. ***Awareness and Use of Language***

Language is a critical element to the identity process for asexuals (Mandigo & Kavar, 2022; MacNeela & Murphy, 2015; Mollet, 2021; Robbins et al., 2016). Most asexual individuals report not encountering language that represents them until adulthood. Participants I spoke with identified a feeling of relief once they were introduced to language that represented their experiences. For helping professionals, presenting language (e.g., asexual, demisexual, graysexual) for patients to consider could be helpful as they process their identities. This suggestion is collaborative and should be presented that way. It is not saying "oh, I think you are asexual," rather, it is saying, "have you ever heard of the term asexuality?" "I am curious if you ever thought that might fit for you?" and/or "why don't we take a look at it together on the internet and see if anything resonates with you?"

Traditional queer affirmative care creates non-judgmental spaces for dialog around sexual orientation and gender identity (McGeorge et al., 2015; Pepping et al., 2018). Learning to create space that embraces asexual sexual orientations is essential to creating a safe space for asexual individuals. Clinicians can present language and education that provides space to consider what individual desires look like, how attraction is formed, or how a person may view themselves within the context of relationships. This space can open conversation and reflection for patients to better understand themselves.

Language should always embrace the multitude of ways that people experience attraction, romance, and sexual experiences. It is critical to not present language that might infer that a person who is not interested in romance, sexual experiences, or intimate partnerships is *broken* or that there might be something wrong. Asexual individuals are often pathologized by health care providers or mental health professionals (Flanagan & Peters, 2020; Foster & Scherrer, 2014). Providing language that embraces the sexual orientation and the experiences of asexual individuals as normal provides an affirming environment (Flanagan & Peters, 2020).

Utilizing asexual patients' language affirms their identities. For participants, microlabels and other queer terminology were common. Queer affirmative care highlights the importance of utilizing patient language in working with queer populations (Bhatt et al., 2022). Constructs around the experiences of asexual individuals are frequently invisible; therefore, using language for how asexual persons describe themselves and learning more about asexual constructs can create an open and inviting clinical setting. In addition, the split attraction model is a great language tool for exploring attraction and desire.

With language comes social pressures and social stigmas that are impactful to many asexuals. Part of cultural competency is recognizing the stigmas that can exist in some asexuals' worlds, and deconstructing these stigmas can be freeing. A couple asexual participants I spoke with had therapists or physicians mention the terminology of asexuality and this really opened a door for understanding. One participant, William, shared that he learned the term "demisexual" from his therapist. After learning the term, he did his own research and said "I never even knew it (demisexuality) was a thing…once you get the word out there…I am now more comfortable with who I am." In thinking about the identity formation process that many asexual participant experiences, the awareness of language is a critical component to feeling whole, complete, and connected. For this participant above, just the mention of a possible term allowed him to dive into researching demisexuality and embracing that label for himself. Emmaline, an asexual participant stated, "I would love if the concept of asexual was mentioned early on during like high school sex ed.…as a valid possibility." Being able to resonate with the language out there is important to asexuals thar I have spoken with.

E. ***Relationships: Biases, Expectations, and De-construction***

Dating and relationships can look different for every single person, despite a plethora of social scripts around heteronormative and monogamous relationships that identify social expectations of healthy vs. unhealthy relationships. Consider a more common relationship form— monogamous, sexual, married, heterosexual— these relationships do not look one way. In addition, there are so many types of relationships, e.g., non-monogamous relationships, kink relationships, nonsexual relationships, short-term relationships, the list is endless. If you intersect queer identities into relationships, that can add another piece to consider. Then, if you become more precise and intersect asexual identities and relationships—that can also look millions of different ways. The part of this recognition in terms of asexuality is—are there things about relationships that you would identify as unhealthy or healthy? What are those things? What is it that leads you to understand relationships in this way? How can you break down some of these contextual elements that could close the door on the many different ways you can support people in all kinds of different relationships? If you have a vision that there is only one way to relationship—and you find yourself conceptualizing treatment plans or clinical interventions to help clients reach this projected *ideal*—you should re-think the pieces of these assumptions.

Participants highlight the perspective that there is no one way to experience connections with people. People vary in their experiences of attraction and their need for intimacy and intimate companionship, which is an important distinction to make when working with any relationship (asexual or otherwise). With asexual spectrum individuals who do desire intimate partnerships, it is important to recognize that this might not look any specific way. Relationship therapies should integrate individual partner's needs and desires and consider them outside of external societal expectations (Barros & Doyle, 2025). Asexual participants were, at times, creative in how they and their partner(s) met intimacy needs (e.g., polyamorous identities were mentioned by a few participants as one way of meeting various intimacy and connection needs). However, building a sense of trust and safety around discussions of intimacy, boundaries around intimacy for all partners, and expectations of intimacy is key to helping asexual individuals and partners best understand how to work together.

Couple therapists and couple researchers historically (and even in present day) have stressed the importance of sexual compromise and sexual intimacy as critical for a fulfilling relationship (Day et al., 2015; Fraenkel, 2019). One participant, Anita, shared that this is the dominant perspective, stating, "too many people think that they (people who may not want sex) should just power through it and that is normal." As a therapist myself, it is fairly common to hear my own supervisees or colleagues discussing a case of sexual incompatibility and hear language that suggests that one person do something sexually that is not comfortable to them. Some current research has begun to challenge the notion or expectation that there is one particular way to create intimacy and highlights normalizing differences in desire in clinical settings (e.g., Fahs et al., 2019).

There is often a focus, in clinical settings, on conversations of dating and long-term relationships and less focus on asking clients what they desire for their future connections to people overall. Recognizing and supporting people who are not interested in relationships and connecting to the things that are important to them is important to providing asexual affirmative care. Helping people overall, but certainly asexuals, who are not interested in relationships, locate things to do that are not "around the meat market mentality" (as one demisexual person summed up their feelings that everything is about dating and sex) can be such a welcoming space for a person who is constantly facing social expectations that they should be finding a relationship. Asexuals experience amatonormative and allonormative messages in daily life, just by flipping through social media, turning on a show, hanging out with family or friends, etc. This constant reminder that relationships must look a certain way can be exhausting. Even for asexuals in relationships, helping them consider other ways of connecting to people overall—hobbies or activities that are not as focused on romantic or sexual connection could be a welcoming addition to affirming care.

Summary of the Asexual Affirmative Care Model

The asexual affirmative care model presents the importance of self-reflection, representation, affirming care, and inclusion in similar ways that queer affirmative care approaches clients (Giammattei & Green, 2012; McGeorge et al., 2015; McKinney et al., 2020; Rock et al., 2010), with the added awareness of asexual experiences and language around asexuality. Traditional queer affirmative models highlight clinical awareness of self and cultural competencies around sexual and gender minorities. The asexual affirmative care model builds on these perspectives while integrating language that can be beneficial to asexual identity process experiences and challenging constructed notions of relationships and intimacy that often factor into counseling and health care environments.

A couple participants shared reflections that nicely summarize part of what asexual affirmative care is. Alex shared that practitioners should,

> Take their (asexual clients') word for it, I remember when I first realized I am ace, I had so many people tell me, 'well, that can't be right.' Just the hurricane of excuses, 'you're too young,' 'how do you know if you aren't interested in sex if you've never had sex,' 'are you sure it isn't a hormone imbalance?'... when I heard the word asexual and it sounded right, it was another year or so before I fully embraced it. Even now, people are saying 'are you sure?' it is disheartening...no one says that about being straight, but I hear that all the time about being ace (asexual) or aro (aromantic). It is just like, trust them...trust that they have done this questioning and the soul searching and it is like what they identify with feels right...just believe what they are and treat their identity with respect.

Amy shared a similar sentiment,

> A lot of therapists could do good by reminding people that other types of relationships, platonic friendships, or romantic relationships without sex or sexual relationships without romance, like all those can exist and those can all be fulfilling in different ways.

Asexual affirmative care embraces asexual experiences and decenters amatonormative expectations and biases.

Queer affirmative care provides a foundation for working with various developmental stages that sexual and gender minorities may experience (McKinney et al., 2020); however, elements of asexuality have not been addressed as clearly in affirmative care research and training. Participants note ways that language has been useful to their own journeys. The asexual affirmative care model indicates ways that clinical or health care professionals can positively contribute to asexual identity formation processes through language and awareness. The model is a supplement to queer affirmative care models in a way that further embraces asexual experiences and identities.

Clinical Commitment

Providing queer affirmative care (inclusive of asexual affirmative care) requires a commitment to life-long reflection and learning. Queer affirmative care begins with knowledge and self-reflection. Programs designed to educate future clinicians and medical professionals should be setting the stage for cultural competency and cultural humility that embraces asexuals (Singh et al., 2025). Education can enhance awareness and understanding of the experiences of asexuals and promote internal processing around personal perspectives and biases. I argue that affirmative care starts the minute an individual begins their graduate program in any helping field and continues on throughout their entire life and professional career (Thacker Darrow et al., 2025). It takes a commitment. Education programs have a responsibility to set the climate for this life-long journey.

Commitment may mean personal activities that allow practitioners to get a better understanding of something by absorbing themselves into an environment. These activities could include attending conferences or seminars with queer/asexual focus, going to pride festivals, locating book clubs with queer topics, attending queer art exhibits or film series, and watching queer-directed/written media content. It is essentially a commitment to develop more comfort, more understanding, and challenge one's own biases or knowledge.

Asexuals as Practitioners

I want to take just a moment for a side journey in talking about asexual affirmative care. I have presented information on how asexuality is different than the norm and some of the nuances of asexuality. What if you are asexual and you are a practitioner working with allosexuals? I feel like this is a notable path to mention. As a demisexual person, sometimes, when I am working with allosexual clients or even writing a book like this, I realize that allosexual experiences, to me, can be confusing. Even though allonormative experiences are very much part of the dominant narrative and everywhere around me (unlike asexual experiences), I find myself pausing and can almost feel my brain trying to understand where allosexuals are coming from to some degree. This is by far not from a place a judgment, most asexuals (including myself) share how sex-positive and relationship positive they are and how supportive they are of those around them who experience attraction, romantic desire, and/or sexual desire. At the same time, I might hear a client tell me of a one night stand where they had the best sexual experience of their lives and yet they hardly remember the person's name. They might go into detail about seeing a person across the room and being immediately aroused. As a demisexual, I can't imagine that feeling. Certainly, I'd be able to have a sexual experience with a stranger, but the feelings around that experience (e.g., the instant arousal and the best sex ever) would not happen for me. Several times during the writing this book, I would pause, squint my eyes, dig around in my brain, and realize I did not know the answer to some ways that allosexuals experience the world. I have found myself asking allosexual friends some of the most bizarre questions (with their permission of course), like, "do you actually get physically aroused sometimes just by looking at a stranger?" or "If you had the time and everything was in order, would you really want to have sex every day?" or "do you really think about sex 19 times a day?" (this is likely some contrived social media thing I heard once). And, as you would expect, all allosexuals I speak with answer these questions differently; there is incredible variability under the allosexual umbrella too.

Obviously, we do not have all the experiences, desires, etc. of our clients, and we can still provide connected and informed care, but there is something to at least pausing to consider how I, as a demisexual, may miss something or may have to take a pause to better understand a dynamic that I do not feel myself. It is possible for asexual practitioners to have blind spots at times with allosexual clients. Considering over 90% of the clients I have worked with (maybe more) have been allosexual, I am guessing I approach this with non-judgment, compassion, and not-knowing that I would with any other difference, and those clients certainly seem to feel validated and heard. But, there is always room to learn and grow.

There were a couple asexual participants that I spoke with who were in helping fields. This theme of "what it is like to work with allosexuals" was not one that evolved from the data, this divergence is merely an acknowledgment, a recognition, that we, as asexual clinicians, do have to open the door to something that is different from our own experience, often frequently in our clinical work. One asexual participant that I spoke with, Riley, shared they were training to be a therapist. They talked about their own internal biases and recognized that. They indicated, "I assume that every person I meet is allosexual and being able to identify that and separate that in my own consciousness." They also shared the importance of "allowing for any possibility with each person." For example, not making assumptions about their sexual orientation or gender identity, but letting those parts of who they are evolve into the sessions as they do. I appreciated Riley's reflections on how we as asexuals still have biases and therapist self-reflection is for everyone, even asexuals.

Along with this, as an asexual practitioner, clearing the way to allow for client's needs and desires to be fully heard by you, even if they don't fit your experience, may require a few head scratching moments. I know I have had a couple clients in my years who expressed shifts in libido or lack of desire for a partner, and I have had to get out of my head about my own identity and really hear out what this impact is like for them. Rather than jumping to "oh, have you ever heard of asexuality?!" I have had to pause and ask more questions.

I am going to guess that many people reading this book are actually on the asexual spectrum or identify somewhere else under the queer umbrella. If you are also a practitioner of sorts, likely you have done a lot of work around social messages and expectations. If you read this book and you are allosexual, you may have found yourself saying a few times "um, they are saying allosexuals do X, that is not me at all." Keep in mind, so much of what I presented in this book about allosexuality represents asexual participant perspectives of allosexual experiences (as well as my own). All this to say, we all come from a context and an understanding of the world. At the same time, there is no one way of representing any sexual orientation or gender identity.

References

Amos, N., Grant, R., Lin, A., Hill, A., Pang, K. C., Skinner, S. R., Cook, T., Carman, M., & Bourne, A. (2025). Mental health and wellbeing outcomes among trans young people in Australia who are supported to affirm their gender. *Society for Adolescent Health and Medicine, 77*, 51–58. https://doi.org/10.1016/j.jadohealth.2025.03.011

An, H., & Kim, E. (2024). Unveiling the stressful experiences faced by asexual individuals in South Korea: A consensual qualitative study. *Psychology & Sexuality*, 1–16. https://doi.org/10.1080/19419899.2024.2408018

Barros, S. P., & Doyle, E. M. (2025). Trans-cending the mononormativity of relationship therapy: An intersectional framework for increasing competency. *Journal of Marital & Family Therapy, 51*(3), 1–10. https://doi.org/10.1111/jmft.70025

Bhatt, N., Cannella, J., & Gentile, J. P. (2022). Gender-affirming care for transgender patients. *Innovations in Clinical Neuroscience, 19*(4–6), 23–32. PMID: 35958971.

Bogaert, A. F. (2015). Asexuality: What is it and why it matters. *Journal of Sex Research, 52*(4), 362–379. https://doi.org/10.1080/00224499.2015.1015713

Boot-Haury, J. W. (2023). Development of the asexual stigma inventory. *Journal of LGBTQ Issues in Counseling, 17*(3), 187–201. https://doi.org/10.1080/26924951.2023.2202354

Bowleg, L., Malekzadeh, A. N., AuBuchon, K. E., Ghabrial, M. A., & Bauer, G. R. (2023). Rare exemplars and missed opportunities: Intersectionality within current sexual and gender diversity research and scholarship in psychology. *Current Opinion in Psychology, 49*, 1–6. https://doi.org/10.1016/j.copsyc.2022.101511

Brunning, L., & McKeever, N. (2021). Asexuality. *Journal of Applied Philosophy, 38*(3), 497–517. https://doi.org/10.1111/japp.12472

Budge, S. L., Abreu, R. L., Flinn, R. E., Donahue, K. L., Estevez, R., Olezeski, C. L., Bernacki, J. M., Barr, S., Bettergarcia, J., Sprott, R. A., & Allen, B. J. (2024). Gender affirming care is evidence based for transgender and gender-diverse youth. *Journal of Adolescent Health, 75*(6), 851–853. https://doi.org/10.1016/j.jadohealth.2024.09.009

Burger, J., & Pachankis, J. E. (2024). State of the science: LGBTQ-affirmative psychotherapy. *Behavior Therapy, 55*(6), 1318–1334. https://doi.org/10.1016/j.beth.2024.02.011

Carlson, T. S., & McGeorge, C. R. (2012). LGB-affirmative training strategies for couple and family therapist faculty: Preparing heterosexual students to work with LGB clients. In J. J. Bigner & J. L. Wetchler (Eds.), *Handbook of LGBT-affirmative couple and family therapy* (pp. 395–408). Routledge.

Day, L. C., Muise, A., Joel, S., & Impett, E. A. (2015). To do it or not to do it? How communally motivated people navigate sexual interdependence dilemmas. *Personality & Social Psychology Bulletin, 41*(6), 791–804. https://doi.org/10.1177/014616721559012

Fahs, B., Swank, E., & Shambe, A. (2019). "I just go with it": Negotiating sexual desire discrepancies for women in partnered relationships. *Sex Roles, 83*, 226–239. https://doi.org/10.1007/s11199-019-01098-w

Flanagan, S. K., & Peters, H. J. (2020). Asexual-identified adults: Interactions with healthcare practitioners. *Archives of Sexual Behavior, 49*(5), 1631–1643. https://doi.org/10.1007/s10508-020-01670-6

Foster, A. B., & Scherrer, K. S. (2014). Asexual-identified clients in clinical settings: Implications for competent practice. *Psychology of Sexual Orientation and Gender Diversity, 1*(4), 422–430. https://doi.org/10.1037/sgd0000058

Fraenkel, P. (2019). Love in action: An integrative approach to last chance couple therapy. *Family Process, 58*(3), 569–594. https://doi.org/10.1111/famp.12474

Freeman-Coppadge, D. J., & Langroudi, K. F. (2021). Beyond LGBTQ-affirmative therapy: Fostering growth and healing through intersectionality. In K. L. Nadal & M. R. Scharrón-del Río (Eds.), *Queer psychology*. Springer. https://doi.org/10.1007/978-3-030-74146-4_9

Giammattei, S. V., & Green, R. (2012). LGBTQ couple and family therapy: History and future directions. In J. J. Bigner & J. L. Wetchler (Eds.), *Handbook of affirmative LGBT-affirmative couple and family therapy* (pp. 1–24). Routledge.

Glass, V. Q. (2022). Queering relationships: Exploring phenomena of asexual identified persons in relationships. *Contemporary Family Therapy: An International Journal, 44*, 344–359. https://doi.org/10.1007/s10591-022-09650-9

Hartwell, E. E., Serovich, J. M., Reed, S. J., Boisvert, D., & Falbo, T. (2017). A systemic review of gay, lesbian, and bisexual research samples in couple and family therapy journals. *Journal of Marital and Family Therapy, 43*(3), 482–501. https://doi.org/10.1111/jmft.12220

Harvey, R., Murphy, M. J., & Laszloffy, T. A. (2022). Evolution of LGBTQ-affirmative couple and family therapy. In R. Harvey, M. J. Murphy, J. J. Bigner, & J. L. Wetchler (Eds.), *Handbook of LGBTQ-affirmative couple and family therapy* (pp. 9–24). Routledge.

Jones, C., Hayter, M., & Jomeen, J. (2017). Understanding asexual identity as a means to facilitate culturally competent care: A systematic literature review. *Journal of Clinical Nursing, 26*(23–24), 3811–3831. https://doi.org/10.1111/jocn.13862

Kahn, S., Alessi, E. J., Kim, H., Woolner, L., & Olivieri, C. J. (2018). Facilitating mental health support for LGBT forced migrants: A qualitative inquiry. *Journal of Counseling & Development, 96*, 316–326. https://doi.org/10.1002/jcad.12205

Lu, R., & Chui, H. (2025). Counseling aces: Experiences of asexual clients in China. *Archives of Sexual Behavior: The Official Publication of the International Academy of Sex Research*, 1–19. https://doi.org/10.1007/s10508-025-03148-9

MacNeela, P., & Murphy, A. (2015). Freedom, invisibility, and community: A qualitative study of self-identification with asexuality. *Archives of Sexual Behavior, 44*, 799–812. https://doi.org/10.1007/s10508-014-0458-0

Mandigo, D. M., & Kavar, L. (2022). The experience of male asexuality: A phenomenological inquiry. *The Qualitative Report, 27*(2), 488–508. https://doi.org/10.46743/2160-3715/2022.5213

McGeorge, C. R., Carlson, T. S., & Toomey, R. B. (2015). Assessing lesbian, gay, and bisexual affirmative training in couple and family therapy: Establishing the validity of the faculty version of the affirmative training inventory. *Journal of Marital & Family Therapy, 41*(1), 57–71. https://doi.org/10.1111/jmft.12054

McKinney, R., Desposito, M., & Yoon, E. (2020). Promoting identity wellness in LGBTGEQIAP+ adolescents through affirmative therapy. *Journal of LGBT Issues in Counseling, 14*(3), 176–190. https://doi.org/10.1080/15538605.2020.1790464

Mitchell, H., & Hunnicutt, G. (2019). Challenging accepted scripts of sexual "normality": Asexual narratives of non-normative identity and experience. *Sexuality & Culture, 23*, 507–524. https://doi.org/10.1007/s12119-018-9567-6

Mollet, A. L. (2021). 'It's easier just to say I'm queer: Asexual college students' strategic identity management. *Journal of Diversity in Higher Education, 16*(1), 13–25. https://doi.org/10.1037/dhe0000210

Mondave, M., Saleska, J., Wang, J. J., Bluma, E., Jackson, D., Tapia, Y., Yashar, L., Zima, B. T., & Choi, K. R. (2025). "Feeling like you matter:" LGBTQ + young adult perspectives on affirmative mental healthcare. *The Journal of Behavioral Health Services & Research: Official Publication of the National Council for Behavioral Health, 52*(1), 155–167. https://doi.org/10.1007/s11414-024-09919-x

Pavanello Decaro, S., Prunas, A., Servi, B., Albanesi, C., & Lorusso, M. M. (2025). Experiences of Italian asexual and aromantic individuals in healthcare settings: From explicitly aggressive to affirming interactions. *Journal of LGBTQ Issues in Counseling, 19*(1), 97–119. https://doi.org/10.1080/26924951.2024.2441293

Pepping, C. A., Lyons, A., & Morris, E. M. J. (2018). Affirmative LGBT psychotherapy: Outcomes of a therapist training protocol. *Psychotherapy, 55*(1), 52–62. https://doi.org/10.1037/pst0000149

Robbins, N. K., Low, K. G., & Query, A. N. (2016). A qualitative exploration of the "coming out" process for asexual individuals. *Archives of Sexual Behavior, 45*(3), 751–760. https://doi.org/10.1007/s10508-015-0561-x
Rock, M., Carlson, T. S., & McGeorge, C. R. (2010). Does affirmative training matter? Assessing CFT students' beliefs about sexual orientation and their level of affirmative training. *Journal of Marital and Family Therapy, 36*(2), 171–184. https://doi.org/10.1111/j.1752-0606.2009.00172.x
Russell, J. (2023). The sex lives of asexuals. In S. Neves & D. Davies (Eds.), *Erotically queer: A pink therapy guide for practitioners* (pp. 59–74). Routledge. https://doi.org/10.4324/9781003260608-5
Schneckenburger, S. A., Tam, M. W. Y., & Ross, L. E. (2024). Asexual competent practices in healthcare: A narrative review. *Journal of Gay & Lesbian Mental Health, 28*(3), 314–334. https://doi.org/10.1080/19359705.2023.2214528
Singh, R. S., Zamarin, K., Eckstrand, K. L., Skyler, M., Sturm, R., & Wilging, C. (2025). Recommendations for promoting affirming healthcare for gender and sexual minorities with intersecting marginalized identities. *BMC Health Services Research, 25*(585), 1–12. https://doi.org/10.1186/s12913-025-12708-7
Thacker Darrow, N. E., Strunk, K. K., & Racelis, T. L. (2025). LGBTQ+ affirmative care training in counselor education: A community-based inquiry. *Counselor Education and Supervision, 64*(3), 341–353. https://doi.org/10.1002/ceas.12346

Chapter 7
Conclusions and Future Directions

Located within the stories and descriptive journeys of asexuals that I have been honored to spend time with is this deep sense of ownership, pride, and re-authorization of self that I did not necessarily expect to find. Asexual participants that I have interviewed have been overjoyed and outwardly thankful toward my creation of an inclusive resource. Their voices and deep introspections have taught me about myself and about life in a vulnerable and humbling way. Their stories impact us all and can change the way we re-center social expectations of relationships.

If we start to consider the various ways people experience connection and validate these ways as equally important and valid, we open the door to so many possibilities. One conclusion I have come to in the midst of my own research is that there is a rich, inner feeling that can exist when a human is connecting to another human. Each of these connections is valuable and holds space. Consider moments in your life where a person has added so much to your life, yet their presence was minimal—like the woman walking by you at the park who said something that warmed you, or the customer at work who comes in frequently and you have developed a bond that lights you up, or a flirtatious encounter, or a life-long deep friendship, or a romantic partner, or a one night powerful sexual experience with someone you never saw before or after… What if we open up our minds to experience the magnitude of these connections to their fullest? What if we stop and realize that these sometimes brief encounters may affect our growth and fulfillment and could be perceived as just as fulfilling as the couple who represents a traditional romantic and sexual expectation? What if we honored all of our human connections differently than we typically do or what if others celebrated those connections for how important they were to us?

Many asexuals and their partners I spoke with valued their movement from considering relationships in traditional ways. Once they were able to deconstruct external messages of relationship expectations—they marveled at the ways they connected. They found a deep sense of comfort, safety, and connection to partners.

V. Q. Glass, *Asexuality, Relationships, and Identity Formation*,
https://doi.org/10.1007/978-3-032-22857-4_7

An analogy comes to mind—as a child, growing up in Charlotte, North Carolina, we had an unusual hurricane, *Hurricane Hugo*. It hit the Charlotte area, which is inland enough that it is generally safe from hurricanes. Hugo left Charlotte devastated in many ways. On top of the city-wide destruction, we were without power in most areas for three or more weeks. This led to a complete paradigm shift in the way we were used to doing things. What was once watching TV in our own living rooms, cooking dinner in our own kitchens, and retiring to bedrooms for music or phone calls completely shifted. For those three weeks, it turned into neighbors crowding around a small battery-powered black and white TV to watch the big game together, or groups of people coming together to grill out food and enjoy each other's company. We went for walks, visited with people, people helped others clean out debris or manage fallen trees, people shared stories, we played board games. It was refreshing, as a child, to learn that people connect and care in those expressly human ways that were not as common in the late 1980s. Asexuality and the journeys of asexuals, if given space and attention, can "flip off" electricity in some ways, allowing new experiences and understandings to emerge to fill those spaces. If we listen, if we allow ourselves to reframe a social structure that looks one way, think of all the new, refreshing ways we can connect with one another and how valuable that could be.

Because a major focus of my research has been asexuals in relationships, I find the ways that asexuals and their partners experience the world and adapt to one another to be especially unique. I think all of us (in particular relationship therapists) can learn a lot from these research participants. One thing I have learned is that in order to best embrace couples that I work with in therapy, I have to tap into ALL that makes them a couple, that connects them. When I start working with a couple, I often ask them to describe their relationship. I ask them to envision a pie chart of their relationship and tell me what makes up the parts of the pie chart. They might say something like "30% building a family together, 20% sharing household chores, 40% having a person to support them, 10% doing activities together." Sometimes, they may say something like "10% arguing" or "10% annoying each other" if they have a good sense of humor or they are referring to what brought them to therapy. *BUT, guess what?* Even with allosexual/allosexual couples, sex and romance are infrequently part of these pie charts! If they are in there, they are minimally represented (e.g., "10% affection"). It isn't that couples do not include sex and sexual intimacy as part of their relationship, or might even tell me that it is a significant part, but it is that they may not be ranking them in there when it comes down to their defining of the relationship. Counteract those possible real-people experiences with the most recent dating reality shows, the drama series on Netflix, or the old sitcom—which nearly always place sex in a very high, very critical space in a relationship.

A recent study that I have come across really opened my eyes around this topic. Heim and Heim (2023) explored the perceptions of couples who have experienced a longevity in their relationship. In this study, 180 couples (maybe allosexual, but this was not defined in this study) who have been together over 40 years were surveyed and asked about what helped their longevity. My absolute favorite thing about this research was that there were 17 notable response categories (themes) and none of these 17 involved sex or even physical affection. The 17 categories were: commitment, altruism, shared values, good communication, compromise, love, never give up, patience, teamwork, respect, family focus, common interests, separate time, friendship, opposite personalities, modeling, and humor (p. 789). Long-term couples, in this research study, are defining critical reasons for their longevity, and the reasons are more about connection, friendship, and commitment. Maybe, just maybe, social messages that highlight this human need for amatonormativity, inclusive of intensive romance and sexual conquests, are not what the focus or social expectation should be on at all. What if we shifted our thinking and our relationship scripts to consider something like "compromise" or "patience" or "humor" as just as, if not more, important than sex or romance? I think this shift in thinking could open an unlimited amount of ways that we as humans and practitioners could embrace all kinds of human connection. Rather than the relationship therapist asking, "how is your sex life?" and placing a large emphasis on this specific question, maybe they could feel out other areas of relationships and ask, "what do you laugh about together?" or "when do you notice your partner being patient with you?"

I relate this shifting of narratives around relationships to some of the ways that social scientists and helping fields have presented feminist shifts and queer shifts in language. This whole book has been about considering how to *center* asexuality as a marginalized identity. Allen, a foundational researcher and theorist in family sciences, has spent decades bridging critical feminism and families (Allen, 2000, 2023). She challenges mainstream expectations of *doing family* that are oppressive and de-centers these expectations in ways that allow for non-oppressive evolutions of families and relationships (Allen, 2000, 2023). Allen (2023) stated:

> Feminist theorizing is embedded in a critical and contentious practice that reflects a shared politics of engagement to decenter patriarchy, capitalism, colonization, racism, white supremacy, heteronormativity, and other systems of oppression and inequality on behalf of social change (p. 900).

From a relationship perspective, de-centering socially constructed norms is especially important for asexual journeys. Being that family is frequently a key variable in the eye of legitimacy in Western (and global) perspectives, valuing complex experiences of relationships allows space for asexual identities to flourish.

Queer theory has also expanded social constructions around family and identity (Bertone & Pallotta-Chiarolli, 2015). Queer theory involves a purposeful and active centering of queerness (Ahmed, 2006; Bertone & Pallotta-Chiarolli, 2015; Moussawi & Vidal-Ortiz, 2020). By presenting queerness as centered, our clinical work, our research, and our personal lives embrace identities and experiences that are often devalued, invisible, or seen as *other*. Birdsong (2020) states:

> As activist Shon Faye (as cited in Birdsong, 2020) puts it queer is about removing labels and replacing them with a question. It is a side eye and a challenge back to mainstream society and politics. It says 'I don't know the answer but why are you asking the question?' Queering relationships is rejecting the restraints of convention, but is also liberatory truth-finding. It allows us to look at a relationship (and so many other things) stripped of preconceptions and ask, what is this really? What are the components? What is happening inside of it? (Birdsong, 2020)

I particularly am drawn to the terminology of "liberating" in this quote. Feminist shifts and queer theory have allowed more space, freedom, and liberation where people once felt confined by one narrative (Ang, 2024). Asexuals in my own personal community and many that I have spoken with in part of my research frequently bring up the concept of "feeling liberated" through language. This understanding of self and the breaking down of expectations that did not fit for them—allows space for them to thrive and grow in their own way. Even more startling are the ways that allosexual partners of asexuals can flourish in this new space, in this new relationship narrative. Partners began to have paradigm shifts in what relationships were expected to look like and found themselves appreciating all the liberating new ways that they could feel connected to another human.

What Happens Now?

By engaging with the asexual voices in this book and considering your own social scripts around relationships, the climate of the expectations present in those around you, and the dominant messages that marginalize asexuals, you are taking a step in this decentering. If these messages are awkward, uncomfortable, or specifically unusual to you—I encourage you to keep working on decentering amatonormative expectations that can feel oppressive to many. The reframing and recentering of relationships and re-narrating relationship directions can be applied to future clinical and training experiences (Few-Demo & Allen, 2020). My own professional identity includes three parts: clinician, researcher, and academic (educator). I am guessing many people reading this fall into one of those categories. To conclude this book, I will break down these professional parts with some parting challenges.

Clinical

If you are a clinician, you have all this new information about asexuality. You have some background on asexual identity processes, asexuals in relationships, some historical elements of asexuality in mental health and medical health fields, and many stories of asexual journeys of resilience, of struggle, and of daily life. This background provides a backdrop for cultural competency in working with asexual clients. The impact of social messages and language leaves this hole for finding one's voice when it may not fit into these expectations. Barros and Doyle (2025) stated, "relationship and family therapy research and resources, however, generally lack flexibility in their application to relationships that aren't captured by dominant discourses of relationship composition" (p. 1). It is through breaking down these dominant discourses that we provide space for all identities. I feel that, overall, our work as practitioners is to walk with people to this *liberation*, to this space where they can express their voices and be authentic. This movement can sometimes be just providing language to asexuality—this can allow for a connection to a community and an identity. Sometimes it is creating a space that breaks down messages around sex, romance, love, human connection, and family forms to open dialog for clients to embrace their own authenticity and their own desires. Sometimes this space could be about supporting partners or other family through education or relationship therapies. Underneath all of this is the importance of the clinicians diving into their own biases and embracing an affirming approach that includes asexual identities.

As practitioners, we all have a perspective. This perspective could be based on our own experience or on the social constructions of the world around us. At times, we are challenged with fighting these messages and recognizing not all people experience or feel the same way allows space to grow and understand new ways of thinking and being. One demisexual participant, Ruby, stated her goals to therapists,

> …do not give in to social expectations, let the couple figure out what works for them. Therapists, even our couple's therapist, have a perspective that is often from the kind of sex fueled society that sex is important to a relationship at all costs…letting therapists learn that these are not acceptable and are actually harmful for many people, not just asexual people. We (Ruby and her partner) were in therapy for a short while and the therapist never said it, but did seem to be subtly pushing me to have sex when it was something I did not want to do.

Consider Ruby and other asexuals and the vulnerability of sitting in a space with a clinician and sharing parts of themselves that may not fit social expectations. This vulnerability is something to embrace and celebrate, not to further repress or judge.

Most helping professions incorporate ethical codes that challenge practitioners to consider power and privilege in their own work. Additionally, clinical work often stresses the importance of cultural humility as foundational to the therapeutic process (Hook et al., 2017). Cultural humility involves so many pieces; it involves an awareness of self, a comfort with difference, a skill in allowing client understanding and identities to emerge, a cultural competence, and a commitment to social justice. My challenge to clinicians is to embrace these expectations and consider what that means for you as a clinician possibly working with asexuals. Some things you might ask yourself:

- Do I have allonormative or amatonormative expectations or biases? What can I do to further grow and challenge these?
- Do I think to myself "any couple void of a satisfying sexual relationship must be unhealthy"? If that thought comes into play at times, what can you do to better allow space for other narratives?
- Am I comfortable in queer spaces, in queer language, in asexual spaces, in asexual language? If you are not sure, what things could you put in place to make yourself more comfortable?
- If a client shares with me, "I have always felt a little different, like never had crushes and am not sure I want to date?" Would I bring up the terminology around asexuality? Would I be comfortable doing this? Explore why or why not? What comes up for me when I think about this dynamic?

- Do I have resources available for asexuals? Check out your local area to see if there are asexual social groups that you can have available for clients. Are there books, articles, podcasts, influencers, etc. about asexuality that might be helpful to you and/or your clients? Also make sure you are aware of the Asexual Visibility & Education Network (AVEN)—asexuality.org. AVEN is a great resource for asexuals and anyone wanting to know more about asexuality.
- How can I create space for all kinds of relationships? For example, does your intake paperwork identify relationships outside of legally recognized persons? Do you ask about chosen family and value all of these?

In general, continue to be open, aware, and affirming. Cultural humility and affirmative care are lifelong commitments.

Research

One of my favorite quotes comes from the book *Queer Phenomenology: Orientations, Objects, Others* (Ahmed, 2006). Ahmed states, "to make things queer is certainly to disturb the order of things…the effects of such a disturbance are uneven, precisely given that the world is already organized around certain forms of living –certain times, spaces, and directions" (p. 161). Queer research can be messy; we are diving into territories that were written through a different, dominant script. I find this messiness to be the reason for research. Research is about building on what is there and adding more! For example, as much as I hate to say it, some of my research would not have been possible without the evolution of the understanding of Freud's perspectives through proving and disproving his assumptions and theories over the years. But, as a queer researcher and a researcher of asexuality, creating theory, practice, and technique through research requires a whole bunch of in the moment paradigm shifts. And, likely, I miss some important ones. Likely, all research misses some important ones. It is a conscious effort to both build off what we know and create new awareness that propels that new research even further.

When it comes to research on asexuality specifically, I think it is important to mention the impacts of research on asexuals (and queer individuals overall). If you are doing research on relationships, consider what inferences you are making and the impact the results could have on those who are asexual. I come across a ton of research, for example, on sex therapy and some of the ways to address challenges in intimacy with couples. Participants in these studies may not be asked about asexuality, or they may not even be aware of asexuality. Given this possibility, if you are doing research or making blanket statements around intimacy, how can you be sure there is not another variable (asexuality) impacting your results? Almost all of the current research that I have read related to relationships, applying theory to relationships, understanding relationships, etc. does not mention asexuality even as a side note. I think this is just a plea for more awareness and inclusivity in relationship research overall.

One aspect I mentioned throughout this book is that the emergence of research on asexuality has a very White/Western voice. I feel that research, in general, should seek out intersectional perspectives (Few-Demo et al., 2014); however, given the limitations in research perspectives on asexuality, I feel intersectionality and asexuality in research is a critical direction because it is lacking. Even with my own commitment to intersectional voices in my research, I have struggled locating intersectional asexual voices. Part of me wants to highlight the evolving nature of language and how maybe asexuality as a term and identity started in White/Western linguistics and culture and perhaps has not found a place in other communities. Or maybe because this term comes from White/Western communities, it is not as embracing of intersectional experiences? This lack of language assumption on my part is merely an educated guess of what I see/do not see in research on intersec tional asexual perspectives. This is not that asexual identities do not exist in all humans, because I feel asexuality is innate and exists everywhere, but that the embracing of language to further define or connect to asexual communities may not have found its way into other cultures and communities or may be defined differently because of differences in relationship scripts. In summary, I think continual research on intersectionality and asexuality is a critical next step.

Academic

It may go without saying that what is taught to emerging clinicians, researchers, and educators highlights what the professions value. Values have certainly shifted over time and what is being taught today, even in fields like gender studies or queer studies looks completely different than it did in the 1990s, during my undergraduate years. Like research, there is value to this constant questioning, re-writing, and re-analyzing of what we bring to others. Education around asexuality is just one more piece in that process.

My mother, who went to an all-women's college in the mid-1960s, shared with me that the social messages for women at the time revolved around the fact that they were going to college for their future husbands. The idea was that they should have "just enough" education to be able to engage in dialog with their future husband's (male) work colleagues. My mom explained that social dictates at the time tended to herd women into either teaching or nursing. Social scripts resisted women in sciences, business-related fields, or analytical fields. She described to me home economics college courses that she took where women in college learned how to cook, clean, take care of babies, and take care of husband's needs. These expectations of women at the time were oppressive, yet education bought into these messages and taught this one way of being and doing family—further reiterating the values expected at the time.

Social construction is an active process. Education is one of the catalysts of this process. Teaching women how to be wives in the 1960s, home economics college courses evolved over time to human development and family studies sciences.

Being that these courses were part of my own teaching background, I can proudly say, instructions on how to please husbands were not part of my curriculum, nor the values of the field. That being said, a focus on forming relationships in one particular way (e.g., romantic/sexual) is still often a major part of these courses. I am not saying these areas should not be in these courses, but a focused representation of queer (inclusive of asexuality) and intersectional elements of family and relationships should also be prevalent parts of all fields of study that involve understanding humans.

By integrating awareness of power and privilege into our understanding of relationships, the entire educational system can be impacted (Few-Demo et al., 2014). Education around family studies, for example, often builds in anti-oppressive language and multiple perspectives on family. As educators, we should be continuously looking internally and challenging social constructions that might be creating environments that leave out or pathologize groups of people. Ask yourself, is what you are teaching inclusive of asexual perspectives? Of queer perspectives? Of intersectionality? If not, what can you do to change your course development, your discussions with students, or your academic focus?

Conclusion

As humans appreciate other humans, the recognition of oppression requires a look at self (Allen, 2000). There is a deep, self-reflection piece where you break down the walls, the narratives, the expectations, the biases, the parts of self that are contributing to this power imbalance. I believe that a shift from the allosexual center of expectations needs to happen, it is assumptive and pathologizing (Busby et al., 2025; Dias Martins et al., 2025). This shift requires a look at the messages that have impacted our views of normality in terms of attraction, romance, and sexual desire.

References

Ahmed, S. (2006). *Queer phenomenology: Orientations, objects, others*. Duke University Press.
Allen, K. R. (2000). A conscious and inclusive family studies. *Journal of Marriage and Family, 62*(1), 4–17. https://www.jstor.org/stable/1566683
Allen, K. R. (2023). Feminist theory, method, and praxis: Toward a critical consciousness for family and close relationship scholars. *Journal of Social & Personal Relationships, 40*(3), 899–936. https://doi.org/10.1177/02654075211065779
Ang, M. W. (2024). Dynamisms of romantic family imaginaries and asexual identity-making. *Journal of Family Studies*, 1–16. https://doi.org/10.1080/13229400.2024.2396440
Asexual Visibility and Education Network. (2022, February 1). https://www.asexuality.org/
Barros, S. P., & Doyle, E. M. (2025). Trans-cending the mononormativity of relationship therapy: An intersectional framework for increasing competency. *Journal of Marital & Family Therapy, 51*(3), 1–10. https://doi.org/10.1111/jmft.70025

Bertone, C., & Pallotta-Chiarolli, M. (2015). Putting families of origin into the queer picture. In C. Bertone & M. Pallotta-Chiarolli (Eds.), *Queerying families of origin* (pp. 1–14). Routledge.

Birdsong, J. (2020, June 20). The queering of friendship: Rethinking platonic relationships guided by LGBTQ models, Salon. https://www.salon.com/2020/06/20/the-queering-of-friendship-rethinking-platonic-relationships-guided-by-lgbtq-models/

Busby, D. M., Allen, C. Z., Leavitt, C. E., & Jensen, A. C. (2025). Physical aspects of sexuality, attachment, and sexual satisfaction. *Journal of Marital and Family Therapy, 51*(1), 1–15. https://doi.org/10.1111/jmft.12760

Dias Martins, C., Vergara, R. C., & Khoury, B. (2025). A machine learning approach for investigating variable importance in relationship and sexual satisfaction: The role of interpersonal mindfulness and psychological safety. *Journal of Marital and Family Therapy, 51*(2), 1–18. https://doi.org/10.1111/jmft.70026

Few-Demo, A. L., & Allen, K. R. (2020). Gender, feminist, and intersectional perspectives on families: A decade in review. *Journal of Marriage and Family, 82*(1), 326–345. https://doi.org/10.1111/jomf.12638

Few-Demo, A. L., Lloyd, S. A., & Allen, K. R. (2014). It's all about power: Integrating feminist family studies and family communication. *Journal of Family Communication, 14*(2), 85–94. https://doi.org/10.1080/15267431.2013.864295

Heim, C., & Heim, C. (2023). "How did you stay together so long?" relationship longevity, a cross-generational qualitative study. *Journal of Marital and Family Therapy, 49*, 781–801. https://doi.org/10.1111/jmft.12656

Hook, J. N., Davis, D., Owen, J., & DeBlaere, C. (2017). *Cultural humility: Engaging diverse identities in therapy*. American Psychological Association. https://doi.org/10.1037/0000037-000

Moussawi, G., & Vidal-Ortiz, S. (2020). A queer sociology: On power, race, and decentering whiteness. *Sociology Forum, 35*, 1272–1289. https://doi.org/10.1111/socf.12647

Glossary

Aceflux/Acefluid A person who describes their asexual orientation as more fluid or shifting (Young, 2023).

Acephobia The fear or hatred of asexuality or asexual people.

Aegosexual Describes a person who does not desire to engage in sexual activity with a person, but does experience arousal from content, masturbation, or fantasy (Young, 2023).

Aesthetic attraction Viewing a person in a way that appreciates their appearance, but this isn't rooted in sexual attraction (Fine, 2023).

Agender A person who does not identify with a specific traditional definition of gender and/or someone that does not feel they connect to ideas of masculinity or femininity/male or female.

Allonormativity The assumption that all people experience sexual attraction and experience the world in allosexual ways.

Alloromantic (romantic interest microlabel). A person that has a romantic identity or romantic attraction (Tessler, 2025).

Allosexuality/Allo A person who does experience sexual attraction, a more commonly reported experience of sexual attraction (essentially people who are not asexual) (Russell, 2023).

Ally A person outside the queer community who notes their support and respect for queer persons. Often associated with a person who may work towards supportive and action-oriented social change efforts.

Alterous attraction When an individual describes a love they have towards a person that does not necessarily fit into traditional definitions of romantic or sexual attraction (Young, 2023).

Amatanormativity The assumption that all people desire a specific kind of love and partnership and that this partnership is valued more than any other relationship (Brake, 2012).

Apothisexual When a person is repulsed by sexual activity or even sexual content (Young, 2023).

V. Q. Glass, *Asexuality, Relationships, and Identity Formation*,
https://doi.org/10.1007/978-3-032-22857-4

Akoisexual A person who feels sexual attraction; however, they do not want others (or the person they are attracted to) to feel it back (Young, 2023).

Aroace A person who is both asexual and aromantic.

Aromantic (romantic interest microlabel). A person who does not experience romantic attraction (Tessler, 2025).

Aromantic spectrum (A-spec) (romantic interest microlabel). Describes a person who mostly does not experience romantic attraction, but can include variations of that experience.

Asexuality A sexual orientation that identifies a continuum of experiences, the primary uniting experience that defines asexual spectrum identities is not feeling sexual attraction (Boegart, 2015).

Asexual Spectrum/Aspec/Ace Commonly used words to describe people who define themselves as under the asexual umbrella of experiences (Mandigo & Kavar, 2022).

Autochorissexualism Where a person is aroused by sexual situations or materials, however, does not experience sexual attraction to a person (Boegart, 2015).

Biromantic (romantic interest microlabel). A person that identifies as having a romantic attraction to more than one gender.

Cisgender A person who feels their gender assigned at birth and their gender identity are congruent.

Coming out The process where a person internally comes to understand their own sexual orientation or gender identity and/or shares this identity in more public ways.

Cupiosexual A person who desires a sexual relationship despite not feeling sexual attraction (Young, 2023).

Demiromantic (romantic interest microlabel). A person who identifies as experiencing romantic attraction only when a deep emotional connection is formed. Sexual interest microlabels.

Demisexual/Demi-asexual/Demiace An individual who only experiences sexual attraction to a person once they form an emotional bond or connection (Hille, 2023).

Emotional attraction A desire to be intimate through emotional connection (sharing, conversation, etc.).

Fluid/Fluidity A description of when a person experiences a fluctuation of sexual orientation or gender identity through time.

Fraysexual A person who feels sexual attraction towards those that they do not know well and sexual attraction fades the more they get to know the person (Young, 2023).

Gender binary Looking at gender as two opposing and different dimensions (male and female or man and woman) and the assumption that all people are one of the two noted genders.

Genderfluid An identity noted when a person feels they are a combination of gendered elements of masculinity and femininity.

Grayromantic (romantic interest microlabel). A person who identifies as experiencing romantic attraction in certain circumstances.

Graysexual/gray-asexual/grayace An individual who only experiences sexual attraction in very specific circumstances (Hille, 2023).

Heteronormativity The assumption that all people are heterosexual.

Heteroromantic (romantic interest microlabel). A person who identifies as having romantic attraction to persons of a different gender (typically used to describe attraction in terms of a gender binary male/female).

Heterosexual A person identifies as having a sexual attraction to persons of a different gender (typically used to describe attraction in terms of a gender binary male/female).

Heterosexism Language, behavior, words, policies, etc. that reinforce the idea that only heterosexual identities are normal or appropriate.

Homophobia A fear or intolerance of queer people or elements in society that could represent anything queer.

Homoromantic (romantic interest microlabel). A person who identifies as having a romantic attraction to persons of a similar gender.

Lithosexual A person who feels sexual attraction;, however, they do not want others (or the person they are attracted to) to feel it back (Young, 2023).

Nonbinary A gender identity that is not exclusively male or female.

Non-desire A notable lack of feeling desire for another person that is a contradiction to heteronormative, allonormative, amatanormative expectations (Fine, 2023).

Omniromantic (romantic interest microlabel). A person who identifies as having a romantic attraction to all genders and considers gender a role in that romantic attraction.

Omnisexual A person has a sexual attraction to all genders and considers gender as a rolc in that scxual attraction.

Panromantic (romantic interest microlabel). A person who identifies as having a romantic attraction to all genders.

Pansexual A person identifies as having a sexual attraction to all genders.

Platonic attraction A desire for a connection without sexual or romantic aspects.

Polyromantic (romantic interest microlabel). A person who identifies as having a romantic attraction to multiple genders.

Queer An umbrella term that identifies all gender and sexual minorities.

Queerplatonic/queerplatonic relationship (QPR) A QPR is a relationship that may not fit into the sexual, romantic, or social norms of a "relationship"; however, they are equally as valid committed and intimate relationships (Young, 2023).

Romantic orientation "An identity or label typically based on the gendered direction of romantic attraction. For example, heteroromantic, homoromantic, biromantic, panromantic, or aromantic are romantic orientations. Some people may have different sexual and romantic orientations (e.g. a biromantic asexual)" (Asexuality Visibility and Education Network [AVEN], 2022).

Sensual attraction Experiencing a desire to physically connect with someone in a non-physical way (e.g., hugging, cuddling, kissing) (AVEN).

Sex-averse (Sexual interest microlabel). A person who is not really drawn to sexual activity.

Sex-favorable/Sex-positive (Sexual interest microlabel). A person who tends to appreciate and desire a sexual relationship.

Sex-indifferent/sex-neutral (Sexual interest microlabel). A person who is open towards sexual activity but maybe not considering it.

Sex-repulsed (Sexual interest microlabel). A person who has a negative reaction to sexual activity. For some, this can be a physical reaction.

Sexual attraction A desire to have sexual experiences with another person (Asexuality Visibility and Education Network [AVEN], 2022).

Sexual normativity The idea that all people have sexual desires and have a need to act on these desires (Schneckenburger et al., 2024).

Sexual orientation "An identity or label typically based on the gendered direction of sexual attraction, or the lack thereof. For example, heterosexual, homosexual, bisexual, pansexual, or asexual are sexual orientations" (Asexuality Visibility and Education Network [AVEN], 2022).

Skoliosexual An individual who is sexually attracted to gender diverse individuals.

Split Attraction Model Highlights that people can experience "sexual attraction" and/or "romantic attraction" separately or differently (Diamond, 2003).

Squish A "non-romantic, non-sexual desire for a potential friend" (Fine, 2023, p. 165). Kind of like a crush, but not a romantic or sexual feeling.

Transgender A person whose gender identity and gender assigned at birth do not necessarily correspond. Often an umbrella term for all gender minorities.

References

Asexual Visibility and Education Network (AVEN). (2022, February 1). https://www.asexuality.org/

Bogaert, A. F. (2015). Asexuality: What is it and why it matters. *Journal of Sex Research, 52*(4), 362–379. https://doi.org/10.1080/00224499.2015.1015713

Brake, E. (2012). *Minimizing marriage: Marriage, morality, and the law*. Oxford University Press.

Diamond, L. M. (2003). What does sexual orientation orient? A biobehavioral model distinguishing romantic love and sexual desire. *Psychological Review, 110*(1), 173–192. https://doi.org/10.1037/0033-295X.110.1.173

Fine, J. (2023). From crushes to squishes: Affect and agency on r/AskReddit and r/asexual. *Journal of Language and Sexuality, 12*, 145–172. https://doi.org/10.1075/jls.22004.fin

Hille, J. J. (2023). Beyond sex: A review of recent literature on asexuality. *Current Opinion in Psychology, 49*. https://doi.org/10.1016/j.copsyc.2022.101516

Mandigo, D. M., & Kavar, L. (2022). The experience of male asexuality: A phenomenological inquiry. *Qualitative Report, 27*(2), 488–508. https://doi.org/10.46743/2160-3715/2022.5213

Russell, J. (2023). The sex lives of asexuals. In *Erotically queer: A pink therapy guide for practitioners* (pp. 59–74). https://doi.org/10.4324/9781003260608-5

Schneckenburger, S. A., Tam, M. W. Y., & Ross, L. E. (2024). Asexual competent practices in healthcare: A narrative review. *Journal of Gay & Lesbian Mental Health, 28*(3), 314–334. https://doi.org/10.1080/19359705.2023.2214528

Tessler, H. (2025). Aromanticism, asexuality, and relationship (non-) formation: How a-spec singles challenge romantic norms and reimagine family life. *Sexualities, 28*(1/2), 514–535. https://doi.org/10.1177/13634607231197061

Young, E. (2023). *Ace voices: What it means to be asexual, aromantic, demi or grey-ace*. Jessica Kingsley Publishers.

Index

V. Q. Glass, *Asexuality, Relationships, and Identity Formation*, https://doi.org/10.1007/978-3-032-22857-4

MIX
Papier aus verantwortungsvollen Quellen
Paper from responsible sources
FSC® C105338

If you have any concerns about our products,
you can contact us on
ProductSafety@springernature.com

In case Publisher is established outside the EU,
the EU authorized representative is:
Springer Nature Customer Service Center GmbH
Europaplatz 3, 69115 Heidelberg, Germany

Printed by Libri Plureos GmbH
in Hamburg, Germany